The writer as liar

The writer as liar
Narrative technique
in the *Decameron*

Guido Almansi

Routledge & Kegan Paul
London and Boston

First published in 1975
by Routledge & Kegan Paul Ltd
Broadway House, 68–74 Carter Lane,
London EC4V 5EL and
9 Park Street,
Boston, Mass. 02108, USA
Set in Monotype Garamond
and printed in Great Britain by
The Camelot Press Ltd, Southampton
© Guido Almansi 1975

ISBN 0 7100 8147 2

Contents

Introduction   *page*   vii

1 Narrative screens   1

2 Literature and falsehood   19

3 Bawdry and *Ars Combinatoria*   63

4 The meaning of a storm   108

5 Passion and metaphor   133

Bibliographical conventions   159

Index   161

Introduction

The present volume is intended as an inquiry into narrative forms and is therefore somewhat removed from the method and scope of standard historical criticism. The general thesis of the book, which assembles a range of critical observations on salient points of Boccaccio's masterpiece rather than presenting a continuous theoretical discussion on the whole of it and imposing its own over-all view, tends to propose an anti-realist and anti-psychological reading of the Hundred Tales. Its purpose is to set this suggested reading of the text alongside the other more traditional interpretations which lay emphasis on the psychological and realist current of the stories, in order to offer an alternative critical viewpoint. If a number of sections may appear polemical, my general intention was not such, and the interpretations which I put forward, even though they follow a formalist line, have only been made possible through a comparison with, and within the terms of, the best tradition of Boccaccio criticism, particularly that of the twentieth century.

The volume presumes a prior acquaintance with the *Decameron* on the part of the reader. I have tried to present a synopsis of each individual *novella* with which I deal, but in doing so I have been far from wishing to give the impression that this treatment is sufficient to follow my own or indeed any other critical discussion of the text in question. Not least of the book's intentions is the hope that it will stimulate a closer reading of the *Decameron*, which in my opinion stands as one of the finest documents of Western literature.

All quotations from the text are given in English, with the Italian original quoted in the notes. At every point in my work I have made use of the recently published translation of the *Decameron* by Harry McWilliam (Penguin, 1972). I would therefore like to take this opportunity to express my regard for the quality of the translation and my gratitude to Penguin Books for having allowed me to quote widely from it. Full bibliographical details for the abbreviated references in the notes are supplied in the section Bibliographical conventions on page 159.

One

Narrative screens

In an essay entitled 'Dante ou la traversée de l'écriture'[1] Philippe Sollers, leader of the *Tel Quel* group, makes the following statement: 'The *Divine Comedy* is the first book entirely conceived and enacted as a book' ('le premier livre pensé et agi intégralement comme livre'). This observation is obviously theoretical and ideological, and as such it calls for an ideological reaction. Yet our response is likely to be emotional rather than ideological, in so far as we are tempted to agree with such a forceful and subversive paradox for emotive reasons. In other words, our sympathy for the remark arises out of our lack of sympathy for other critical stances, rather than from an inner conviction about the validity of Sollers's assumption.

One might argue that little can be done, in the field of criticism, until the vestiges of sundry outdated positions are swept away. In this sense, Sollers is of great help. Everything is debunked by his outrageous statement: the tiresome legend of Dante the Man, the time-honoured and yet inept myth of Dante the Pilgrim, the superfluous epic of Dante the Poet, and with them, all the paraphernalia of the Man of Genius, the pangs of creation, the moral duties of realism, the ethical essence of any masterpiece. All we are left with is a text in the process of composing itself ('un texte en train de s'écrire'), a verbal icon drawing on its own tautological evidence, confirming its own existence by reiterating the simple fact that a text is a text is a text.

There is only one way to approach this text: we must go through the narrow gate of our reading process. On the far side of the text, in the miasmic crater of human emotions and ideas, where all new creations are hatched and brought to life, nothing is left: only a void, or a question mark, which must remain as it is, for ever lacking an answer. A text is thus doomed to be an autonomous entity owing its right of existence to itself, and constituting its own criteria of validity.

It is hardly possible to deny, at least as far as we are concerned here, the seductiveness of the above approach, which repels all the counter-attacks of the old schools in their pristine or renewed disguises. The self-contained text rejects the immodest claims of psychocriticism; the fearsome threats of the spelaeologists of psychic depth, chewing over their data about the author's or the character's life and childhood; the obnoxious interventions of the hagiographers upholding national glories; the inane discoveries of cleaning women in the poet's laboratory, and so on and so forth. The critic becomes a passive gynaecologist who attends the mysterious process of a text's parthenogenesis, thus witnessing a divine birth.

Yet, at the very moment when we are most enticed towards Sollers's theories, we also know that he is wrong: at least partially wrong. His method cannot work. Surely he is not partially, but impartially wrong when he tries out his ideas on the *Commedia*. For this is a text which stubbornly refuses this sort of approach, and for the following reasons:

(*a*) It is not permissible to reduce the cosmological invention of the *Divine Comedy* to a purely linguistic and literary structure, independent of the ethical design that Dante wanted to impose on the contemporary world, and on Italy in particular. Surely it is neither advisable nor indeed necessary to dispense with the extraordinary parallelism in Dante between the forms of the physical world and those of the moral world, which amounts to a transformation into ethical terms of his topography and cosmogony. This ethicization, if one may coin the word, forces the reader to accept Dante's terms either in good or in bad faith (and what else is the 'suspension of disbelief' but an acceptance of the author's terms in bad faith?). In other words, the *Divine Comedy* would not look as much like 'un livre pensé comme un livre' ('a book programmed as a book') as 'un livre pensé comme un exemple' ('a book conceived as an *exemplum*').

(*b*) If Dante's arrangement of the Afterworld into the three kingdoms is the objective correlative of the individual soul's path towards salvation, then the book must be a reflection or image (however it may have been distorted or blurred by way of the linguistic, metrical or narrative adjustments forced upon it by the sequence of the text) of the ethical plan which is germane to Dante's thought, but not necessarily determined by the structure of the work itself. Ethico-political activity and the literary act itself are so closely knit in Dante that the text cannot be considered independently, 'chiuso e parvente del suo proprio riso' ('hidden and revealed by its own smile')[2] or be separated from the uninterrupted moral commitment which can be felt in every line of the *Comedy*. Therefore the work turns out to be not so much 'un livre pensé comme un livre' as 'un livre pensé comme engagement' ('a book conceived as moral commitment').

(*c*) The immediate identification between the author and the main character of the *Comedy* represents a strong temptation to the reader to construct (in good or in bad faith) a further identification between Dante the character and that Everyman Dante which is the reader himself. The result is that all three of them, the author, the character and the reader, are caught up and involved in a mysterious operation which conducts their collective soul from damnation to salvation. Once again, then, we are faced not by 'un livre pensé comme un livre', but rather by 'un livre pensé comme expérience' ('a book conceived as moral experience').

(*d*) I am not at all sure if it is permissible to apply such a fanatic and inflexible concept of formalist orthodoxy to an energetically committed and anti-literary text like the *Divine Comedy*. The relationship in Dante between the complementary experience of art on the one side and the *Erlebnis* on the other does not work in terms of certain fixed or codifiable canons, as with pure realists and straight formalists, because all too often the factual lived experience can break through that type of aesthetic model and impose an absurdly personal message on a text which should by its very nature (i.e. by virtue of the literary conventions inside which it operates) be moving towards the impersonal representativeness of allegory.

So perhaps Dante's *Comedy* is not the 'texte en train de s'écrire' according to the formula excogitated by Sollers. If I were to name an Italian literary masterpiece which fulfils the definition 'un livre pensé et agi intégralement comme livre' ('a book conceived and enacted as a book'), I would have no hesitation in opting for the *Decameron* rather than the *Comedy*. Now we can go back over the four problems I have just posed in relation to Dante, and see how they work for Boccaccio.

(*a*) The *Decameron* may well be a cosmological invention, a *comédie humaine,* or so forth, but it is certainly not 'un livre pensé comme un exemple' ('a book conceived as an *exemplum*'). By this

I do not want to imply that its internal ethical structure is irrelevant to the society it describes (or rather, to any society, be it Boccaccio's or twentieth-century Britain); the point is that the applicability, or relevance, of moral laws (which ultimately turn out to be chiefly a taxonomy of human behaviour, a practical summary of modes of conduct rather than a *corpus* of laws) is never imposed from above, as is the case with Dante. Instead it is left up to the reader to choose whether to use an ethical model, or, at times, a discordant and occasionally contradictory series of ethical models, and to use them in the way he sees fit, by learning his lesson from Cepperello in the very first *novella*, or from Griselda in the last.

(*b*) The *Decameron* is not the objective correlative of some entity, sensation or idea external to the text. It exists by and for itself, and its ethical organization is an internal function of the book, and has little to do with some preordained system of values.

(*c*) The *Decameron* is by no means 'un livre pensé comme expérience' ('a book conceived as moral experience'), and it would be quite unjustified to posit some kind of identification between the author and his characters, or between the characters and the reader. The mystic union of author–protagonist–reader in the *Comedy* is quite out of the question in Boccaccio's *Hundred Tales* (and again I should like to insist that this union takes place during our reading of the *Comedy* even where we are acting in a disingenuous way).

(*d*) The *Decameron* lends itself to a rigidly formalist interpretation, in so far as the author always keeps the sphere of the *vécu* sealed off from that of narrative inventiveness.

So the *Decameron* would seem to be the ideal text for the formalists to get their teeth into: a completely self-sufficient text, a book 'qui s'écrit et s'invente à l'intérieur de ses propres règles' ('which writes itself, continuously generating its own structure and rules'), a book where all references to some external reality, which it might be supposed to convey in a mimetic sense, are in fact passed through a filtering process which deforms their everyday recognizability. This process forces the reader to adopt a quintessentially literary and non-*engagé* technique for absorbing the text. This is because the *Decameron* invites us to take part in an artistic game with fixed rules, while at the same time it forces the reader to be continuously aware of the fact of its being literature, part of the genre of story-telling.

Some other literary works, such as the *Divine Comedy*, tend to require from their readers a kind of blind faith in a reality of a different order which has nothing to do with artistic requirements: something which is chronologically prior to the text itself (as for example the ramifications of Florentine politics) or posterior to it (celestial salvation). But the *Decameron* poses no such questions to the reader: the only faith which it asks of him is at an aesthetic level. It calls for a patient and trusting concentration on the gradual revelation of secrets which it unearths from the chaos of human adventure: this is the source which supplies all those *novelle* preaching an *exemplum*, those models of a conduct which is disgraceful or sublime, generous or mean, noble or base.

The lesson provided by the text will certainly be available for an extraneous classroom, outside the written page, *au dehors* of the book-binding which incorporates its private universe of types and print, *l'univers du texte*. Certainly the reader can, if he cares to, abstract a message from the *Decameron* and take it home for his private moral, social, political, or psychological edification. However, at the heart of the matter we are left, in the *Decameron*, with an inflexibly aesthetic message, one which stands at a considerable distance from mimesis and real life representation. The text strains at the task of carrying to the point of exasperation the very intentionality of its rôle as a text: it desires to appear exactly what it is: 'un livre pensé comme un livre' ('a book programmed as a book').

There is a splendid picture by Magritte which shows an enormous pipe, precisely reproduced on a large canvas. The pipe assumes a menacing and alarming reality in the composition because the size of the picture and the isolation of the single object represented in it serve to magnify the pipe's presence and make it even more striking and eccentric. However, at the bottom of the painting the following words are written in large characters: CECI N'EST PAS UNE PIPE (This is not a pipe).

The *Decameron* presents us with a pipe and at the same time denies its existence *qua* pipe: it presents us with a portrait of contemporary society, the epic of a mercantile age, the minor vicissitudes of the next-door neighbour, of the middle-class citizen, the urban gentleman, all the trivial preoccupations of everyday life, the deeds and achievements of local worthies and historical figures from the near and distant past, while at the same time underlining their romanesque existence, their essence as pure products of pen and ink, their unspoilt presence as literature. The text invents a world which has the same reflecting properties as Alice's mirror: the copy is never quite exact. What comes out is a model of the *vécu*, and of contemporary society, while at the same time we find a statement emphasizing the fact that everything to be found in the text is part of a world of narrative rather than lived experience, a world of words and not a world of action, a world of sounds and symbols, not of flesh and blood.

This is the cliff against which a goodly proportion of Boccaccio criticism (especially in the nineteenth century) was shipwrecked. Like Pinocchio, people were obstinately attempting to fry eggs on a fire which was painted on the wall. So they looked for historical and realistic accuracy, exact mimesis, factual objectivity and psychological plausibility in a text which, on the contrary, represents a colossal prevarication in the face of these good old-fashioned human concerns. This book is intended as a record and critical appreciation of Boccaccio's art as prevarication.

The usual technique employed by writers and artists to release their work from the constant pressure of the *vécu* consists in an effort to create an artificial distance between the subject and the reader. A classic example of this would be the opening formula: 'Once upon a time in a far-away country, on the other side of the sea, there was a king.' In this single sentence we have three elements which combine to set up a distancing effect: distance in terms of the time at which the story occurs, the place where it took place, and the social class which is involved. But the *Decameron* is not a fairy-tale; indeed, to a certain extent it is the exact opposite of a fairy-tale. In terms of time, space and social class the world of the *Decameron* is very close to that of the author, and this proximity between *vécu* and narrative colours the whole text, so that even today, six hundred years on, the narrative language of the *Decameron* sounds familiar to a reader's ears. It is a world of known rather than unknown elements, as in fairy-tales. It is a social and symbolic universe in which we come to recognize ourselves and our own everyday concerns, the privileged obsessions of our or any age.

If we were to take some of the commonest themes in the

Hundred Tales, such as the Mediterranean saga, the *comédie des mœurs* in Florentine or Neapolitan society, the convent story, the rake's progress, or the unscrupulous merchant's fortunes, we would inevitably be reminded of a familiar universe, one based on symbolic keys which are well inside our grasp, even though laws, customs, morality and patterns of social kinship have altered vastly since the time of Boccaccio. And yet this familiar world is another world, it is *autre*: everything in it takes place on the other side of the barrier. For we are faced by a narrated world, where the narrators, locked inside the stylized refuge of their *cornice*, are simultaneously able to link up and separate the fictional characters and us readers. In this way the *cornice* becomes a far more effective barrier than the gateway to Inferno, or the threshold between life and death which we are presented with in the *Divine Comedy*, because the *Decameron* rules out any possibility of a mystical link-up, of our crossing over the barrier. The narrator is continuously in a position to remind the reader that this is a narrative universe, placed at two removes from the lived universe which is familiar to all of us, namely the world of the *vécu*. Readers, story-tellers and characters all come to form a linked series of imaginary moments which imposes a unique and unrepeatable mode of reading on the end product.

Possibly we are justified in hazarding the view that every work of art is bound to contain some secret device for ensuring the due distance between itself and its consumer. We have the physical stage in works for the theatre, the frame for pictures and drawings, the linguistic alteration of the main characters' names in a story taken from real life experience, the creation of an artistic entity where *nomina sunt numina*. Then we have the special techniques involving *ostranenye* (estrangement) listed by Sklovsky in the works of Tolstoy, and so on. In fact, art is the invention of rhetorical constructs that command a permanent mixture of belief and disbelief. It may well be difficult to make the audience believe in what is going on by frightening him with Hellfire or Purgatorial penances in a fresco or the tabernacle at the corner of the street. Yet it is probably an equally hard task to make him disbelieve in art, by reminding him of the inherent mechanism which would in fact allow him to gain a respectable distance from what he is witnessing. Real artistic experience is not in fact achieved, as our critical predecessors fondly imagined, at the

point when we view a still life in a painting and this still life
presents such apple-like apples that we are tempted to reach forward with a knife and sample them. This amounts to a gastro-
nomical hypnosis, certainly not artistic experience. Art consists in
a process of forcing the spectator to look at the apples, not in
inviting him to salivate at the prospect of chewing one.

Amongst the infinite possible ways of reminding the spectators
of their real rôle as consumers of a work of art, the device employed by Boccaccio in the *Decameron* is surely one of the most
effective. If I had to think of a contemporary work which exploits
a similar distancing technique from the subject, I would probably
go to a children's book, and more specifically to *Winnie-the-Pooh*
(though this would almost certainly condemn me as one of the
exegetical monsters put to rout by Frederick Crews in his *The
Pooh Perplex*[3]). In actual fact A. A. Milne's famous classic follows
a strikingly different technique from the narrative of a traditional
fairy-tale ('Once upon a time there was a king, who . . .'). The
teddy-bear protagonist of *Pooh* appears in the very first words of
the story as essentially a toy creature, an inaminate object,
'coming downstairs now, bump bump bump on the back of his
head. . . . It is, as far as he knows, the only way of coming downstairs.' In this quotation every word serves to emphasize the fact
that we are going to deal with an inert and lifeless hero.

However, this first version of Winnie-the-Pooh is instantly
compared with another Winnie-the-Pooh, a different creature who
lives in the Hundred Acre Wood. Let us take an example from the
first chapter:[4]

> 'What about a story?' said Christopher Robin.
> '*What* about a story?' I said.
> 'Could you very sweetly tell Winnie-the-Pooh one?'
> 'I suppose I could,' I said. 'What sort of stories does he like?'
> 'About himself. Because he's that *sort* of bear.'
> 'Oh, I see.'
> 'So could you very sweetly?'
> 'I'll try.' I said.
> So I tried.
> 'Once upon a time, a very long time ago, about last Friday,
> Winnie-the-Pooh lived in a forest all by himself under the
> name of Sanders.'

At this point we have reached a second level of the narrative; we have come through and beyond a further distortion and alteration of the original reality. The reader's conception of a first and second version of Winnie-the-Pooh, and of a subtle relationship which connects the two narrative levels, will be strengthened by another passage, still in the opening chapter of the adventure: [5]

He [Winnie-the-Pooh] crawled out of the gorse-bush, brushed the prickles from his nose, and began to think again. And the first person he thought of was Christopher Robin.

'Was that me?' said Christopher Robin in an awed voice, hardly daring to believe it.

'That was you.'

(Christopher Robin said nothing, but his eyes got larger and larger, and his face got pinker and pinker.)

So Winnie-the-Pooh went round to his friend Christopher Robin, who lived behind a green door in another part of the Forest.

'Good morning, Christopher Robin,' he said.

'Good morning, Winnie-*ther*-Pooh,' said you.

Consequently, we have two Winnie-the-Poohs and two Christopher Robins, who coexist at two different levels of narrative reality. And the dividing-line between these two levels presents the author with an extraordinary freedom of expression in handling his material, allowing him to create a fantastic superstructure which is generated inside a familiar, non-fantastic world. The teddy-bear, one of the most familiar and everyday of all possible objects, thus becomes a character with strikingly mythical dimensions, without at the same time losing its hold on the familiar environment which has produced it.

If we return to Boccaccio with these reflections in mind, perhaps we can formulate the following theorems:

(*a*) The action in the *Decameron* takes place 'a very long time ago, about last Friday'.

(*b*) The *Decameron* succeeds in setting up an astonishing relationship between the reader on the one hand, and the characters inside their narrative material on the other. This connection is modified by a series of screens which divide the first narrative level from the second, i.e. the world of the story-tellers' *cornice* from that of the tales which they actually tell.

(*c*) The *Decameron*, like *Winnie-the-Pooh*, is a text which lives entirely inside the dimensions of narrative interplay.

(*d*) The characters in the *Decameron* are familiar, everyday presences, which are capable of assuming mythical proportions and qualities in the passage between one narrative level and the other.

The term *cornice*, or 'frame', usually employed by critics to distinguish the narrative material in the *Decameron* which concerns the male and female story-tellers from the actual stories which they relate, is a particularly felicitous one. This *cornice* presents us with a gay company of young ladies and gentlemen, seven and three of them respectively, who leave the city of Florence under the menace of the plague to take refuge in the grounds of a country villa, far away from the infectious epidemic, and cut off from the general deterioration in civil and moral codes of conduct which had attended the spread of the disease. They move in a serene and peaceful aristocratic ambience, where, amongst all the other manifestations of gracious living and refined entertainment, a special rôle is played by the ancient and noble art of story-telling. This is all-important, and the following chapter will attempt to show more fully one of our underlying convictions: namely that the art of relating stories and the awareness of the difficulty of telling them is continuously present in the text.

This awareness intrudes not just at the primary aesthetic level, in the sense in which every work of art exalts itself and the artifices it uses, but also at a structural level, since this is a case where we have to pay special attention to the technique of story-telling. This latter is presented to us in a double guise: not only do we have the stories themselves, which vary in their deployment of narrative skills, but we also have the courtly contest which the story-tellers fight in an atmosphere of idyll and good taste in order to entertain and compete with the rest of the company. This means that it would certainly be an oversimplification of the Tenth Day to treat it simply as a progressive ascent towards virtue. We should also look at the decisive parallel ascent towards narrative inventiveness, in other words the creative process involved in attempting to invent ever more convincing examples of human magnanimity and virtue. And this is valid both for the author and for the narrators.

We could begin by looking at the work under two headings, which can be labelled conveniently as a social and a narrative mode. The social mode of the *Decameron* falls into three stages: the plague, the noble company, and their stories. Seen from this point of view, it is not so much that the *cornice* frames the stories as that it stands as an intermediate point separating the historical reality of plague-ridden Florence and the fictional reality of the stories as an expression of contemporary society.

Midway between these two aspects of the *Decameron* as a realist depiction, we are faced by a paradoxical hypothesis, namely the tranquil existence of a joyful company of young aristocrats which provides an ideal model of graceful living and courtly behaviour in contrast with the torment and corruption of the fictional characters in their stories, and of the inhabitants of Florence in the introduction. The historical world (contemporary Florence) is morally and physically bankrupt, contaminated by a decay in customs and the spread of a noxious plague. The fictional world of the stories is equally corrupt, since pride, envy, greed and debauchery seem to dominate all possible adventures, so much so that only the constant restraint of human intelligence and the impact of the art of living[6] can put a curb on it and restore a measure of worldly common sense. The other world, the world of the story-tellers themselves, is in flight from the historical world, and content to relate the vicissitudes of the fictional world, while at the same time denying the evidence of both by virtue of its uncorrupt life-style.

The foregoing, in fact, constitute the essential data which we can derive from a social reading of the *Decameron*, and correspond with the view expressed by standard Boccaccio criticism where it is concerned with the plague and the *cornice*. But it is possible to embark on a different type of reading, the one that I have already labelled 'the narrative mode'. This would restore to the *cornice* its function as a framing device, an outer circumference which encloses and delimits the possibilities of the internal narrative circle, and actually comments on its implications and effectiveness. It throws emphasis on the vital zone of the ten days and their narrative content, while toning down the extraneous picture of Florence and the plague presented in the introduction to the book. The gay company thus acquires a central rôle, which is to act as a go-between relating the reader to the stories which he has before him. The friendly discussions and picnic parties of the ten story-tellers act as a background from which they *compère* and interpret the tumultuous world of the *Decameron's* hundred tales for the benefit of their readers.

In other words, we are no longer dealing with a kind of triadic view which places the ideal standard of the gay company in an elevated position at the centre, surrounded on both sides by the humbler realities of the plague and of the narrative material. Instead we shall come to visualize a concentric structure, with the gay company of story-tellers on the outside and the stories on the inside: in other words, a *cornice* which is literally a *cornice*, an enclosing frame.

If we accept the validity of this way of looking at the *cornice*, we can move on to a discussion of its practical advantages. We could rely on the views of a series of celebrated scholars who have considered the question of the functionality of the *cornice* with illuminating results.[7] Evidently the *cornice* serves to hold the hundred tales together; it supplies a structural coherence and a unifying rhythm to the exposition of extremely heterogeneous material: in short, it turns the hundred stories into a single book, almost a novel. The *cornice* also provides unity where there is variety, consistency where there is a chaotic miscellany of themes; using the flimsy pretext of the story-tellers' petty preferences, one minute accepting, at the next minute trying to evade, the subjects which they impose on each other, Boccaccio actually renders their subject-matter more assimilable and less difficult to understand, without reducing it to a single tone or emotional tension. The *cornice* offers moments of relaxation and solace, it smoothes out the reading process for a few pages with a more relaxed syntax and a less frenetic sense of action compared with the unrelenting drama of what surrounds it. The *cornice* provides the reader with a breathing-space (at times a highly entertaining one, as at the end of the Sixth Day) to counter the suspense of the stories.

The *cornice* serves pre-eminently to instruct the reader as to how the stories are to be read and understood, since they do not exist as separate entities but are conditioned and reflected by the stories that precede and follow them, by the themes for the day and the personality of the individual story-teller,[8] and even by the young company's own jokes, comments, tears and sympathy for their fictional creations. Thus we are justified in saying that the figures in the *cornice* provide an informal commentary on the text: footnotes, interpretative glosses which are all designed to assist the eager but dilettante reader.

The *cornice* also acts as a subtle lever, gradually transferring the complex material of the stories towards a model of ascent, commencing with the scandalous turpitude of Ciappelletto and progressing through to the apparently sublime humility of Griselda, going by way of the worldly promptings of human intelligence and exploiting the interventions of chance and virtue. It is an ideal model which is hinted at but not exemplified in the *Decameron*, since among the many other levels at which the author plays with the readers' reactions, he is content to allow a glimmer of this ascent to come through to them, while at the same time severely curtailing the triumph of virtue and goodness by a number of doubtful examples of saintly behaviour in the Tenth Day itself.[9] The *cornice* manages to insert even the most fantastic stories into a recognizable human dimension, so that a patina of almost domestic familiarity is allowed to tone down the purest flights of imagination.

So far so good; in my own words I have expressed a number of views which are still in fact recognizable as those of the main twentieth-century critics of the *Decameron*. Yet perhaps there is a further, different and possibly opposite function, which needs to be given a wider airing. Suppose the *cornice* actually serves the purpose of a standard picture-frame, i.e. a reminder that what is inside is an artistic object? What if one were to see the *cornice* of the *Decameron* as a deliberate statement declaring that everything within it is a stylized narrative creation, a sum of narrative items which the *cornice* thus automatically sets apart from the items of the everyday world which the reader lives in and knows about? Thus the *cornice* becomes an 'estranging device', an *ostranenye*, to use the Russian term which is gaining wide currency in contemporary criticism on the continent.

Let us consider a situation where there are two salt-cellars laid at the table where I am about to eat, one of them worked by Benvenuto Cellini, the other picked up from a counter at Woolworth's. If they are filled with regular salt, I can use either of them to add salt to my main dish. From a purely functional point of view the two salt-cellars are indistinguishable. Indeed, it would be hard to grade them at an aesthetic level, whatever this really means, since when all is said and done there is no such thing as an absolute normative criterion which can set apart the unique artifact of a master craftsman from its humble counterpart in the consumer market.

In order to isolate Cellini's salt-cellar from any mortifying comparison with the Woolworth's bargain product, I am obliged first to define the *objet d'art* (and therefore frame it) specifically as an *objet d'art*.[10] I shall have to state that it is worth a certain sum of money, which means that I shall be framing it in terms of its market value, its rarity, its antiquity, noble origin, and so on. Or I must lay it under a glass cover in a museum; or provide it with a dignified location on a mantelpiece, outside the contact of other merely functional artifacts, so that by a kind of unwritten semantics of space I achieve a situation where the object states, by the very fact that it is removed from comparable objects, the more intangible fact that it is artistic and of great value. Similarly, a simple water-colour or drawing stuck on a wall is differentiated from the wallpaper as and when we place a frame round it. In other words, we need mere emptiness or a surrounding convention to set apart the *objet d'art* as such.

In this sense, the *cornice* in the *Decameron* comes to fulfil two parallel functions: first, it vouches for the artisticness of everything that goes on within it by reminding the reader/spectator that the framed object must be considered according to the standard conventions which we are prepared to ascribe to artistic experience; second, it maintains the necessary distance (cerebral, visual and temporal) between the world of fable and the lived, everyday world which I label elsewhere in the pages that follow as the *vécu*. The *cornice* comes to be identified with the medium, as McLuhan might say; it stamps the seal of art on what it contains.

In my view the gay company of story-tellers plays this rôle in helping to establish the difficult compromise between the episodes related in the text and the experiences which the readership has had directly. Without for a moment denying the various other rôles which are played by the busy narrators in the course of the well over 800 pages of the *Decameron*, we still have to take into account the possibility that they are also there for the 'estranging' purpose of preventing too close and dangerous a contact between the text and the act of reading it. In the long narrative cycle of the *Decameron*, these ten figures crop up continually as screens which protect the frontiers of narrative experience from irrelevant incursions by importuning interpreters who would invoke historical objectivity, or psychological plausibility, or mimesis of real world occurrences. Between us readers and the events and characters of the *novelle*, there is this continuous stylistic artifice which acts as a screen to filter out any direct confrontation between ourselves and the stories which we are supposed to be reading as an artistic construct.

Such a confrontation might, for example, lead us to query the excessive generosity of Nathan (X, 3) the excessive wickedness of Ciappelletto (I, 1), the improbability of the adventure that befalls Nicostrato (VII, 9), or the psychological implausibility of the story of Tito and Gisippo (X, 8). The ten story-tellers cajole us into acceptance, constantly reminding us of the play element, the entertainment factor to which we subscribe by the act of taking up and reading the hundred stories which they in turn have provided for our delectation.

The most extreme and decisive case of this attitude is surely to be found in the *novella* of Federico degli Alberighi and the Falcon (V, 9). Federico, a rich young nobleman spends all his estate on his love for a married woman, Monna Giovanna. He is reduced to poverty and thereafter retains a single, splendid falcon, which consoles him because at least he can still go out hunting. However, the son of the woman falls gravely ill and the only thing that would cure him, apparently, is to satisfy his wish to possess the falcon. In order to obtain the falcon for her son, Monna Giovanna has herself invited to lunch by the impoverished nobleman so that she can find an opportunity to formulate the request. Federico, however, is unaware why she has come, and because he cannot afford good food for this still-loved guest, he kills his falcon and presents it to her as the meat dish.

This is the story, reduced to its essentials, and it is one of the most attractive and moving *novelle* in the whole *Decameron*, despite the banality of the subject-matter, based on the day-to-day preoccupation of how to make ends meet in the shopping basket. The *novella* turns out to be embarrassingly close to the world of unpaid bills and shopkeepers unwilling to advance credit. Despite the fairy-tale dimension provided by the silent presence of the splendid falcon, it is all too easy for the down-to-earth problems of this bachelor housekeeper to ring an approximate chord in the heart of Everyman reader, who is only too familiar with the experience that is apparently being related.

Yet it is precisely in this dangerously familiar story that the narrative screens between reader and subject-matter are multiplied. Fiammetta, who is queen of the Fifth Day, is required to make her contribution at the critical moment of the ninth *novella* of the Day. This is how she begins the actual material of her story:[11]

> You are to know, then, that Coppo di Borghese Domenichi, who once used to live in our city and possibly lives there still, one of the most highly respected men of our century, a person worthy of eternal fame, who achieved his position of pre-eminence by dint of his character and abilities rather than by his noble lineage, frequently took pleasure during his declining years in discussing incidents from the past with his neighbours and other folk. In this pastime he excelled all others, for he was more coherent, possessed a superior memory, and spoke with greater eloquence. He had a fine repertoire, including a tale he frequently told concerning a young Florentine called Federico, the son of Messer Filippo Alberighi.

Every item in the extraordinary passage serves to distance and defamiliarize this too familiar drama. We are presented with Boccaccio, who has a character called Fiammetta, who tells of a person named Coppo di Borghese Domenichi, who among other stories narrates the adventure of Federico. Coppo himself is inserted in the distant past not so much by means of the biographical data given on him ('and possibly lives there still') as by the past tense 'fu' ('was'); he is inserted in the distance of his social class, by his nobility, and in the isolation of his rôle by his virtue; he is also set apart in the aristocracy of his intellect by the ornate choice of words ascribed to him.

The slow and dignified progress of this intermediary passage between Fiammetta's opening remark and the start of the story about Federico, serves to soft-pedal the otherwise alarming familiarity and irksome realism of the incidents which are going to be described. They are isolated in a mythical, even if fairly recent, period of the past; they are rendered fairy-tale, even though they are factual and contemporary; they are covered with a patina of legendary antiquity, even though they amount to little more than the daily gossip of housewives.

This also serves to explain the reason for Boccaccio's choice of Federico degli Alberighi's name, which has nothing to do with realistic depiction of known incidents or local gossip, but is filled with an aura of remote and classical distance by the fact that it occurs in Dante. The Alberighi in fact flourished at the time of Cacciaguida, Dante's ancestor:[12]

> Io vidi li Ughi, e vidi i Catellini,
> Filippi, Greci, Ormanni e Alberichi,
> già nel calare, illustri cittadini.

> (I saw the Ughi, I saw the Catellini, / Filippi, Greci, Ormanni and Alberichi, / illustrious citizens already in decline) (*Paradiso*, XVI, 88–90)

The age of Coppo, his authority, the memory of him, the reference in Dante: these are all elements which serve to put a distance between Federico and the sphere of everyday housekeeping problems. They help to bathe him in the glow of the classical *raconteur*. 'In Firenze fu già' ('once used to live in our city'): the shopping-list has been deftly transformed into myth.

Notes

1 Philippe Sollers, *Logiques*, Éditions du Seuil, Paris, 1968.
2 Dante, *Paradiso*, XVII, 36; Sinclair's translation, 1971.
3 Frederick Crews, *The Pooh Perplex*, Barker, London, 1964.
4 A. A. Milne, *Winnie-the-Pooh*, Methuen, London, 1972, p. 2.
5 *Ibid.*, pp. 7–8.
6 See Getto's concept of 'l'arte di vivere', the art of living, in Getto, 1958.
7 See Getto, 1958; Russo, 1970; Branca, 1970; Baratto, 1970; etc.
8 The personalities of the various narrators were studied by Carducci and his school with meagre results. Only bawdy Dioneo survives as a real character on close analysis.
9 This is one of the crucial problems of the *Decameron*. There is no doubt, however, that the protagonists of the Tenth Day are not as saintly as they are usually supposed to be.

10 This example is taken from Morse Peckham, *Man's Rage for Chaos: Man, Biology and the Arts*, Chilton Books, Philadelphia, 1962.

11 McW, p. 463.

Dovete adunque sapere che Coppo di Borghese Domenichi (il qual fu nella nostra città, e forse ancora è), uomo di grande e di reverenda autorità ne' dí nostri, e per costumi e per virtù, molto più che per nobiltà di sangue, chiarissimo e degno di eterna fama et essendo già d'anni pieno, spesse volte delle cose passate, co' suoi vicini e con altri, si dilettava di ragionare. La qual cosa egli meglio, e con più ordine e con maggior memoria e ornato parlare che altro uom seppe fare. Era usato di dire tra l'altre sue belle cose, che in Firenze fu già un giovane chiamato Federigo di messer Filippo Alberighi (*Dec.*, V, 9).

12 Sinclair's translation, 1971.

Two

Literature and falsehood

Perhaps it is true that a book, any book, contains its own inbuilt reader's guide: instructions to the recipient about what to expect, how to interpret what he has before him. This idea of the book containing the key to itself is in a wide sense already implicit in any definition in terms of literary genre, since the initial classification constitutes a powerful and complex cultural influence on the way books are accepted. At its simplest level the notion can be summarized in a tautology: satire is satirical – it predisposes its reader to a satirical world view, it requires a satirical attitude to the text, it smoothes the way for the satirical gambit, and so on.

Here we are dealing with the most elementary manifestation of the reader's manual, i.e. the genre, one which invites a rough preliminary scrutiny of the various ways in which a particular book can be received. But it hardly provides an adequate account of the major masterpieces of literature, which usually stray far beyond the confines of a codified literary genre. Any revolutionary new work may find it convenient and advisable to give the reader a measure of assistance in the guise of a preface, or an introductory statement of intent. Alternatively, it can adopt the tactic of concealing such hints in the context, like a cryptogram, and tacitly inviting the reader to take part in an informational treasure hunt. Clearly this latter method already implies a special *modus legendi*. It becomes the reserve of readers sufficiently involved in the quest for the deep structure or idiosyncratic manner of a particular work to be prepared to spend the necessary time in locating and decoding its hidden cypher.

Nevertheless, the author's location of this key inside his work can hardly be chosen at random, unless he deliberately wants to unleash the patient scholar across the length and breadth of his text like the bookworms searching for the name of God in Borges' Library of Babel.[1] Under these circumstances it is the text itself which must develop a system of signposting capable of guiding the reader through a series of clues to the vital treasure. (The process is akin to the children's game where distance or closeness in relation to a hidden object is revealed by the cry 'cold' or 'hot'.) The system can be varied by adopting a spatial solution and locating the message at a key point in the material of the text. It can be placed, for example, at the beginning of the lines, as in an acrostic, or at the exact centre point of the whole work.

The latter is very probably the case with Dante's *Divine Comedy*. Several of Dante's commentators have in fact noticed how the seventeenth Canto of *Purgatorio* is the fifty-first out of the hundred of the whole *Comedy*, but that it acquires the central position if you eliminate for the purpose of calculation the opening Canto of the *Inferno* which stands as a *Proemium* to the whole poem. Now *Purgatorio* XVII also contains at its own centre a theoretical disquisition on Love (*l'amor naturale* and *l'amor d'animo*), and this complex analysis could be considered an interpretative key to the *Comedy* as a whole.

Strangely enough nobody seems to have transferred this kind of attention from the *Divine Comedy* to the *Decameron* (this worldly reflection of the other-worldly *Commedia*), which would seem to contain in the same central position of the text a *novella* which reads as a coded invitation to approach the whole book in a *special way*.

The *novella* in question is the first of the Sixth Day, and hence the fifty-first of Boccaccio's hundred. It is the relatively little known story of Madonna Oretta which initiates the series of 'witty sayings' for the Sixth Day. Oretta, a Florentine lady of noble birth, has taken part in a long walk through the countryside with a group of other ladies and knights. At a certain point she finds herself being entertained by one of the distinguished men of the party, who offers her a ride on his horse and insists on combining it with 'one of the finest tales in the world'.[2] The man's story, says Boccaccio, 'was indeed excellent'[3] but the knight, who was more skilful at sword-play than the art of story-telling, 'ruined it completely'.[4] Madonna Oretta is overcome, not so much by the story itself as the way it is being told: 'She began to perspire freely, and her heart missed several beats, as though she had fallen ill and was about to give up the ghost.'[5] Therefore, with the dual purpose of saving herself from the boredom of listening and offering a dignified escape-route to the knight, who 'had tied himself inextricably in knots',[6] she interrupts him 'in affable tones'[7] with the following *boutade*: 'Sir, you have taken me riding on a horse that trots very jerkily. Pray be good enough to set me down.'[8] At this, the knight, 'who was apparently far more capable of taking a hint than of telling a tale',[9] accepts her witticism and turns to telling her different stories, leaving the first unfinished.

From the point of view of content, this story (obviously I am referring to the one in which Oretta is protagonist rather than the unknown one which she has to put up with on horseback), is one of the weakest in the *Decameron*. The episode is banal almost to the point of total insignificance. There is no characterization whatsoever of the two people who figure in it; even the closing *riposte* falls rather flat. The critics, following their habitual tendency to concentrate on the subject which is communicated by way of the narrated facts rather than on the message enclosed in their stylistic treatment, have paid little attention to the story. In the analyses of the Sixth Day of the *Decameron* we usually have a rapid skirting of Madonna Oretta's horse-riding encounter in order to move to more weighty episodes. Muscetta can be taken as typical of this attitude: 'Madonna Oretta, the wife of Pope Boniface VIII's banker, is witty. But much more arresting is the quick-wittedness of Cisti the Baker. . . .'[10] It was Getto who provided the first exception, for he seemed to have sensed the exceptional rôle of the story (even though he has omitted to pick out its strategic placing) and dealt with it in the first four pages of the chapter 'Culto della forma e civiltà fiorentina nella sesta giornata' in his book on the *Decameron*.[11] Yet even Getto seems to insist a little too strongly on the content of the *novella*, when he builds up a somewhat implausible range of social and psychological meanings to redeem the story from the grey zone of narrative mediocrity into which he feels that it is otherwise bound to fall. The critic finds that Madonna Oretta's story is a 'delightful miniature which offers a momentary glimpse into the aristocratic life'.[12]

However, at this particular level it is not really clear how the *novella* is different from any number of other minor *vignettes* which feature either in the narrative or the *cornice* of the hundred *novelle*, and are equally effective as portrayals of the genteel existence of a group of well-born young Florentine friends. Many of these episodes are sketched with an equally vivid 'miniaturist's skill', and here it is enough to think of the games and jokes which the ten story-tellers indulge in at the end of several of the Days. Nor again is it much help to invoke Getto's celebrated concept of the 'art of living' in the *Decameron*, which leads him to find that 'that *novella*, rejoicing in its own delicate lyricism, finds its justification in the taste of a refined way of life, which in this case is presented as the art of conducting oneself elegantly in society, talking to the point and telling stories pleasantly'.[13] Against this view, it seems to me that the invention of Madonna Oretta (i.e. the words she utters) is on too restricted a level to make her story function as part of the complex social and ethical questions of the individual in society which is one of Boccaccio's major considerations in the *Decameron*.

Also I find that Getto's closing observations on the link between the historical situation and the psychological comment which might be drawn from it go further than the *novella* itself can justify:[14]

> The failure of this story-teller not only annoys the noblewoman, it really causes her profound discomfort. In a society that cultivates an exquisite sensitivity for form, this sort of aesthetic blunder transposes into a moral lapse and ultimately a physical disquiet, eliciting, as it does, reactions of irritation and consummate pain.

But this commentary is contradicted by the actual ending of the *novella*, where the lady graciously accepts a change of subject and welcomes other stories, which the knight will evidently make an effort to tell more fluently. It also misses the irony that runs through the whole narrative. What is misleading the critic, in the view of the present writer, is a determination to interpret at all costs what goes on inside the content of the *novella*. Getto is investigating the insignificant actions which the characters pass through; he is not responsive to the aesthetic information which the story in itself diffuses over the rest of the *Decameron*.

One is bound to admit that Getto comes close to an intuition on these lines in the final paragraph of his discussion of Madonna Oretta:[15]

The ideal which the ten story-tellers are living at that precise
moment, the nine who are listening no less than the single
one who is narrating, is the ideal of elegant presentation and
intelligent handling of the spoken word; this is also the ideal
stated by the tone and effect of the *novella* itself.

This is surely a much more fruitful line of approach. But I think
it can be extended a good deal further. If we follow the stylistic
message of the *novella* rather than its content, we may arrive at the
following overall interpretation: the story of Madonna Oretta,
in its strategic location at the very centre of the *Decameron*'s
hundred stories, is a story about how to relate and how not to
relate a story. It is therefore a *meta-novella*; in other words, a
novella dealing with the art of telling a *novella*.

As for the actual story which the knight tells his passenger on
the horse, we do not in fact know the plot; but we do know all
the details from it which are essential to the construction of the
meta-novella. We know, for example, that the knight's story 'in
itself was indeed excellent' (which is the vital point), but that it was
poorly related. In other words, the fifty-first *novella* of the
Decameron confirms in its readers a fact which they have only
just begun to realize: art is the enjoyment of forms, not of things.[16]
The beauty of the knight's story resides purely at the level of the
content, of its *signifié*. Thus it is nullified by the absence of a
corresponding beauty at the level of forms, of the *signifiant*. In
fact it is the latter element which determines the value and
effectiveness of this and any other story. Hence the force exerted by
the *signifiant* over the *signifié* operates at different levels: it affects
the relationship between Madonna Oretta and the knight; it
influences that between the narrator and his listeners in the
'lieta brigata' of the *Decameron*, as Getto suggests; and it tempers
the attitude of the readers of the *Decameron* to the work which they
have in their hands. At the very centre of the surface of its text
the *Decameron* provides us with a simple explanation of how the
Decameron is supposed to be read. It permits us to open a secret
chink in the book's construction and glimpse the internal strategy
which Boccaccio followed in its composition.

Thus one could go so far as to say that Madonna Oretta's
novella is an implicit invitation to conduct a formalist reading of the
Decameron.[17] Perhaps a deep-rooted intellectual perversion or

aesthetic prejudice has prevented the *Decameron*'s readers from perceiving this message for 600 years. Our forebears in criticism were therefore perverse in their determination to absorb facts and information from a literary text, as though the author were a reliable chronicler of events instead of the sly old charlatan we knew all along, doling out infamous hints which we were forced to take seriously. Why should we be different and act any better? The fact is, our perversion will be of another kind, leading towards excess of interpretation, unabated exuberance, captious exegesis: in short, an over-ambitious hermeneutics. Hence the following pages.

So the exact centre of a literary work can be chosen for the location of the message, which in any case cannot be too well hidden if the author is so concerned that it should reach his readership. Its secrecy also consists in the fact that it is not an addition to the text, as is the case with the introduction to the Fourth Day, but rather a possible adjustment to our way of reading the text.

Alternatively, the author can slip the reader a surreptitious *billet doux* with his first hand-shake, by enclosing the message in the opening *novella*. Edgar Allan Poe's example of the purloined letter calls to mind a model of concealment, but could also suggest the possibility of false concealment, one of the innumerable forms of peekaboo which any self-respecting writer knows how to play against his readers. In the story of Cepperello which rings up the curtain on Boccaccio's hundred tales, we may well be dealing with an advance notice to the book's readers[18] concerning the content of the whole work. This message may well be stating what the book is: a tapestry of falsehood, a pack of lies.

Perhaps at this point we should sum up the plot of *Decameron*, I, 1: Cepperello, a crook, killer, sodomite, counterfeiter, drunkard, blasphemer, and trickster, 'il piggiore uomo che mai nascesse' ('the worst man ever born')[19] is selected by an important financier for the difficult mission of recovering moneys owed by bad debtors in Burgundy. He takes shelter in the home of two Florentine brothers, money-lenders by profession, falls ill while there, and very shortly finds himself at death's door. To avoid causing his hosts any trouble, he makes his confession to a friar, inventing himself a completely fictitious personality as a man who has been pious and devout, chaste, honourable and scrupulous to the point of excess in his duties towards his neighbour and his religious devotions. As the confessional dialogue proceeds, a picture is gradually formed of a saintly figure who could be taken as a paradigm of the Christian life-style. This in fact is what the friar ends up doing: when Cepperello dies, he promotes the life of this arch-sinner as a model for imitation, and once Cepperello has been triumphantly buried in a local chapel, he is revered by the populace of the town and his body becomes the means by which God performs a whole series of miracles.

It is a *novella* which has elicited from the various critics who have approached it some widely conflicting interpretations. At times they have advanced personal views which, once imposed on the text, seem to make it into a kind of theological portent. Without burrowing too far back into the past and resuscitating the views of a Leonardo Salviati, a Voltaire, Olimpia Morato, Vincenzo Borghini, Cardinal Bellarmino or Francesco De Sanctis, it is enough to consider the range of twentieth-century interpretations of the *novella* to see completely contrasted theories holding at one moment that the story is a carefully worked-out theological statement, at the next that it is a farcical satire against sainthood. At any rate, it will be easy to imagine the present writer's smirk of complicity as he offers yet another account of the story to confuse the situation even further.

The main dividing-line between the standard critical positions concerns the rôle of Cepperello, the protagonist: is he a sinner or a virtuoso artist? The point is, which is the more important? On which of these two facets of the scoundrel is the author concentrating? It will be as well to use these two convenient terms, 'sinners' and 'artists' to label the two divergent schools of thought on the story.

According to the 'sinners', the splendid opening portrait of Cepperello 'is a sinister piece of writing, among the finest ever produced by Boccaccio . . . a harsh painting in black brush-strokes'.[20] Cepperello sums up within himself the three basic mortal sins (meanness, lust and pride):[21] he is evidently a modern version of Judas, and the sentence 'he was perhaps the worst man ever born'[22] suggests as its model the Gospel text referring to history's greatest traitor.[23] This would make the *Decameron* into the model itinerary of a soul progressing towards eventual salvation, and follows the influential mediaeval tradition established by Dante in the *Divine Comedy* and by countless authors of rhetorical and erudite works. So Boccaccio is conducting his readers from the Judas/Cepperello image of *Decameron*, I, 1 to the Mary/Griselda figure of *Decameron*, X, 10 in a continuous ascent from the depths of Hell to the heights of Heaven.[24] 'The story of Ser Ciappelletto is the one which, in its links to the *cornice* [the external frame] of the *Decameron*, succeeds in touching on the most exalted theological problems.'[25] To be a proper sinner Cepperello is bound to believe in God[26] and yet live out his wickedness until death.[27] Therefore he is presented as a believer, and this faith which he professes is what arouses the admiration of the Florentine brothers, since they are amazed by the sacrifice which he is making by placing at risk the salvation of his immortal soul.[28] Cepperello, in accordance with his *éthique noire*,[29] chooses his perdition 'with a complete awareness that he is going to be damned'.[30] This damnation seems to follow on inevitably since at the end of the story it is stated that Cepperello is now 'in Hell, in the hands of the devil':[31] 'a terrifying comment', says a critic.[32]

The 'sinners' read the ending of the story with even richer extravagance: in the mad challenge hurled by the supreme malefactor against the divine rules that control the sacrament of confession, they argue that it is Cepperello himself who comes out of it humiliated and vanquished: his artistry has availed him nothing. Not only does he end up in Hell to pay the penalty of his feckless contempt for the Creator, but also his sacrilege is transformed into a pious and worthy deed. God, in his infinite wisdom, converts the irreligious canonization of a Judas not into a triumph for Cepperello and a humiliation of the Church, but rather into the posthumous defeat of the evil notary and a fresh glory for Church and Deity; the relics of the sinful body in fact become a secret link between Divine Providence and the prayers of the devout.[33]

The 'artists', as a school of interpreters of *Decameron*, I, 1, do not take Ser Ciappelletto to be a believer: 'the story is neither positive nor negative on the subject of religion.'[34] There is no question of irreligiousness: religion as such is neither present nor absent in the *Decameron*: there is merely a serene indifference to anything connected with religious practices.[35] If the focal point of the story is not in fact the denigration of cult worship of saints, as De Sanctis held,[36] then we shall have to shift our attention to Cepperello's art of living, to the stylistic exuberance which parallels the abomination of his misdeeds.[37] 'Qualis artifex pereo' are the words of the Emperor Nero which Croce would ideally place in the mouth of the dying sinner.[38]

No moral judgment is passed in the *novella*,[39] except perhaps for Boccaccio's enthusiastic comments on the hypocrisy and intellectual games-playing of his created character. Clearly Boccaccio has a more than sneaking admiration for Cepperello, as he has for the other great spinner of yarns in the *Decameron*, Frate Cipolla.[40] The *Decameron* exalts the art of living; its first *novella* praises the art of dying.[41] Cepperello is not an atheist,[42] or a Vanni Fucci[43] (and not even a modern bourgeois Capaneo, as one critic suggests):[44] he has the untroubled disposition of an artist.[45] The opening page is far from sinister; but is rather pervaded with a bewildered and casual gaiety.[46] The illness, death and sacrilege in the story arouse neither compassion, scandal nor horror in its characters or readers:[47] there is only a vague feeling of the poetic effect of the skilful manœuvring of the protagonist,[48] the pure hero of the power of human words.[49] And so the 'artists' tend to argue.

Meanwhile, on the death mask of Cepperello, now revered by the ingenuous citizenry of Burgundy, there survives an enigmatic and indecipherable grin.[50] Believer or atheist? Is he one of the damned or one of the blessed? An instrument of evil or a saint who performs miracles? Cepperello's features give nothing away, while his *novella* gives way to oddly conflicting interpretations. Its greatness seems to me to consist precisely in the way it can ride high over the poking curiosity of critics such as ourselves and include our most injudicious proposals and embarrassing advances to this text with which we are trying to flirt.

If we turn our attention to the marginal areas of the *novella*, its *incipit* and its *finis*, and pretend for a moment to take the text *au pied de la lettre* where it exalts the mysterious ways of divine benevolence, then all of a sudden we are faced by a vanquished sinner instead of a triumphant one, and his farcical miracles become full-fledged miracles with a divine seal of authenticity. This interpretation turns an amoral story into a model of morality, and any residual amusement on the part of its audience into hushed awe at the mysteries of faith. In a way this could be seen as the latest trick the villain Cepperello has succeeded in pulling off on us through the agency of his contemporary recorder and his not so contemporary critics who have turned things so remarkably upside down in their exegesis (yet it seems to me that the stylistic evidence of the text still points firmly in the opposite direction). One seems to be left with a potential *novella*, reinforced by all the actual *meta-novelle* which can be added as glosses to it. In the present chapter I should like to jot down one such *meta-novella*.

If the fifty-first *novella*, at the centre of the collection, is a signpost directing us towards a particular way of reading the whole, it also seems plausible that the first story in the *Decameron* may have a similar function. This is, after all, the story which opens and sets the tone for a whole collection; it establishes a way of narrating and a way of reading. Thus it could well be a cryptic piece of information concerning the *Decameron*; it may stand as a symbol for a literature which is metaphorically exemplified in Cepperello.

It is a story which instructs us in some of the techniques which can operate transformations on reality by the mere power of words. The whole range of Cepperello's heinous sins is transformed, as it passes through the filter of his confessional voice, into a set of their opposite virtues. The worst man who ever lived is transformed into a saint, and wickedness becomes the ability to generate miracles. Words, the diabolic instruments of falsehood, overturn reality by offering us a picture in which everything is false: our pleasure as readers comes from enjoying this sensation of total falseness. One by one we sample a set of untrue notations, testing their guaranteed mendacity against the previous fictional reality which was provided for us at the opening of the story: Cepperello's consummate villainy. This parallels the standard literary process which adopts the elements of everyday reality and converts them into fiction. Stories use men, women, houses, streets, fields, animals, trees, plausible events and possible adventures, meetings, wars, kidnapping and love affairs. All these ingredients are then transformed into a tissue of lies, into massive accumulations of false and erroneous information, of adventures which never took place performed by human beings who never existed in ways that have little bearing on human experience. And however hard we try to argue, following Picasso, that art is not truth, but a falsehood which helps us to come nearer to truth, the fact still remains that our aesthetic palate is greedy for this type of falsehood which we read off against the grid of things as we actually know them to be. The story of Cepperello suggests itself as a model of art's systematic and high-handed deformation of the truth.

In other words, it seems obvious that the hero's false confession can be read as an analogue of the literary process. It remains to be seen if it is useful to try to use it as such. We wish to know whether the implicit parallel will actually help us to read the story with greater enjoyment and awareness of what is going on; will it help us to appreciate the key for our reading which Boccaccio seems to have suggested at the outset of the Hundred Tales? In my view the answer is 'yes', and for this reason I shall venture to propose a new angle of approach to *Decameron*, I, 1. Perhaps the duty of the critic is not that of clearing the waters by imposing a rigid interpretative scheme on the text with which he is dealing, but rather to muddy things up and suggest a contradictory plurality of readings which draws both the attentive and the careless reader into the realm of hermeneutical delectation.

Cepperello, therefore, is not merely an artist and master of verbal inventiveness with a genius for deception, but also a negative print of the writer, who is the master of all deceptions. Cepperello's amazing ability to create a fictitious universe and seat himself at its centre on the throne of sainthood parallels the writer's ability to create the far larger fictitious universe of the *Decameron* which shines with the unabated radiance of lying. Cepperello's final victory is the victory of word over deed, false over true, unreal over real; thus it bears a straight resemblance to the *Decameron* itself, which is a glorious defence of the prevarications of writing.

This gives the initial position of the *novella* its real significance, not just in the way which Branca indicates (the long path from Cepperello/Judas to Griselda /Virgin Mary, the process from the worst man in the world to the best possible woman), but because it comes to represent a guide to the reader informing him how to manipulate the complex narrative machinery of the hundred stories in the *Decameron*. Cepperello lies to the gullible friar while at the same time winking at us not-so-gullible readers and communicating the very fact that he is lying. Boccaccio, in his turn, is lying, but by way of the first character in his book he lets us know that this is so, and that his whole creation must in fact be read as a magnificent edifice of interlocking falsehoods.

Thus the first *novella* becomes an aesthetic model of literature as falsehood, and the artist as counterfeiter: it is a reminder of the irrevocable immorality of art (*Plato docet*). This is not all that far from the opening of *La vie très horrifique du Grand Gargantua,* miraculously discovered in a little volume which was 'gros, gras, grand, gris, joly, petit, moisy . . .' ('large, fat, big, grey, nice, small, mouldy'):[51] here the alliterative and assonantic series of epithets serves to determine, with its own internal contradictions, the fatal mendacity of the work.

The story, as its narrator Panfilo expressly says, is one of God's 'marvellous works', and it is right that God, who is 'immutable'[52] should open the *Decameron*, which deals with the infinite muta- bility of His creation (from Cepperello to Griselda). Certainly God's creation also includes the incredible tactics of a divinity who 'answers those who pray him'[53] even if 'we appoint as our advocate in His majestic presence one who has been cast by Him into eternal exile'.[54]

But part of this creation is also the sinner and the liar, hence the art of lying, or art *tout court*. 'It is proper, dearest ladies, that everything done by man should begin with the sacred and admirable name of Him that was maker of all things.'[55] If God is the maker of all things, he must also be the maker of literary art, and it represents a suitably pious step on Boccaccio's part to commence his great work with this exaltation of fiction and falsehood, which are, after all, further manifestations of God's greatness.

I have deliberately pushed my interpretation to the point of paradox in order to set it against the other paradoxical position which sees the episode as an *exemplum* of the inevitable defeat and punishment of sin. Panfilo's opening statements are so vague that they could be taken any way the reader likes. In any case, I would argue that my line of approach to the *novella* is backed up by firmer stylistic evidence than that of some of the 'sinners'.

Boccaccio's writing is often enigmatic and impassive (as at the close of the present *novella*, but I shall discuss this aspect further on): yet here it is open and frank, and uses a wide range of

stylistic devices[56] to exalt the glorious mendacity of Cepperello's
confession: Boccaccio is out to uphold the dignity of falsehood.

> It is said, then, that Musciatto Franzesi, having become a
> fine gentleman after acquiring enormous wealth and fame as a
> merchant in France, was obliged to come to Tuscany with
> the brother of the French king, the Lord Charles Stateless,
> who had been urged and encouraged to come by Pope
> Boniface. But finding that his affairs, as is usually
> the case with merchants, were entangled here, there, and
> everywhere.[57]

This quotation represents the beginning of the story of Cepperello proper. It offers an imposing historical documentation[58]
with precise accuracy of chronological, personal, geographic,
economic and political details. Not only are the King, Pope and
other important characters presented with all their dates and
particulars in order. Even Musciatto Franzesi is a historical figure
and his life can be documented. In fact, literary criticism has
gone to great lengths to gather information about his various
vicissitudes.[59] But even the figure of Cepperello is historically
documented: there is a Cepperello Dietaiuti da Prato, who did
actually have business relations with Musciatto Franzesi.[60]
Apparently, however, he was not a notary and therefore not
entitled to the title *Ser*:[61] this is the first chink in the factual
presentation of the story.

At the opening of the *novella* the narrator is offering us the basic
pattern of a historical chronicle with its implied impartial presentation of actual occurrences. Such sturdy guarantees put the seal of
authenticity on the true facet of the story and set up the pseudo-
legitimacy of its false elements, which in fact amount almost to the
whole *novella*. So the story and its documentation are prostituted
to the purpose of providing a semblance of truth to what is
resoundingly untrue: what is false is transformed into something
faintly plausible by the astute introduction of historically verifiable
data.

It is hard to agree with Getto, where he argues that while the
chronological location of events is intentionally precise, their
geographical location (the town in Burgundy where the two
Florentine brothers are living) is left unstated so that nobody can
actually check up on the worship of a Saint Cepperello.[62] In the

Decameron Boccaccio seems quite unconcerned with this type of consideration: the problem is not so much one of inventing a true and real situation (which would immediately be rendered pointless, if my interpretation is correct, by the fact that Cepperello's story is a grandiose metaphor), but rather the task of predisposing the readers' minds to a passive enjoyment of the big lie. In other words, the narrator is saying to his readers that his story is a complete yarn, but the way he is going to tell it is such that the reader will forget this fact and fall under the persuasive influence of fiction. We are not concerned whether the story about Madonna Oretta, the apotheoses of Cepperello and Griselda (the central, first and last *novella* in the *Decameron*; all in a strategic position, yet firmly rooted in quasi-contemporary reality and the Italian geography which would be familiar to Boccaccio's readers) are true and really happened: what matters is that they should be acceptable. The only operative criterion is an aesthetic and artistic one: it is not art which stands as *ancilla historiae*, but history which is *ancilla artis*.

Musciatto Franzesi is looking for a man without any scruples who can go and collect the debts owed to him by the difficult and unwilling people of Burgundy. All of a sudden a certain Cepperello occurs to him, a man wrongly called 'Ciappelletto' by the French 'thinking that . . . the word Cepperello signified chapel, which in their language means garland'.[63] In a way this already puts what amounts to a saintly halo around the hero at the very start of his story which is going to end with sainthood.[64] The bizarre figure of Cepperello is presented to us in a portrait which in its perverse and brilliant subtlety can hardly have a parallel in the whole of the *Decameron*:[65]

> This Ciappelletto was a man of the following sort: a notary by profession, he would have taken it as a slight upon his honour if one of his legal deeds (and he drew up very few of them) were discovered to be other than false. In fact, he would have drawn up free of charge as many false documents as were requested of him, and done it more willingly than one who was highly paid for his services. He would take great delight in giving false testimony, whether asked for it or not. In those days, great reliance was placed in France upon sworn declarations, and since he had no

scruples about swearing falsely, he used to win, by these
nefarious means, every case in which he was required to
swear upon his faith to tell the truth. He would take
particular pleasure, and a great amount of trouble, in stirring
up enmity, discord and bad blood between friends, relatives
and anybody else; and the more calamities that ensued, the
greater would be his rapture. If he were invited to witness a
murder or any other criminal act, he would never refuse,
but willingly go along; and he often found himself cheerfully
assaulting or killing people with his own hands. He was a
mighty blasphemer of God and His Saints, losing his temper
on the tiniest pretext, as if he were the most hot-blooded man
alive. He never went to church, and he would use foul
language to pour scorn on all of her sacraments, declaring
them repugnant. On the other hand, he would make a
point of visiting taverns and other places of ill repute, and
supplying them with his custom. Of women he was as
fond as dogs are fond of a good stout stick: in their opposite,
he took greater pleasure than the most depraved man on
earth. He would rob and pilfer as conscientiously as if he
were a saintly man making an offering. He was such a prize
glutton and heavy drinker, that he would occasionally suffer
for his over-indulgence in a manner that was highly
indecorous. He was a gambler and a card-sharper of the
first order. But why do I lavish so many words upon him?
He was perhaps the worst man ever born.

The whole description is exceptional and unusual in the
authorial strategy of the *Decameron*. Normally the characters of
the book are, as I suggest in chapter 3,[66] 'voyageurs sans bagage',
'travellers without luggage', totally immersed in a grammatical
and narrative present tense; about their past, or their physical
and emotional make-up, we readers are vouchsafed precious little
information. The typical *Decameron* character is born and invents
his identity inside the narrative that concerns him. The adjectives
that qualify him at the commencement of his story are stinted and
non-specific. As examples of this we could take four descriptions
from the stories immediately following Cepperello: 'an extremely
upright and honest man';[67] 'a strikingly beautiful girl,
perhaps some local farmhand's daughter';[68] 'more beautiful and

worthy of esteem than any other woman in the world';[69] 'a certain law-abiding citizen, endowed with far more money than common sense'.[70] After such a perfunctory description provided about him at the opening of his story, the Boccaccio character tends to grow into being by means of the continual accumulation of precise details that spring directly from his conduct inside the narrative. The character is not, therefore, described, but describes himself by his line of conduct. In this sense the Andreuccio of *Decameron*, II, 5, one of Boccaccio's most celebrated *novelle*, is absolutely typical: he is a horse-dealer who comes from Perugia to Naples to buy some stock. This is all we are told about Andreuccio. The character is constructed by his actions inside the story of which he is the protagonist.

But this is clearly not the case with Cepperello. We need a maximum amount of information on this particular character, since all his subsequent declarations in the confession will need to be weighed up and compared against his initial description. But what is the precise effect of the description? In what way do we readers record the moral turpitude in Cepperello's extraordinary portrait? I have mentioned already that the 'sinners' among its critics emphasize the sinister qualities of the story's opening portrait. Branca, in particular, bases his polemic against Auerbach's rather hurried reading of the story[71] (which holds that there is no element whatsoever of moral judgment in it), precisely on the interpretation of the opening section on Cepperello's portrait.[72]

Yet I would still like to disagree with the 'sinners' line: for at least one reader, namely myself, Cepperello's portrait does not exert a sinister or frightening effect, but rather an exhilarating fascination. Far from representing a dire warning against the gloomy perils of sin, it stands as a lusty reminder of how attractive it can be to be wicked. It is not so much a sermon on morals as a propaganda statement on behalf of vice. The psychological test can be phrased very crudely as follows: the description instils the desire to live like Cepperello, and not the wish to take holy orders and become a friar.

To illustrate my point I should like to take a similar occurrence which gives rise to an episode in the *Divine Comedy*. In the twenty-fourth Canto of *Inferno* Dante is faced by one of the most shockingly wicked characters in the Afterworld, Vanni Fucci, a thief and blasphemer who directly challenges God's punishment by making an absurdly vulgar gesture towards the Creator ('Le mani alzò con ambedue le fiche',[73] i.e. he is turning to God and telling Him 'Up yours!'). In presenting his credentials as one of the damned to Dante, Vanni Fucci says that he had stolen sacred articles from a church:[74]

in giù son messo tanto perch'io fui
ladro alla sagrestia de' belli arredi.

In John Sinclair's translation of the *Comedy* this becomes: 'I am put down so far because I was a thief in the Sacristy of the Fair Ornaments.'[75] At the elementary level of our poetic reception of these lines, we readers are bound to feel the attraction of those 'Fair Ornaments' whose beauty is being exalted by the text. None of us could confidently declare that he is quite immune to the temptation of stealing such inviting articles from the Sacristy himself. The fascination of this *fair* line is bound to catch us up in a feeling of sympathetic involvement with Vanni Fucci, and makes us unconscious accomplices in his sacrilegious crime. At a literary level, crime is poetically convincing when it succeeds in disposing the reader to accept the hypothesis of his own complicity in what is being evoked on the page. The inevitability of a poetic crime (Andreuccio stealing the ring in *Decameron*, II, 5; Raskolnikov murdering the old woman; Mersault killing his Arab, and so on) implies a silent but operative involvement on the part of us readers. The same thing has happened in the quoted passage from Dante's *Inferno*, where the sacrilegious robbery becomes a *datum* of our imagination, not an entry in the penal code.

The catalogue of Cepperello's vices falls under the same heading: each of them shrieks out from the page, vibrant with life and underlined by the author's impassioned interest in the sinful details. This sense of joyous involvement and full-blooded vitality is transferred from the fictional sinner to the sinner lurking inside every reader by a marked emphasis on the pleasure experienced in Cepperello's acts of transgression: '... willingly ... great delight ... particular pleasure ... the greater would be his rapture ... cheerfully ... always willing to visit taverns and other places of ill repute ... greater pleasure. ...'[76] Oh, what a great life, the life of a sinner! The seven capital sins, and also the venial sins tacked on to them, turn into a parade of urbane delights. Forging documents and presenting false witness become moral duties, causing extreme discomfort in anyone who fails to abide by them. Sowing discord becomes a promise of endless amusement; theft and murder are a joy to perform. Blasphemy is a triumph of human speech, and this is stated with a gloriously solemn rhythm in the words: 'as if he were the most hot-blooded man alive'.[77] Sacrilege becomes something to boast about, and assiduous visits to drinking taverns and brothels constitute a triumph of the flesh. Sexual deviation becomes pure enchantment, and moves outside the ambit of moral condemnation. Even the nasty effects of Cepperello's gluttony and drunkenness fail to evoke a sense of disgust and in fact invite energetic human participation from the reader. When Cepperello gives way to vomiting ('tanto che alcuna volta sconciamente gli facea noia'),[78] his sickness has a glorious Rabelaisian quality: it achieves the epic dimension. But at this point I could mimic Boccaccio himself and say 'But why do I lavish so many words?[79] Cepperello is a dynamic model for human imitation. He invites our enthusiastic allegiance, and has little to do with a sinister picture designed to remind us of the perils of the flesh.

His portrait, like the rest of the story, is based on a constant device of turning things back to front so that facts and forms present the double aspect characteristic of the mediaeval *topos* which showed *il mondo alla rovescia*, a topsy-turvy world. There is a Cepperello-villain and a Ciappelletto with the halo of a saint. There is his physical portrait with brief information, the emphasis falling on the splendid diminutive *assettatuzzo* (see below, p. 38); also, his moral portrait, drawn in strong and decisive lines, with heavy accentuation on the adjectives in the superlative: 'this elegant little figure is a monster of the most enormous perversion.'[80] Furthermore, there is a remarkable insistence on antiphrasis, which couples together positive adverbs and expressions of satisfaction ('volentieri', 'allegrezza', etc.) with the most unspeakable and negative actions.[81] Again, there is a constant reversal of professional ethics: the notary, whose job is to vouch for the truth, in fact becomes a guarantor for falsehood; the merchant is a perjurer; the banker is a crook.[82]

What is more, we expect the sentences to work out in a certain way, and then the narrator completely alters and mocks our anticipation: 'There is an unexpected dissonance between the premiss and its conclusion'.[83] For instance, we know that Cepperello was a notary, and are told that 'he would have taken it as a slight upon his honour if one of his legal deeds. . . .'[84] Here the next words we might expect are something like ' . . . one of his legal deeds showed some irregularity'. In fact the sentence continues: 'were discovered to be other than false'.[85]

This technique of the world upside down runs through the rest of the *novella*: the sodomite turns out to have been a virgin all his life; the blasphemer of the Lord and the Saints has become a devout man of the church; the trickster was an ultra-scrupulous businessman; the glutton and drunkard was an occasional sinner who happened to crave 'for those dainty little wild herb salads',[86] and so on. All this means that the final metamorphosis of the arch-sinner into a holy man of God is in perfect keeping with the stylistic make-up of the *novella*.

Let us concentrate for a moment on the last touch in Cepperello's splendid portrait, 'Egli era il piggiore uomo che mai nascesse', which Branca insists is modelled on a verse from the Gospels:[87]

Ciappelletto's sinful excesses are all merged in one by an expression which is clearly allusive, referring to the man who has proverbially been considered the most wicked, hypocritical and treacherous in history, the man who sold Christ himself with a kiss: 'Egli era il piggiore uomo forse che mai nascesse' (I, 1, 15); 'Bonum erat si non esset natus homo ille' (Gospel of St Mark, XIV, 21, and compare St Matthew XXVI, 24).

Branca also argues[88] that we are dealing with:

an itinerary 'a principio horribilis et fetidus, in fine prosperus, desiderabilis et gratus'; a grand design which 'inchoat asperitatem alicuius rei sed eius materia prospere terminatur.' A gallery of figures ranging from Ciappelletto/ Judas to Griselda/Virgin Mary.

I find these analogies somewhat bewildering. The sentence from the Gospels is fairly far from the phrase in the *Decameron*, and is for that matter equally applicable to Judas or to Job: 'Let the day perish wherein I was born.'[89] It could also recall the man in

Ecclesiastes: 'Wherefore I praised the dead which are already dead more than the living which are yet alive. Yea, better is he than both they, which hath not yet been.'[90] The sentence from the Gospels condemns the supreme traitor with the worst possible insult available to human experience: 'it was better if he had not been born'. The expression in the *Decameron* is surely sly, and hand-picked to close Cepperello's grand portrait on a note of epic farce. This superlative of degree, 'piggiore uomo che mai nascesse', is being applied to a little chap pernickety in his sartorial habits ('assettatuzzo') and can only render him that much more likeable by extolling his incredible vitality. Hence the word 'piggiore' has come to be a complimentary epithet, and this is implied by the stylistic evidence of the passage under consideration. And one has only to think of another 'horrible man', Guccio Balena, the servant of Frate Cipolla,[91] who had 'nine failings, any one of which, had it been found in Solomon or Aristotle or Seneca, would have sufficed to vitiate all the ingenuity, all the wisdom, and all the saintliness they ever possessed'.[92] Yet nobody would consider Guccio as a counterpart of Judas.

Perhaps it is time to define what I mean by 'stylistic evidence' in the case of such a refined stylist as the author of the *Decameron*. Where every stylistic effect is calculated, the critic will clearly be looking for subtle edges and tiny alternative senses in the discourse; he will register any unusual device which seems to move the overall meaning of a passage in a different direction from the way its simple content is moving. Obviously only the crudest writers would actually interrupt the flow of their narrative to turn to the readers and make a theatrical wink inviting them to scoff at some event or character in his text, or to read it allegorically, as Dante sometimes requires of his reader:[93]

Mirate la dottrina che s'asconde,
sotto 'l velame delli versi strani.

A writer's tongue-in-cheek should never become painfully visible; it is best for it to lurk just inside the humorist's mouth.

Suppose we take as an example *Decameron*, VII, 7 (the splendid *novella* of Lodovico and Beatrice):[94] a young nobleman called Lodovico falls in love in the best courtly tradition (e.g. Jaufré Rudel)[95] with Beatrice, a Bolognese lady married to Egano de Galluzzi, simply on the basis of what he has heard about her

beauty. He goes off to Bologna, where he succeeds in becoming
the favourite servant in the Galluzzi household. During a trip
away from home by the husband, Lodovico starts playing chess
with Beatrice and lets her win several times, though he never
stops emitting long and mournful sighs. Beatrice asks him the
reason for all this sighing, at which Lodovico tells her the whole
story of his love for her: the lady yields to the young man's
desires and Boccaccio makes the following comment:[96]

> Ah, how singularly sweet is the blood of Bologna! How
> admirably you rise to the occasion in moments such as these!
> Sighs and tears were never to your liking: entreaties have
> always moved you, and you were ever susceptible to a
> lover's yearnings. If only I could find words with which to
> commend you as you deserve, I should never grow tired of
> singing your praises!

The content of this declaration can be taken literally,[97] and still
fits into a thematic *continuum* in the *Decameron* which includes the
stories of Nastagio degli Onesti[98] and Tedaldo degli Elisei.[99]
None the less there is a stylistic presence in the passage which
hints at a different overall message from that conveyed by the
sum of all the words' meanings. The traditional sexual availability
of women in Bologna, already mentioned in classical literature (it
is enough to think of Catullus' *Bononiensis Rufa*)[100] is being
ironically underlined here by the exaggerated opening invoca-
tion: 'O singolar dolcezza'; it is also suggested by the pedantic
symmetry of the clause patterns: 'né di lagrime nè di sospiri . . .
a' prieghi pieghevoli e agli amorosi disideri arrendevol'; by the
linguistic exuberance of the closing sentence: 'mai sazia etc.;
and finally by the odd and otherwise unjustifiable synaesthesia:
'vedrebbe la voce', 'to see the voice'.[101] Such an excessive
concentration of stylistic effects must convey a special message of
its own, suffusing the passage with a subtle veil of irony which
really comes to provide the following meaning: 'The ladies of
Bologna are worthy of all praise; they are to be credited for being
femmes de petite vertu; all honour to such beautiful creatures',
or something along these lines. This makes it less surprising when
Madonna Beatrice's behaviour in the second part of the *novella*
turns out to be among the most wicked and scandalous in the
whole *Decameron*. Yet both readings are legitimate.

To return to the opening portrait of Cepperello, I think we can
now see how important it is to distinguish between the straight
evidence of single words and the strategic impact of word-
placement and linguistic resonances. The choice of words itself,
and even single sentences taken on their own, tend to confirm the
sinister qualities of the portrait; but the overall structure of the
page subverts and makes a mockery of this impression.[102] The
sum has turned out to be a contradiction of all its parts.

The story of the first *novella* continues with Cepperello accepting
the debt-collecting job offered by Musciatto and going off to
Burgundy: 'And there, in a gentle and amiable fashion that ran
contrary to his nature, as though he were holding his anger in
reserve as a last resort . . .'[103] Cepperello's initial moves
are cautious: 'he suggests a cat holding in its claws',[104] says
a critic who follows a psychological approach to the story. But
a tactical interpretation of the *novella* would see this muted
mood at the beginning as a deliberate contrast to Cepperello's
unforeseeable and capricious behaviour as it will be revealed
later in the narrative. He takes lodgings in the house of two
Florentine brothers, money-lenders and friends of Musciatto
Franzesi, but falls sick with an illness that Boccaccio casually and
dismissively defines as 'il male della morte',[105] literally, 'the
sickness to death'. 'His illness, like his subsequent death, does
not arouse the slightest compassion',[106] is the comment of another
critic. However, this is not a sign of 'aesthetic imperturbability'[107]
on Boccaccio's part, but clear evidence that he is conscious of the
symbolic and functional rôle of the short story character,
who is not, fortunately, a worshipped idol, a 'Madame-Bovary-
c'est-moi', as in a nineteenth century-novel. Even if Cepperello
seems to be revered and exalted into a grand figure in a scene
such as the opening portrait, this does not imply that the author
need indulge elsewhere in irrelevant sentimentality about the
untimely illness of a being who after all exists only as a creation of
paper and ink. Such sentimental involvement is invited neither
from the writer nor from his readers.

The story continues with Ciappelletto lying in his bed and
overhearing a conversation between the two money-lenders, who
fear that if the arch-sinner dies in their home they are bound to
suffer inevitably: if he confesses his many sins or if he dies
without receiving the Sacrament, either way he is not going to be

welcome in any church, and his body will be tossed into a ditch. This in turn might cause a popular outcry against 'these Lombard dogs',[108] the heretical and despicable money-lenders which the brothers are conscious is their class and label. They conclude that either way things will go badly for them.

Now Branca, who sees the whole *Decameron* as a grand epic celebration of fourteenth-century Italian mercantile enterprise, has rightly drawn attention to the ruthless business ethos which runs through the story, and to the painful picture of the merchants' life in France, profiteers subjected to the constant hatred of the populace.[109] The alarm which the brothers feel conveys something of the terror and xenophobia which had caused endless persecution towards the end of the thirteenth and in the first half of the fourteenth century.[110] Mercantile interest is an absolute law to which all must submit; it is in this sense that the two brothers must weigh up the possible consequences of the sinner's death as it might affect their business activity, let alone whether it might cost their lives ('stealing our goods')[111] and are objectively conscious of the reason for such general hostility to them ('because of our profession which they consider iniquitous').[112]

Even Cepperello reacts to the money-lenders' anxiety with a proposal that seems to match the requirements of a business situation, and his relationship with God is ironically cast as a series of entries in a ledger-book: 'I have done our good Lord so many injuries while I lived, that to do Him another now that I am dying will be neither here nor there.'[113] The speech suggests a businessman who has had dealings with the authorities in Heaven, or at least it has the tone of one who can conceive of no other relation except the familiar layout based on two columns of debit and credit in an accounts book. It can hardly convey a total awareness of damnation, as Branca insists.[114] Cepperello is toying with a plan that involves a certain risk but is undertaken out of loyalty to colleagues and compatriots.[115] The concept of a divine entity is missing; God has become a worldly figure and one's relationship with Him involves a degree of aggressive frivolity.

This, surely, is the psychology and sociology of the scene, and represents the point of departure and not a point of arrival in the *novella*. To save his colleagues from a tricky situation, a regular confession *comme il faut*, i.e. with an adequate amount of deceit, would have been sufficient.[116] It wasn't necessary to develop Cepperello into a saint and have him causing miracles. The stylistic exuberance of Cepperello's utterance goes considerably further than merely underlining the sociological point I have been labouring. And to take it on a purely psychological level would fail to account for its very exuberance and weaken the story until it presented a merely psychotic figure.

Whatever happens, we must not lose sight of the other, vital dimension in the *novella* (existing side by side with the sociological and psychological version of events which are by no means negated by it). This is the level at which the narrative has a symbolic suggestiveness that converts a given event or observation into something subtler, or in any case different, from what it appears to mean. There is no other way of justifying the sense of outrage that runs throughout the story. It is this suggestiveness which transforms a sinner into a saint, his confession into pure farce, a piece of contemporary news-reporting into a fabled legend, and the *novella* itself into a *meta-novella*.

Cepperello asks the money-lenders to summon 'the holiest and ablest friar you can find, if there is such a one'.[117] This in fact will give the protagonist a worthy figure to play opposite him. So there arrives on the scene 'an ancient friar of good and holy ways who was an expert in the Scriptures and a most venerable man, towards whom the townspeople were greatly and specially devoted, and they conducted him to their house'.[118] The author seems to exert a control over his narrative at two simultaneous levels, both by concentrating on the psychological plausibility of his characters and by sustaining the psychological persuasiveness of our reading. He will, in other words, be constantly manipulating the fictional character and the hypothetical readership. The friar is a venerable and distinguished churchman because this renders him a worthwhile foil to the protagonist. Cepperello's brilliance will be all the greater if his victory is not to be gained at the expense of some gullible half-wit.[119] The friar is 'of good and holy ways', partly to satisfy the reader's love of symmetry, since this sets a holy and virtuous way of life in contrast with a fiendishly depraved one. But it also satisfies the reader's desire for scandal (or the desire to be scandalized, surely one of the prime motives for picking up a novel or collection of stories?). It does this by setting things up so that the reversal of rôles between the two main characters in the course of the confession can turn out to be that much more wicked and shocking.[120]

The fact that the friar is venerated by the local citizens simply puts the reader in the mood for a canonization at the end of the story; his prestige at the beginning makes Cepperello's cult at the end more convincing. The friar is an 'expert in the Scriptures' to accommodate Cepperello's intellectual versatility where he elaborates a fascinating idiom of unctuous piety. We witness a linguistic process in which the stylistic rigour of the 'Scriptures' declines towards the debased oleograph of the Legends of the Saints. Indeed, with all these devices operating together, we can say that at times in his major work Boccaccio's seemingly fluent choice of language conceals what is in fact a stylistic and compositional strategy which goes to the most extraordinary lengths of subtlety to convey a series of subsidiary effects.

The confession itself has been held by critics to be one of the finest comic *pièces* in the Italian language.[121] I find that the pages of the confession are still obstinately narrative, despite the immense vitality of a number of sections of dialogue. The introductory clauses, for example, have a markedly rhythmic quality: 'Whereupon Ser Ciappelletto replied', 'said the friar', 'To which . . . Ser Ciappelletto replied', 'To which the holy friar replied', etc.[122] These clauses tend to tone down the natural impetus of dialogue, which usually calls for a more immediate and spontaneous response by the reader since he always wants to be ready for the next line. The clauses help to enfold the dialogue in the more leisurely tempo of narrative material which requires an accurate and highly developed mode of reading. And wherever the responses in direct speech might seem to follow on from each other too frenetically, there is always indirect speech ready and waiting to curb the rhythm and stimulate a more reflective mode of reading:[123]

Next he asked him whether he had displeased God by committing the sin of gluttony; to which, fetching a deep sigh, Ser Ciappelletto replied that he had, and on many occasions. For although, apart from the periods of fasting. . . .

And it is in fact indirect speech which Boccaccio chooses to express Cepperello's rigid moral code where he mentions his passionate craving for 'cotali insalatuzze d'erbucce', 'those dainty little wild herb salads'[124], and this is followed by a highly intricate phrase, all set in totally implausible and *ad hoc* syntax: here the word repetitions, and especially the variations on conjugated forms of the verb *parere* ('to seem') contrive to suggest, as one critic has pointed out,[125] the see-saw motion of a scruple-ridden conscience: ' . . . e alcuna volta gli era *paruto* migliore il mangiare che non *pareva* a lui che dovesse *parere* a chi digiuna per devozione, come digiunava egli.'[126] Hence we can say that the literary inventiveness of Cepperello's confession is not merely a product of the liveliness and spontaneity of its dialogue: in fact it is derived from the sheer force of its style and manipulation of syntactic devices. Nor it is quite true to say that the action represents a triumph of the human word, in the sense of words pronounced in the course of a dialogue.[127] In Cepperello the word triumphs because of its specific contribution to a complex narrative setting.

Apart from the basic contrast between the well-documented portrait of Cepperello the sinner and the unfolding confessional revelation of Ciappelletto the saint, there is a further contrast in these pages between the legalistic punctiliousness of the holy friar and the moral concern of the hallowed sinner. The friar performs the job that he is there for, which requires him to review all the mortal sins and put forward a series of possible impediments (which are ultimately of little substance) to the sinner's eventual absolution. After his opening question on how Cepperello has respected the sacrament of confession, the friar examines him on debauchery, gluttony, avarice, wrath, violence, false witness and fraud. This presentation of confessional practice is perfectly orthodox and conformist; not so Cepperello's extraordinarily varied responses, which by their very zeal and conscientiousness seem to imply a re-enactment of devotional practice and a heartfelt reappraisal on Cepperello's part of the moral dilemma which the sacrament poses. It appears to be a straight conflict between the tired old conformity of devotional ritual and the real devoutness of an individual layman who sees the moral obligation entailed by that ritual. But it only appears to be like this, since we readers are in the privileged position of knowing that the seeming conformist is the real 'holy' figure, and the spokesman for an intimate personal crisis of conscience is just a blackguard. Here again the analogy between the episode being narrated and the whole game of literature seems to hold good: literature has always claimed the right to invent its own internal moral issues and then adapt them as it pleases.

It was Getto[128] who noticed that Cepperello's first six answers to the friar's interrogation are alternately negative and affirmative: 'Debauchery?' 'No.' 'Gluttony?' 'Yes, but . . .' 'Avarice?' 'No.' 'Wrath?' 'Yes, but . . .' 'Violence?' 'No.' 'False witness or speaking ill of thy neighbour?' 'Yes, but . . .' Yet even this pattern in the responses is broken: Cepperello says 'Yes' to the last question on fraud, for, according to the rules of the literary game, Cepperello's answers must be unpredictable.[129]

The sinner's 'No' to debauchery gives rise to the most important phrase in the whole confession: 'I am a virgin as pure as on the day I came forth from my mother's womb.'[130] The sodomizer who frequented places of ill repute is now not merely redeemed from all his vices and wicked habits. He is actually cleansed of impurity, of all the *peccata mundi*, by the insane notion of a return to the maternal womb.[131] Not only does the confession of a specific sin become transformed, here as elsewhere in the answers of the confession, into a declaration of the opposite virtue:[132] Cepperello's words suggest the perfect innocence of a saint that the world has been unable to corrupt. His is the glorious return to the 'anima semplicetta che sa nulla',[133] a myth of the individual's biography which harks back to the other grander myth of pre-lapsarian virtue. The rest of the story follows on inevitably after this decisive release of the protagonist from the taint of original sin.

The answer to the friar's question about gluttony is in the affirmative, but only involves the admission of banal peccadilloes committed during fasting or pilgrimages and religious devotions. So the admission of guilt in this instance is converted into a statement of innocence. And once again Cepperello's reference to his sins ('he had drunk the water as pleasurably and avidly . . . as any great bibber of wine')[134] is superimposed, in the reader's mind, over the belching drunkard with his wine-soaked appetite who was presented at the opening of the story.

In the meantime, however, the rôles of the two protagonists are subtly reversed,[135] with the pious confessor increasingly reminding the friar of the exact obligations attendant on religion and Christian morality: 'I know that things done in the service of God must all be done honestly and without any grudge.'[136] The Italian text has: 'senza alcuna ruggine', which literally means 'without any rust'. And here the choice of the word *ruggine* is very apt, as Momigliano has observed in his notes on the passage.[137] In his fictional account of himself, Ciappelletto is a perfectionist in spiritual purity, just as his portrait showed a perfectionist in hypocrisy and vice; pedantically virtuous, he now wants to purify every item in his life and to cancel out the tiniest blemishes of rust that might tarnish his immortal soul. His immaculateness is also bound to have an effect on his opposite number, reducing the friar's spotlessness in proportion to his own: ultimately everything around Ciappelletto, even the habits of the holy friar, gains a patina of dirt in contrast with the lily-white virtue of this newly constituted saint.

Asked about avarice, Cepperello replies with a good imitation of the pious life stories in the *Legenda Sanctorum*:[138] 'my father left me a wealthy man, and when he was dead, I gave the greater part of his fortune to charity. Since then, in order to support myself and enable me to assist the Christian poor. . . .'[139] And then he returns to the 'Christian poor', 'my Creator',[140] where the hagiographic language, based on the recurrent words indicating the Deity, is imitated almost too perfectly, like a forger's work when he has forgotten to leave a minuscule error as his trade mark. Clearly at this stage the psychological level of the narrative becomes increasingly unimportant: as far as the plot goes, Cepperello is taking an implausible risk. The exaggerated innocence of his self-portrait ought by now to be arousing the suspicions of the venerable friar. Cepperello's desire to overdo his victory and triumph in full spate over the conventions of the sacrament is losing touch with reality. By now his story is soaring towards epic heights, with a proportional loss of psychological viability for both the characters and the way they are dealing with each other.

What counts now is precisely the sheer incredibility of the story,[141] since the literary game of falsehood is being exaggerated to a point of no return. We have a writer called Boccaccio, who has invented a story-teller called Panfilo, who has invented a character called Cepperello, who has re-invented his own biography. The reader is being required to follow this sequence from one liar to the next, along a cumulative falsification of the truth.

Hence it is probably no accident that this *novella* provides the only case in the *Decameron* where the story-teller reappears at the last paragraph in the third person, rather than offering a comment on his story in the first person: 'E qui si tacque' ('And there the narrator fell silent').[142] As a minor device, this little touch serves to distance the second liar in the narrative chain even further from reality. In this *novella* on literature as falsehood, or falsehood as literature,[143] it is of paramount importance that each separate stage of the lie should be clearly marked as such for the reader: this explains the device of the manifestly fictitious narrator ('And there the narrator fell silent'), which multiplies the scope of the deception.

After Cepperello's impassioned admission that he had been guilty of the sin of wrath, though it was a question of pious anger directed against those who frequent places of low repute instead of going to church (one should notice how the descriptions in the opening portrait are being picked up and followed step by step during the confession), the friar asks if he ever committed homicide or did injury to anybody. Cepperello's vehement denial becomes a reproof of the friar's little faith: 'voi mi *parete* uom di Dio' ('you, that *appear* to be of man of God')[144] since he had been able to entertain the mere suspicion of a scoundrel's behaviour in such a virtuous man. 'S'io avessi avuto pure un pensieruzzo' ('If I had thought for a single moment'):[145] 'pensieruzzo' is another example of the story's eccentric use of diminutives: we had 'assetta*uzzo*'[146] in the opening portrait, 'insalat*uzza* d'erb*ucce*' in the answer concerning gluttony, and now 'pensier*uzzo*'. The very thought (pensiero) of violence is inconceivable to the saintly Ciappelletto. The diminutive permits a kind of reduced and miniaturized thought to infiltrate the spotless mind of the saint and then be immediately dismissed by it. If he ever had the 'pensier*uzzo*' to commit 'any of the things you mention, do you suppose I imagine that God would have treated me so generously', '*credete* voi che io *creda*...'[147] Modelled on the famous line from Dante ('Io credea che ei credesse ch'io

credetti'),[148] this presents a further sentence with distorted syntax
suggesting the tortuous, ever-vigilant and pedantic scrupulous-
ness of the character. The recurring stylistic device of diminutive
words, on the other hand, functions antiphrastically[149] as a
contrast with the grand dimension of a story which involves
Heaven and Hell, monstrous crimes and stupendous miracles.

Next comes the inquiry about false witness and ill report, and
then the friar asks the penitent if he had ever deceived anyone as
merchants commonly do: 'Gnaffe, disse Ser Ciappelletto' ('Faith,
sir, I did'),[150] and he reports a banal error involving a few coins
which were subsequently given away as charity. 'Gnaffe', the
comic plebeian corruption of the phrase 'In fede mia', provides a
curious contrast with the sustained language of the rest of the
confession, which combines the tones of catechism, sermon and
hagiography. Such a racy and plebeian expletive with its vulgar
resonance has a distinct air of emerging from the old sinner
Cepperello rather than the dying saint. It is one of the many
about-turns in a story which is itself a commentary on the art of
reversing the truth rather than a carefully thought-out construction of an individual character, i.e. a psychology.

Yet the high point in the course of the 'virtuous' confession,
after the amusing little sermon Ciappelletto gives the friar for
having spat in church, comes when he admits to a sin committed
in youth, or rather in early childhood: once upon a time he
cursed his mother. The despair of the penitent as he pretends that
he cannot dredge up such a shameful memory from the depths of
his past, and the watchful insistence of the friar who is trapped
inside his opponent's sacrilegious trickery, combine here to
form a scene of splendid comedy which is also supremely blasphemous: nothing escapes the iconoclastic assault of literature and
falsehood.[151]

> Ser Ciappelletto pur piagnea e nol dicea, e il frate pur il
> confortava a dire; ma poi che Ser Ciappelletto piangendo
> ebbe un grandissimo pezzo tenuto il frate così in sospeso,
> ed egli gittò un grande sospiro, e disse: 'Padre mio, poscia
> che voi mi promettete di pregare Iddio per me, e io il vi
> dirò: sappiate che, quando io ero piccolino, io bestemmiai
> una volta la mamma mia.' E così detto ricominciò a piangere
> forte.

(Ser Ciappelletto went on weeping, without saying anything, and the friar kept encouraging him to speak. But after Ser Ciappelletto, by weeping in this manner, had kept the friar for a long time on tenterhooks, he heaved a great sigh, and said: 'Father, since you promise that you will pray to God for me, I will tell you. You are to know then that once, when I was a little boy, I cursed my mother.' And having said this, he began to weep loudly all over again.)[152]

'Ed egli gittò . . . e disse': here the parahypotaxis (the redundant 'and' before the main verb) underlines Ciappelletto's skill as a clown: it shows him allowing the never previously confessed secret to trickle out slowly. Yet we must not forget that the subject-matter has now become extremely gross, and the pleasure and amusement which the reader derives from the text has to do with the process of reading as total transgression, as the ultimate sacrilege.[153]

Oimé padre, mio, che dite voi? La mamma mia dolce che mi portò in corpo nove mesi il dí e la notte, e portommi in collo più di cento volte! troppo feci male a bestemmiarla, e troppo é gran peccato.

(Oh alas, father, what are you saying? My dear, sweet mother, who carried me day and night for nine months in her body, and held me more than a hundred times in her arms! It was too wicked of me to curse her, and the sin is too great.)[154]

The critic Muscetta has argued in a revealing passage that the grief of the hardened old paederast over the way he offended his mother shows great psychological finesse.[155] But what does this last formula really mean? In whose particular brain is this finesse supposed to be located? In Cepperello's? In Boccaccio's? Or in that of Muscetta and myself and thousands of other readers ogling and salivating at the outrageous spectacle of a nasty old queer weeping make-up tears over his poor dead mother who bore him inside her for nine long months? This is the critical point: if this one story sanctions literature as falsehood, then this particular scene sanctions the act of reading as a descent into transgression and indecency.

By now it should be obvious that the friar is the opposite of the heavy and slow-witted character that De Sanctis dreamed up for him.[156] He merely follows the convention of a Christian world that requires a truthful confession from a man who is at death's door. Therefore he performs his duty, absolves Cepperello (perhaps the most heretical part of all his behaviour), and sets him up as a model of Christian living in his sermon, thus contributing to Cepperello's eventual veneration as a saint. The two brothers are governed by a similar set of conventions: they hear his false confession and are amazed by Cepperello's sustaining his part so consistently at such a short step from the tribunal of God. They can only admire ('What manner of man is this . . .')[157] the moral stature of Cepperello's sacrilege. But these are not Cepperello's own criteria, or rather, we should say that the reader is not entitled to extrapolate from the character's behaviour the fact that he believes in God and is therefore conscious of his impending damnation.[158] His confession is bound to be taken as truthful by the friar ('who is there who would not have been convinced, on hearing a dying man talk in this fashion?').[159] It is taken to be splendidly and extravagantly false by the two money-lenders, whereas for Cepperello it is simply bound to be false. Cepperello stands, therefore, completely outside any conventions, or at least it is he who creates the laws that govern the ethical behaviour of the individual.

The closing section of the *novella* is the part which has given rise to the most unlikely critical fantasies. It presents two main problems: in which pigeon-hole of the afterworld can we assume Cepperello from Prato is now located? And how are we to interpret the fact that 'it is claimed that through him God has wrought many miracles, and that He continues to work them on behalf of whoever commands himself devoutly to this particular Saint'?[160] Panfilo began this story by stating that God 'paying more attention to the purity of the supplicant's motives than to his ignorance or to the banishment of the intercessor, answers those who pray to Him exactly as if the advocate were blessed in His sight'.[161] Now, with Cepperello dead, 'it is claimed' (this verb serves to make the miracles seem a little less immediate, since those who believe in them are making a personal assumption) that Cepperello is a means by which God performs miracles for the devout. How far are we to take these statements seriously? Has the tongue popped back into the writer's cheek? Or must we really read it all *au pied de la lettre,* and arrive at the truly bizarre ponderings of Giorgio Padoan:[162]

> In my view, however, the canonization of Ciappelletto is not a triumph for him. . . . The rascal who is at death's door and takes advantage of the friar's innocence, 'perhaps the worst man ever born' . . . 'a mighty blasphemer of God and His Saints' who 'never went to church and . . . would use foul language to pour scorn on all her sacraments, declaring them repugnant' turns out to be – that very man – a new source of glory for the church and for God; after his death, almost certainly condemned to Hell, it is actually he who strengthens with his own 'example' the religious faith of others, who are misguided enough to attribute the working of miracles to him.

This brilliant interpretative somersault (though untenable in my opinion) is backed up by an observation by Padoan concerning what he alleges is a *leitmotiv* running through the *novelle* of the First Day, *novelle* in his opinion based on a conclusion which is the opposite of what the protagonist expected:[163]

> In any case, the *novelle* of the First Day follow the same ideal line, because they are all based (though nobody seems to have noticed this fact up to now) on a conclusion which is the opposite of what the protagonist expected, almost as if Boccaccio was deliberately following the favourite mediaeval technique of the world in reverse. Giannotto da Civigni, by giving 'good' advice to Abraam, tells him lies to stop him from going to Rome. But it is the very fact of going there that causes the Jew's conversion to Christianity. The Saladin thinks he is going to play a trick on Melchisedec: instead he ends up giving him valuable gifts. The abbot strongly criticizes the young monk, thinking that by so doing he'll be able to have the young woman all to himself: instead they both have to share her. The King of France wants to go through Monferrato in order to enjoy the body of the Marchioness: he goes away in fact without having obtained anything from her. The Inquisitor orders an unjust punishment: but at the end he is severely criticized in the public presence, and eternal damnation is forecast for his

friars. Can Grande and Ser Grimaldi behave meanly: but
they are sharply reproved and subsequently become
open-handed men. The woman who despaired of getting
her revenge because of the cowardice of the King of Cyprus
is in fact given a harsh revenge on her malefactor through
his agency. Ciappelletto, the first and triumphant example
of the process, who had decided to deceive the gullible
friar by blaspheming and saying untruth . . . ends as a
public model of goodness and religious devotion.

This reading is an interesting one, but seems to me to rest on an
excessive categorization of the *novelle* by theme. The only clear-
cut cases of 'opposite conclusion' are *novelle* 2, 3, and 10. In the
fourth, the real protagonist is the monk, and he achieves the
exact purpose he had in mind when handing over the keys to the
Abbot. In the fifth, the protagonist is surely the Marchioness, not
the King of France, and she achieves what she wanted from her
original plan of preparing chickens for their banquet. In the
sixth, the protagonist had no precise purpose or outcome in
mind. In the seventh and eight *novelle*, Bergamino with his
parable and Guglielmo Borsiere with his *riposte* do obtain what
they wanted. In the ninth, the woman from Gascony has no
particular plan in mind when she makes her remark. For all these
reasons, I find Padoan's proposal of a structural reading of the
First Day as a whole unconvincing.

As I have argued already, the greatness of this *novella* derives
among other elements from the legitimate co-existence of so
many discordant interpretations. My reading is clearly far removed
from that of Padoan (which is also shared by Vittore Branca). It
seems to me that the *novella* is serious in its dedication to blasphemy
rather than devoutness. 'The ladies were full of praise for
Panfilo's story, parts of which they had found highly amusing.'[164]
Those are the words with which the following *novella* (*Decameron*,
I, 2) commences. But why does Boccaccio just say 'parts'? What
anxiety is concealed behind the listeners' laughter? Apart from
the triumphant humour of the text (the opening portrait, the
confession, the friar's sermon, etc.) the story leaves both narrator
and reader perplexed and a little bewildered by the daring
sacrilege and perhaps by the moral implications of the literary
game which has just been played out for him: but his concern

has little to do with the life after death of the fictional character Cepperello, or the logical coherence of miracles achieved by the arch-sinner. Furthermore, the stylistic evidence hardly points in the direction suggested by Padoan. Take a passage like the following:[165]

> And that evening they went to the place where Ser
> Ciappelletto's body lay, and celebrated a great and solemn
> vigil over it; and in the morning, dressed in albs and copes,
> carrying books in their hands and bearing crosses before
> them, singing as they went, they all came to the body,
> which they then carried back to their church with tremendous
> pomp and ceremony, followed by nearly all the people of
> the town, men and women alike.

Here the general line is close to the scene of Frate Cipolla with the coal from the grill of St Lawrence:[166]

> So Friar Cipolla took the coals between his fingers and began
> to scrawl the biggest crosses he could manage to inscribe
> on their white smocks and on their doublets and on the
> shawls of the women, declaring that however much the
> coals were worn down in making these crosses, they
> recovered their former shape when restored to the casket,
> as he had often had occasion to observe. At considerable
> profit to himself, therefore, having daubed crosses on all the
> citizens of Certaldo.

The solemnity of Cepperello's religious funeral is grotesque, like Cipolla's generous distribution of coal. But the huge crosses daubed by the crafty monk have no other effect than that they dirty the white smocks and the doublets and the shawls of the women. They certainly don't cause the occurrence of miracles.

And again, after the friar's sermon, which puts the reader in a mood for satire and irony rather than for theological meditation on the mysterious ways of the Lord, there is the hysterical description of the crowd's behaviour:[167]

> Everyone thronged round his body to kiss his feet and his
> hands, all the clothes were torn from his back, and those
> who succeeded in grabbing so much as a tiny fragment felt
> they were in Paradise itself.

This resembles the tone of scornful criticism of men's general wickedness and stupidity which we find in the harsh story of Martellino.[168] As we read the text, we can hardly expect that the crowd's desire for miracles will be rewarded. This is not just because the figure who is supposed to act as intercessor with the Deity is in fact a sacrilegious sinner, but also because the crowd that tramples round his wretched body and tears the clothes off it deserves neither a genuine nor a false saint's favours. In other words, Boccaccio's presentation inclines the reader to expect the non-occurrence of the miracles, and to consider as vain and pointless the votive offerings and figures made of wax which decorate the chapel devoted to San Ciappelletto. Nor is it the case that the sentence 'it is claimed that through him God has wrought many miracles'[169] invalidates the view that the reader is being invited to expect a non-occurrence, or at least a refusal on God's part to accept the entreaties of the praying flock: this statement is put out by the flock itself ('it is claimed'); it is a declaration of what they want to believe rather than an objective fact expressed by the author.

The second problem, basically an irrelevant one, concerns the after-life of our hero. According to Padoan and Branca, Cepperello is condemned to Hell. Betrayed by his own choice of action, he plunges 'in Hell, in the hands of the Devil'[170] in a phrase which Branca reads as sinister and terrifying[171] (but which seems to me all gaiety and *insouciance*). 'Così adunque visse e morì Ser Cepperello da Prato, e santo divenne, come avete udito' (It was thus, then that Ser Cepperello of Prato lived and died, becoming a Saint in the way you have heard.')[172] This serene and compelling final formula summing up the life and the death of the hero is not a premonition of infernal punishment. The author is not denying the possibility that 'God has blessed him and admitted him to His presence'.[173] A place for the sinner in Heaven may well be unlikely, but that does not mean that it is totally excluded. Perhaps it is more likely that the scoundrel is down in Hell, in the Devil's hands. The simultaneous possibility of both alternatives settles the question: there is no way of knowing Cepperello's precise address in the kingdom of the dead. Whether he is in residence up there or down below does not concern the narrator, who wants to close the story with one last *boutade*, imagining San Ciappelletto blessedly enjoying the ineffable delights of Paradise. He refuses to be the spokesman for a divine condemnation.

Nor is the reader particularly concerned with Ciappelletto's blessedly enjoying the ineffable delights of Paradise: we are merely fascinated by the irony of the suggestion that it might just be the upper of the two. He hardly cares which flames might be devouring the sacrilegious scoundrel he has just finished reading about. Last but not least, Cepperello himself is indifferent to his fate: his existence came to an end at the ninety-first paragraph of the first *novella* in the *Decameron*, since his status as a character in fiction does not allow him any extra-textual existence whatsoever, not even in Hell. Instead, the problem of a future Hell might at a personal level concern a reader who has been peering into the scandalous fascinations of the *novella*.

Notes

1 J. L. Borges, 'La biblioteca de Babel', in *Ficciones*, Buenos Aires, 1942.
2 McW, p. 484 '. . . una delle belle novelle del mondo' (*Dec.*, VI, 1, 7). The Roman number refers to the Day, the first arabic number to the Story in the Day, the second to the paragraph in Branca's edition.
3 McW, *ibid.* '. . . nel vero da sé era bellissima' (*Dec.*, VI, 1, 9).
4 McW, *ibid.* '. . . fieramente la guastava' (*Dec.*, *ibid.*).
5 McW, *ibid.* '. . . spesse volte veniva un sudore e uno sfinimento di cuore, come se inferma fosse stata per terminare (*Dec.*, VI, 1, 10).
6 McW, *ibid.* A fairly free translation of the original: '. . . era entrato nel pecoreccio' (*Dec.*, VI, 1, 10).
7 McW, *ibid.* '. . . piacevolmente' (*ibid.*).
8 McW, *ibid.* 'Messere, questo vostro cavallo ha troppo duro trotto, per che io vi priego che vi piaccia di pormi a piè' (*Dec.*, VI, 1, 11).
9 McW, *ibid.* '. . . il qual per avventura era molto migliore intenditore che novellatore' (*Dec.*, VI, 1, 12).
10 Muscetta, 1965, p. 436. The *novella* of Cisti is *Dec.*, VI, 2.
11 Getto, 1958.
12 *Ibid.*, p. 139.
13 *Ibid.*, p. 140.
14 *Ibid.*
15 *Ibid.*, p. 142.
16 'If we still needed extra proof that style achieves a complete primacy over plot, this story would give it to us most unequivocally' (R. Barilli, 'Semiologia e retorica nella lettura del Decameron', *Il Verri*, nos 35–6, 1971, pp. 27–48), The quotation is at p. 44. Barilli uses this *novella* to criticize the misguided semiological approach of Tzvetan Todorov (1969) who, by concentrating purely on the deep syntax of the stories, ignores the concrete ways in which the *novelle* come to life.

17 Cesare de Michelis in his recent 'Rassegna Boccaccesca' (*Lettere Italiane*, January–March, 1973, XXV, 1, pp. 88–129) makes a number of interesting observations about my interpretation of this *novella*, which has already appeared as a short article in Italian, 'Lettura della novella di Madonna Oretta', *Paragone*, no. 270, August, 1972, pp. 139–42. De Michelis's objections to my thesis can be summed up as follows: if there is a message at the centre of the whole work, it cannot only be an invitation to pay closer attention to its form. We should not lose sight of the fact that the story told by the unaccomplished horseman is related to a woman, who belongs in other words to the ideal audience which the *Decameron* is addressed to (this is an important observation which I had omitted to make in my original article). De Michelis also thinks that the defects in the horseman's technique at telling a story can hardly be considered purely 'formal', but are rather 'full-scale threats against the very comprehensibility and plausibility of whatever story he is trying to tell'. Here I find it more difficult to agree. Given the fact that we readers do not know the story he tries to tell Madonna Oretta, we can never find out whether it becomes incomprehensible or implausible at the hands of this poor speaker. We are bound to accept only the information which the author has provided us, namely that the story was told badly. De Michelis's last observation is the following: if this *novella* were the vital key to the whole work, then it would have to be seen as 'an apology for the poet and man of letters'. This interpretation is eminently acceptable, as will become evident from my approach in the rest of this chapter.

18 Perhaps we should say the *female* readers, to whom the *Decameron* is expressly dedicated (see the *proemio*, the preface to the work), not just for conventional reasons nor as merely a gesture of gallantry.

19 McW, p. 71; *Dec.*, I, 1, 15.

20 Momigliano, 1970, p. 38, footnote 1.

21 Branca, 1970, p. 95.

22 McW, p. 71. '... era il piggiore uomo che mai nascesse' (*Dec.*, I, 1, 15).

23 Branca, 1970, p. 96.

24 *Ibid.*, p. 18.

25 Getto; 1958, p. 38 (although Getto belongs to the 'artists' rather than to the 'sinners').

26 Branca, 1970, p. 158.

27 'It is what Sartre interprets as "il faut vivre le Mal jusqu'a la mort" ("one must live Evil right through one's death"), as he sees it in Genet's experience, that has lost, however, Ser Ciappelletto's hedonistic quality of enjoying evil' (Cottino-Jones, 1968, p. 24, footnote 1).

28 Branca, 1970, p. 158.

29 See Cottino-Jones, 1968, p. 24.

30 Branca, 1970, p. 158.

31 McW, p. 81. '... nelle mani del diavolo in perdizione' (*Dec.*, I, 1, 89).

32 'Note d'orrore' (Branca, 1970, p. 158).

33 Padoan, 1964, pp. 162–3; and Branca, 1970, pp. 98–9.

34 Croce, 1967, p. 90.

35 Russo, 1970, p. 51.
36 De Sanctis, 1949, I, p. 282.
37 Baratto, 1970, p. 297.
38 Croce, 1967, p. 89.
39 Auerbach, 1953, pp. 200–1.
40 Russo, 1970, p. 51. The *novella* of Friar Cipolla is *Dec.*, VI, 10.
41 See Getto, 1958, p. 40.
42 Russo, 1970, p. 61.
43 The character from *Inferno* XXIV who makes an obscene gesture towards God (see this chapter, pp. 34–5).
44 Capaneo, one of the seven kings at Thebes, is to be found in *Inferno* XIV, challenging God's power with defiant words. Baratto (1970, p. 299) suggests that Cepperello is 'un Capaneo borghese', but the expression is meaningless: how can one have a defier of divinity in a middle-class man, respectful of laws and regulations?
45 Russo, 1970, p. 61.
46 Getto, 1958, p. 46.
47 *Ibid.*, p. 49.
48 *Ibid.*, p. 51.
49 *Ibid.*, p. 68. Getto makes an interesting comparison between the hypocritical behaviour of Cepperello, all based on the power of the word, and that of the picaro in *Guzmán de Alfarache* by Mateo Alemán, where words are only part of the action.
50 See Getto, 1958, p. 34.
51 Rabelais, *Œuvres complètes,* Garnier, Paris, 1962, vol. I, p. 13.
52 McW, p. 69. '. . . una delle sue meravigliose cose'; '. . . cosa impermutabile' (*Dec.*, I, 1, 2).
53 McW, p. 69. '. . . esaudisce colore che 'l priegano' (*Dec.*, I, 1, 5.)
54 McW, p. 69. '. . . dinanzi alla sua maestà facciamo procuratore che da quella con etterno esilio è scacciato' (*Dec.*, I, 1, 5).
55 McW, p. 68. 'Convenevole cosa è, carissime donne, che ciascuna cosa la quale l'uomo fa, dallo ammirabile e santo nome di Colui, il quale di tutte fu facitore, le dea principio' (*Dec.*, I, 1, 2).
56 These stylistic devices are carefully listed by Cottino-Jones (1968, p. 23): 'The verbal texture of the *novella* of Ser Ciappelletto is basically composed of figurative devices such as indecision, correction, paralipsis, aposiopesis, as well as periphrasis, catachresis, antonomasia, and metonymy. All of these devices, together with antithesis of language and thought, succeed in presenting an indirect and equivocal form of language perfectly indicative of the narrative mood of the *novella* interwoven around a hypocritical and ambiguous character. Devices such as transplacement, epanaphora, antistrophe, interlacement, epanalepsis, anadiplosis, paronomasia, as well as synonymy, dwelling-on-the-point, and emphasis by hyperbole recur very often in order to create a propitious climate for the persuasion motif underlying the confession scene.' I doubt, however, that reading this paragraph makes us gladder or wiser men.
57 McW, p. 69. 'Ragionasi adunque che essendo Musciatto Franzesi di

ricchissimo e gran mercatante in Francia cavalier divenuto e dovendone
in Toscana venire con messer Carlo Senzaterra, fratello del re di Francia,
da papa Bonifazio addomandato e al venir promosso, sentendo egli
gli fatti suoi, sí come le piu volte son quegli de' mercatanti, molto
intralciati in qua e in là . . .' (*Dec.*, I, 1, 7).

58 See Getto, 1958, p. 41.

59 See Branca, footnote 1 to *Dec.*, I, 1, 7, and the texts which he mentions.

60 See Branca, footnote 1 to *Dec.*, I, 1, 1.

61 A title which was reserved for members of certain professions.

62 Getto, 1958, p. 43.

63 McW, p. 70. '. . . credendo che "cappello" cioe "ghirlanda" secondo
il lor volgare a dir venisse' (*Dec.*, I, 1, 9).

64 See Getto, 1958, p. 44.

65 McW, pp. 70–1.

> Era questo Ciappelletto di questa vita: egli, essendo notaio, avea
> grandissima vergogna quando uno de'suoi strumenti, come che
> pochi ne facesse, fosse altro che falso trovato; de quali tanti avrebbe
> fatti di quanti fosse stato richiesto e quelli volentieri in dono che
> alcun altro grandamente salariato. Testimonianze false con sommo
> diletto diceva, richiesto e non richiesto; e dandosi a que' tempi in
> Francia a' saramenti grandissima fede, non curandosi fargli falsi,
> tante quistioni malvagiamente vincea a quante a giurare di dire il vero
> sopra la sua fede era chiamato. Aveva oltre modo piacere, e forte vi
> studiava, in commettere tra amici e parenti e qualunque altra persona
> mali e inimicizie e scandali, de'quali quanto maggiori mali vedeva
> seguire tanto piu d'allegrezza prendea. Invitato ad un omicidio o a
> qualunque altra rea cosa, senza negarlo mai, volonterosamente
> v'andava, e più volte a fedire e ad uccidere uomini colle propie mani
> si trovò volentieri. Bestemmiatore di Dio e de' Santi era grandissimo;
> e per ogni piccola cosa, sí come colui che più che alcun altro era iracundo.
> A chiesa non usava giammai e i sacramenti di quella tutti come vil
> cosa con abominevoli parole scherniva; e cosí in contrario le taverne e
> gli altri disonesti luoghi visitava volentieri e usavagli. Delle femine
> era cosí vago come sono i cani de' bastoni, del contrario più che
> alcun altro tristo uomo si dilettava. Imbolato avrebbe e rubato con
> quella conscienzia che un santo uomo offerrebbe. Gulosissimo e
> bevitore grande, tanto che alcuna volta sconciamente gli facea noia:
> giucatore e mettitore di malvagi dadi era solenne. Perchè mi
> distendo io in tante parole? egli era il piggiore uomo forse che mai
> nascesse (*Dec.*, I, 1, 10–15).

66 See in particular p. 74.

67 McW, p. 82. '. . . diritto e leale uomo' (*Dec.*, I, 2, 4).

68 McW, p. 89. '. . . una giovinetta assai bella, forse figliola d'alcun de'
lavoratori della contrada' (*Dec.*, I, 4, 5).

69 McW, p. 93. '. . . donna tra tutte l'altre del mondo . . . bellissima e
valorosa' (*Dec.*, I, 5, 6).

70 McW, p. 96. '. . . un buono uomo assai più ricco di denari che di senno'
(*Dec.*, I, 6, 5).

71 Auerbach, 1953, pp. 200–1.
72 Branca, 1970, p. 28, footnote 1.
73 *Inferno*, XXIV, 2.
74 *Inferno*, XXIV, 137–8.
75 Sinclair's translation, 1971.
76 McW, pp. 70–1 (with a slight modification to his translation). '. . . volentieri . . . con sommo diletto . . . aveva oltre modo piacere . . . tanto più d'allegrezza prendea . . . volonterosamente . . . gli altri disonesti luoghi visitava volentieri . . . si dilettava' (*Dec.*, I, 1, 10–14).
77 McW, p. 71. The translation loses some of the force of the original: '. . . sí come colui che più che alcun altro era iracundo' (*Dec.*, I, 1, 13).
78 *Dec.*, I, 1, 14. No translation can convey the impact of the open sounds of the adverb *sconciamente*. McWilliam translates 'in a manner that was highly indecorous' (p. 71).
79 McW, p. 71. 'Perchè mi distendo in tante parole?' (*Dec.*, I, 1, 15).
80 Baratto, 1970, p. 294.
81 On this antiphrastic device, see Branca, 1970, p. 96.
82 See Branca, 1970, p. 98.
83 Russo, 1970, p. 60.
84 McW, p. 70. '. . . aveva grandissima vergogna quando un de'suoi strumenti . . .' (*Dec.*, I, 1, 10).
85 McW, p. 70. '. . . fosse altro che falso trovato' (*Dec.*, I, 1, 10).
86 McW, p. 74. '. . . cotali insalatuzze d'erbucce' (*Dec.*, I, 1, 41).
87 Branca, 1970, p. 96.
88 Branca, 1970, p. 18.
89 *Job*, 3, 3.
90 *Ecclesiastes*, 4, 2–3.
91 *Dec.*, VI, 10.
92 McW, p. 507. '. . . nove cose tali che, se qualunque è l'una di quelle fosse in Salamone o in Aristotile o in Seneca, avrebbe forza di guastare ogni lor virtù, ogni lor senno, ogni lor santità' (*Dec.*, VI, 10, 16).
93 *Inferno*, IX, 62–3. Sinclair's translation: 'Note the teaching that is hidden under the veil of the strange lines.'
94 On this *novella* see Branca, 1970, pp. 127–33.
95 But see Branca, 1970, p. 128 and relative footnotes.
96 McW, p. 557. 'O singolar dolcezza del sangue bolognese! quanto se' tu stata sempre da commendare in cosí fatti casi mai nè di lagrime nè di sospiri fosti vaga, e continuamente a' prieghi pieghevoli e agli amorosi disideri arrendevol fosti: se io avessi degne lode da commendarti, mai sazia non se ne vedrebbe la voce mia' (*Dec.*, VII, 7, 21).
97 I disagree with Branca (1970, p. 130) for whom this paragraph is clearly 'comico-scanzonato'.
98 *Dec.*, V, 8.
99 *Dec.*, III, 7.
100 See also Benvenuto da Imola, *Commentum super Dantis Aldigherij Comoediam,* Florence, 1887, II, p. 16; quoted by Branca, 1970, p. 131, footnote 1.
101 The synaesthesia is lost in the translation.
102 See Russo, p. 1970, p. 60.

103 McW, p. 72. '. . . quivi fuor di sua natura benignamente e mansuetamente cominciò a voler riscuotere e fare quello che andato v'era, quasi si riserbasse l'adirarsi al da sezzo' (Dec., I, 1, 19).
104 Getto, 1958, p. 49.
105 Dec., I, 1, 21.
106 Getto, 1958, p. 49.
107 Russo, 1970, p. 57.
108 McW, p. 72. 'Questi Lombardi cani' (Dec., I, 1, 26).
109 Branca, 1970, p. 157.
110 Ibid.
111 McW, p. 73. 'l'avere ci ruberanno' (Dec., I, 1, 26).
112 McW, p. 72. '. . . per lo mestiere nostro, il quale pare loro iniquissimo' (Dec., I, 1, 26).
113 McW, p. 73. 'Io ho, vivendo, tante ingiurie fatte a Domenedio, che, per farnegli io una ora in su la mia morte, nè più nè meno ne farà' (Dec., I, 1, 28). This explanation of his behaviour is not 'stupid', as Auerbach suggests (1953, p. 201). It is simply blasphemous, as with the nun in the story of Masetto (Dec., III, 1) who believes that, if God is so keen on virgins, 'he can always find other girls to preserve their virginity for Him' (McW, p. 238). The blasphemy arises out of a hybridism between a mundane and an ultramundane standard.
114 Branca, 1970, p. 158.
115 See Baratto, 1970, pp. 79–80.
116 See Padoan, 1964, p. 165.
117 McW, p. 73. 'un santo e valente frate, il più che aver potete, se alcun ce n'è' (Dec., I, 1, 29).
118 McW, p. 73. 'un frate antico di santa e buona vita, e gran maestro in Iscrittura e molto venerabile uomo nel quale tutti i cittadini grandissima e speziale devozione avevano, e lui menarono' (Dec., I, 1, 30).
119 See Getto, 1958, p. 56.
120 See Getto, 1958, p. 59 and 74 and earlier on in this chapter, p. 46.
121 Getto, 1958, p. 54. But see also Baratto, 1970, p. 295; and Russo, 1970, pp. 61–2.
122 McW, pp. 73–4, 'Al quale Ser Ciappelletto . . . rispose . . . Disse allora il frate . . . Al quale Ser Ciappelletto . . . rispose . . . Al quale il santo frate disse . . .' (Dec., I, 1, 32–8).
123 McW, p. 74. 'E appresso questo il domandò se nel peccato della gola aveva a Dio dispiaciuto. Al quale sospirando forte, ser Ciappelletto rispose di sí, e molte volte; perciò che, con ciò fosse cose che egli, oltre a digiuni . . .' (Dec., I, 1, 41).
124 Dec., I, 1, 41; McW, p. 74. This reference to food represents, in the words of one critic, 'un brivido di rinascente concupiscenza' ('a shiver of resurgent lust', Fassò, 1947, p. 42).
125 Getto, 1958, p. 62.
126 Dec., I, 1, 41. The italics are mine. Here is McWilliam's translation: '. . . and sometimes the thought of food had been more attractive to him that he considered proper in one who, like himself, was fasting out of piety' (McW, pp. 74–5).

127 Getto, 1958, p. 68.

128 *Ibid.*, p. 60.

129 'A good habit to acquire, if you are interested in disciplining your strength, is the habit of habit-breaking; to change your habits deliberately on occasion prevents you from being entirely consistent (I believe I explained the virtues of limited inconsistency earlier?) . . . You have hundreds of habits: habits of dress, of manner of speech, of eating, of thought, of aesthetic taste, of moral conduct. Break them now and then, deliberately, and institute new ones in their places for a while. . . . To be sure don't break *all* your habits. Leave some untouched forever; otherwise you'll be consistent.' (John Barth, *The Floating Opera*, Avon Library, New York, 1969, p. 132).

130 McW, p. 74. 'Io son così vergine come io uscí del corpo della mamma mia' (*Dec.*, I, 1, 39).

131 Commenting on this passage, Cottino-Jones (1968, pp. 39–45) says that the periphrasis used to indicate Cepperello's birth introduces sexual connotation. But I hardly think that a mother's womb ('il corpo della mamma mia') can generate such suggestions.

132 See Getto, 1958, p. 59.

133 Dante, *Purgatorio* XVI, 88. 'The little simple soul that knows nothing' (Sinclair's translation, 1971).

134 McW, p. 74. '. . . con quello diletto e con quello appetito l'acqua bevuta avea . . . che fanno i gran bevitori il vino' (*Dec.*, I, 1, 41).

135 See Russo, 1970, p. 64.

136 McW, p. 75. 'Io so che le cose che al servigio di Dio si fanno, si deono fare tutte nettamente e senza alcuna ruggine d'animo' (*Dec.*, I, 1, 43).

137 Momigliano, 1970, p. 45, footnote 1.

138 See Getto, 1958, pp. 60–1.

139 McW, p. 75. '. . . mio padre mi lasciò ricco uomo, del cui avere come egli fu morto, diedi la maggior parte per Dio; e poi, per sostentare la vita mia e per poter aiutare i poveri di Cristo' (*Dec.*, I, 1, 46).

140 McW, p. 75. '. . . poveri di Dio . . . il mio Creatore' (*Dec.*, I, 1, 46).

141 I am intentionally comparing the psychological incredibility of the climactic point in the confession scene, with the greater plausibility of the beginning. Needless to say, this does not reduce the aesthetic impact of the scene.

142 *Dec.*, I, 1, 91 (McW, p. 81).

143 See G. Manganelli, *Literature as Falsehood* (trans. by B. Merry), in *London Magazine,* October–November, 1972, vol. 12, no. 4.

144 McW, p. 76. The italics are mine. (*Dec.*, I, 1, 51.)

145 *Ibid.*

146 'Used to dress very neatly' is McWilliam's rendering of this difficult adjective.

147 McW, p. 76. '. . . qualunque s'è l'una delle cose che voi dite, credete voi che io creda che Iddio m'avesse tanto sostenuto?' (*Dec.*, I, 1, 51). The italics are mine.

148 Dante, *Inferno* XIII, 25. Sinclair's translation: 'I think he thought I thought'.

149 Cf. Cottino-Jones, 1968, p. 30.
150 *Dec.*, I, 1, 55 (McW, p. 76).
151 *Dec.*, I, 1, 71.
152 McW, p. 78.
153 *Dec.*, I, 1, 73.
154 McW, p. 78.
155 Muscetta, 1965, p. 382. On the question of sodomy, see the rather unconvincing argument put forward by Scaglione, 1963, p. 201.
156 De Sanctis, 1949, p. 282.
157 McW, p. 79. 'Che uomo è costui . . .' (*Dec.*, I, 1, 79).
158 Branca, 1970, p. 158.
159 McW, pp. 78–9. 'Chi sarebbe colui che nol credesse, veggendo uno uomo in caso di morte confessandosi dir cosí?' (*Dec.*, I, 1, 74).
160 McW, p. 81. '. . . e affermano molti miracoli Iddio aver mostrati per lui e mostrare tutto giorno a chi divotamente si raccomanda a lui' (*Dec.*, I, 1, 88).
161 McW, p. 69. '. . . più alla purità del pregator riguardando che alla sua ignoranza o allo esilio del pregato cosí come se quegli fosse nel suo cospetto beato, esaudisce coloro che 'l priegano' (*Dec.*, I, 1, 5).
162 Padoan, 1964, pp. 162–3.
163 *Ibid.*, pp. 164–5.
164 McW, p. 82. 'La novella di Panfilo fu in parte risa e tutta commendata dalle donne' (*Dec.*, I, 2, 2).
165 McW, p. 80.

   E la sera, andati tutti là dove il corpo di Ser Ciappelletto giaceva,
   sopr'esso fecero una grande e solenne vigilia; e la mattina tutti
   vestiti co' camisci e co' pievali, co' libri in mano e con le croci
   innanzi, cantando andaron per questo corpo e con grandissima festa
   e solennità il recarono alla loro chiesa, seguendo quasi tutto il popolo
   della città, uomini e donne (*Dec.*, I, 1, 84).

166 McW, p. 513.

   Per la qual cosa Frate Cipolla, recatisi questi carboni in mano, sopra
   li lor camisciotti bianchi e sopra i farsetti e sopra li veli delle donne
   cominciò a fare le maggior croci che vi capevano, affermando che
   tanto quanto essi scemavano a far quelle croci, poi ricrescevano
   nella cassetta sí come molte volte avea provato. E in cotal guisa non
   senza sua grandissima utilità avendo tutti crociati i Certaldesi . . .
   (*Dec.*, VI, 10, 54–5).

167 McW, p. 80. 'Con la maggior calca del mondo da tutti fu andato a basciargli i piedi e le mani, e tutti i panni gli furono indosso stracciati, tenendosi beato chi pure un poco di quegli potesse avere' (*Dec.*, I, 1, 86).
168 *Dec.*, II, 1.
169 McW, p. 81. 'Affermano molti miracoli Iddio aver mostrati per lui' (*Dec.*, I, 1, 88).
170 McW, p. 81. '. . . nelle mani del diavolo in perdizione' (*Dec.*, I, 1, 89).
171 Branca, 1970, p. 158.
172 *Dec.*, I, 1, 89 (McW, p. 81).
173 McW, p. 81. '. . . lui esser beato nella presenza di Dio' (*Dec.*, I, 1, 89).

Three

Bawdry and
Ars Combinatoria

If we are prepared to accept the proposition that the task of literary criticism is to explore the whole of the *lisible*, then it might seem strange that critics have shown a marked reluctance to come to terms with obscenity in the text. Furthermore, the tendency to move towards a cautious bowdlerization of the text has often been reinforced by an indirect bowdlerization achieved by simple keeping silent on the subject of certain daring works. The fig-leaf has in fact been one of the secret icons of literary as well as of art criticism.

The result of all this has been particularly damaging in the case of Boccaccio. Outside Italy the *Decameron* tends to be relegated to the zone of the *outré*, where works may be artistically reliable but are morally ambiguous, while in Italy the most Boccaccesque element in Boccaccio, the licentious *novella*, has been exiled outside the critic's happy hunting ground, which prefers to include works or stories with a less salacious power of fascination. [1] Hence it is no accident that the favourite *Decameron* adventures of established Boccaccio criticism (Andreuccio, II, 5; Cepperello, I, 1, etc.) are permitted to touch the bounds of decency but preferably without being concentrated round an obscene narrative subject (the Monk and the Abbot, I, 4), or on metaphorical references to the sexual act (the story of Alibech, III, 10).

'I shall narrate a hundred stories or fables or parables or histories', [2] says Boccaccio in the *Proemio* to the *Decameron*. And the first fable (*fabel*) which we find in the *Hundred Tales* is in point of fact the fourth of the collection (for the opening story may be defined as a *novella*, a story, while the second and third are, strictly speaking, parables). The fourth narrative composition in the *Decameron* is the admittedly well-known but scarcely studied story of the Monk and the Abbot, of which I here summarize the plot.

A sturdy young monk takes a young country girl to his cell. Once he has realized that the Abbot is eavesdropping at the door,

he decides to take desperate remedies by going to his superior and
handing him the key to his cell with the excuse that in the meanwhile he has to go to the wood 'to bring in all the faggots'.[3] The
Abbot goes to the cell and makes love to the girl, but, in order
not to injure her with his weight, 'he settled down beneath her
instead of lying on top'.[4] The young monk, who has seen
everything through a chink in the wall, is later accused by the
Abbot of mortal sin but manages to escape punishment by
pleading ignorance of the fact that 'monks must bow themselves
down with the burden of women, as well as that of fasting and
vigils'.[5]

A close analysis of this *novella* should enable us to identify a
number of recurring functions in the erotic episodes of the
Decameron and to suggest that there is a solid structure lying
beneath their superficial flippancy of vocabulary and manner.

Coming on the heels of the tight logical architecture displayed by
the first three *novelle*, the *fabel* of the Monk and the Abbot is
connected to the preceding story only by an artificial and tenuous
link:[6]

> So having heard how Abraham's soul was saved through the
> good advice of Jehannot de Chevigny, and how Melchizedek
> employed his wisdom in defending his riches from the wily
> manœuvres of the Saladin, I intend, without fear of your
> disapproval, to give you a brief account of the clever way
> in which a monk saved his body from very severe
> punishment.

With this *novella* Boccaccio can be said to set in motion a new
manner in his repertoire: as the work progresses this manner
will split into two clearly distinguishable lines of development.

The first harks back to the classic models of the *fabliaux*, moving
towards stories with a predominantly (though by no means
exclusively) salacious tone. These illustrate the tidal wave of
sexual appetite as it sweeps and overwhelms the moral consciousness of the individual (as in the stories of Alibech and Rustico,
Masetto, the Abbess with the Priest's trousers), and thus tend
to operate a kind of ethical vindication of the amoral plebeian
subject-matter which is typical of the French tradition. The most
celebrated and striking example of this latter tendency can be

found in the *novella* of Carlo il Vecchio,[7] where we are no longer faced by an exercise in the *fabliau* but something which is much closer to full-scale socio-ethical meditation.

The second line of development in the new manner tends to adopt the *boutade* as resolving factor in the narrative construction of a story (Cisti the Baker,[8] Chichibio,[9] Madonna Filippa[10] and so on). The first example of this category can be found in the splendid *double entendre* which hangs on the verb 'priemere' in the closing dialogue between the monk and the abbot in the *novella* under consideration (*Dec.*, I, 4).

The literary precedents which have been proposed for this story are of little help. There is, for example, the *fabliau*, *L'évêque qui bénit le con*,[11] which is all in a farcical manner and concludes with a superbly blasphemous *grossièreté* in the *benedictio vulvae* of the final episode. None the less, this *fabliau*, of little weight, is profanely and blandly unconcerned with the treatment of moral issues. Again, story LIV of the *Novellino*[12] bears a certain relationship to the *fabliau* but it is extremely slight in construction and little can be made out of the analogue.

The only precise convergence of the three stories lies in the fact that in each case it is the senior member in the ecclesiastical hierarchy (the bishop in both the *fabliau* and the *Novellino*, the abbot in the *Decameron*) who commits the same carnal sin of which he has already accused his subordinate. However, the situation in the Boccaccio story involves a good deal more than crude polemics against the hypocrisy of ecclesiastical authorities. Perhaps the text bearing the closest resemblance to the story in question is another *novella* in the *Decameron* itself, namely IX, 2, the ever-popular adventure of the nun who clasps the priest's breeches on her head, mistaking them for her veil.

The fourth *novella* of the First Day would therefore seem to be linked by its thematic content to a certain mediaeval tradition of short story and yet to stand apart from any specific example of it. This entitles us to imagine that *Decameron*, I, 4 is an original invention by Boccaccio. But it leaves unanswered the more pressing question: why did he invent such a story? This is, of course, the rhetorical question *par excellence*. At the same time, however, this enforced speculative stance gives the critic a certain advantage: it frees him from any historicist qualms and invites him to advance a pure working hypothesis on which to base his choice as to how the text should be treated. Such a hypothesis can be summed up as follows: Boccaccio created this *novella* because the plot excited his passion for combinative possibilities. In other words, it provided an ideal range of action for his *ars combinatoria*.

In order to get a clearer picture of what I mean by this, it will be useful to make a brief digression and consider another story from the *Decameron*: IX, 6. Boccaccio summarizes the plot as follows: [13]

> Two young men lodge overnight at a cottage, where one of them goes and sleeps with their host's daughter, whilst his wife inadvertently sleeps with the other. The one who was with his daughter clambers into bed beside her father, mistaking him for his companion, and tells him about it. A great furore then ensues, and the wife, realizing her mistake, gets into her daughter's bed, whence with a timely explanation she restores the peace.

This story must be taken in conjunction with its immediate precedents, namely, the anonymous *fabliau*, *Le Meunier et les II Clers*, [14] the *fabliau* by Jean de Boves *De Gombert et de deux Clers*, [15] and their illustrious descendant, *The Reeve's Tale*, by Chaucer. To simplify a comparison between these four different versions, I shall adopt the following symbols:

Le Meunier et les II Clers	M
De Gombert et de deux Clers	G
Decameron, IX, 6	Dec.
The Reeve's Tale	R

In all four versions of the story we find the following arrangement of beds:

Bed (a)   The two *Clers* in the French and English versions. The two young men, Pinuccio and Adriano, in the Italian version.

Bed (b)   Husband and wife (Miller and miller's wife in *M* and in *R*; inn-keeper and inn-keeper's wife in *G* and *Dec.*).

Bed (c)   The daughter (of the miller or the inn-keeper) in all four versions. In *M* her bed is located in a 'huche', a baking cupboard which the miller uses a key to lock up.

Cradle   This is at the foot of the parental double-bed in all four
           versions.

The actual movements made between the various beds by some
of their occupants can be presented as follows:

(*a*) In all versions the initial
      transfer is made by the first
      youth, who removes from
      Bed (a) to Bed (c).

(*b*) In *M*, *Dec.* and *R*, the wife
      gets up from Bed (b). In *M*
      and *R* this is because she
      wishes to satisfy a call of
      nature; in *Dec.* it is because
      she has heard a noise made
      by their cat.

(*b*¹) In *G* it is the husband, Sire
       Gombert, who gets up at
       night and 'S'ala a l'uis
       pissier toz nuz' ('went to the
       door to piss all naked').

(*c*) In all versions, the second
      youth transfers the cradle
      from the foot of Bed (b) to
      the foot of Bed (a). In
      addition, in *M* we find the
      youth pulling at the baby's
      ear to cause the returning
      mother's attention to be
      attracted.

(*d*) In *M*, *Dec.* and *R*, in the
      dark the wife is misled by the
      displacement of the cradle.
      and instead of getting back
      into Bed (b), she slips into
      Bed (a) where the second
      youth is lying.

(*d*¹) In *G* it is the husband who,
       because he is used to feeling
       for the cradle normally at
       the foot of his bed before
       getting back into it, returns
       to Bed (a) instead of (b).

(*e*¹) In *G*, the second youth
       transfers from Bed (a) to (b)
       where the wife is lying.

(*f*) In *M*, *Dec.* and *R*, the first
      youth transfers from Bed (c)
      to Bed (a) where the husband
      is already lying himself.

(*f*¹) In *G*, the first youth
       transfers from Bed (c) to (a)
       where the husband is already
       lying by himself.

At this point, the two French versions and the English version
call a halt to the removals from bed to bed, which in fact culminate
with the husband getting a beating at the hands of the first youth.
It is only Boccaccio who seems to aim at a point of aesthetic
exasperation by adding a further transfer, which I shall call (*g*):

(*g*) In *Dec.* the wife transfers
  from Bed (a) to Bed (c) and
  is thus enabled to vouch both
  for her daughter's and her
  own innocence by declaring
  that they have been together
  all the time.

Boccaccio has in fact presented three characters who keep the
same bed throughout, the daughter, husband and second youth,
and two characters of unfixed bed, namely the first youth and the
wife. These latter two exhaust the full combinative possibilities
of the various beds, since in the course of the night they end up
by having occupied at one time or other each of the three
available beds.[16] The authors of the *fabliaux*, on the other hand,
seem to stay firmly inside the range of the obscene joke, and
Chaucer is clearly out to build up his tale into a professional
dispute between the 'Carpenteer' and the 'Millere', so much so
that it ends inevitably with the miller being vanquished and
beaten up.

Boccaccio is the only one who relishes the authorial delights of
pure combinative versatility, since he exploits to the utmost any
possible variations on the narrative material which he has taken
in hand.[17] Furthermore, by allowing this combinative process
to go the full distance, Boccaccio also manages to re-establish
harmony in a situation which had been fractured by adultery
and carnal violence. As at the close of Machiavelli's play
Mandragola, which combines a similar measure of optimism with
cynicism, at the end of *Decameron*, IX, 6, all the characters
turn out to have achieved what they wanted, and are content with
the result, including the inn-keeper, of whom Boccaccio says that
he 'began to laugh and make fun of Pinuccio and his dreams'.[18]
Ultimately, there has been a restoration of social order, which
has survived the violent claims of the sexual appetite and owes
its reinstatement to the connivance of human intelligence,

represented in this case by the skilful alibi improvised by the inn-keeper's wife.

If we come back to the story of the Monk and the Abbot, it will now be clearer that we have a case where Boccaccio moves the three protagonists of his *novella* through a finite but mathematically exhaustive series of burlesque amorous duets. By this means, the combinative possibilities and comic resources of the subject are fully played out. In the first part we have monk and peasant-girl; in the second we have abbot and peasant-girl; in the third we have monk and abbot. All three of these characters are, as is so often the case in the *Decameron*, deliberately shorn of potentially distracting and therefore superfluous psychological attributes. They are reduced to the level of efficient but limited agents of a specific narrative pattern. Such agents can only act convincingly inside the artificially restricted context of their individual story. It is the *récit*, rather than the character, which moves beyond the bounds of the narrative to suggest a social or moral issue to its reader.

What kind of fictional existence do the three characters enjoy? The monk is lively and energetic; he can easily stand up to the rigours of fast and vigils; he is quick-witted. This is all we know. It seems as if the final *boutade* falls into place with a momentum of its own: the text has written his remark for him. His closing words bear little relation to his personality in the story; he simply helps along a favourable situation which lends itself to the kind of felicitous intuition which he comes out with at the end. Since the monk is unencumbered by psychological complexity, he turns into a paradigm of the functional narration. He is little more than a felicitous justification for the way the narrative has developed.

The figure of the young woman is even more emblematic and functional. Description is whittled down to a single conventional notation concerning her physical appearance ('strikingly beautiful')[19] and a psychological detail after the Abbot's advances ('The girl, who was not exactly made of iron or of flint, fell in very readily for the Abbot's wishes');[20] and this, within the terms of the *Decameron*, provides very little information indeed about the girl. She is a character possessing neither face nor personality; a passive victim of a 'texte en train de s'écrire' ('a text in the process of composing itself').

The case of the Abbot might seem to be somewhat different. Here we are tempted to look for psychological ramifications, since he holds higher rank and performs a more complex sequence of actions than the monk. Yet even the Abbot ends by revealing himself as a non-individual living in a psychological void throughout the *novella*.

As a character he appears to be constructed along a contradictory (and correspondingly more convincing and realistic) succession of psychological co-ordinates representing different stages of self-deception. Hence at first sight the Abbot might be taken as one of the recurring types of modern literature, one that is frequently overlooked by academic criticism, the self-deceiver, the *heautonapatoumenos*.[21] It is symptomatic, for example, that the only critic who has paid special attention to this story, Letterio Di Francia, was thoroughly alarmed by the character of the Abbot 'qui s'abuse sur lui-même' and therefore fails to fit into the critic's rationalizing account of his psychology:[22]

> One can actually admit that the Abbot, once he has become aware that there is a woman in the monk's cell, might prefer to wait until the monk comes out rather than ordering the door to be opened immediately so as to punish his guilt. What requires a larger effort to understand is why he should remit the deserved punishment at the point when the monk comes 'con un buon volto' to hand over the keys to the cell, and it is still harder to understand why he inflicts a punishment on his subordinate after he has fallen into the same sin himself, allowing the temptations of the flesh to overcome his resistance in the same way.

What is so difficult for Di Francia to understand is far clearer to a later generation of readers, who have been brought up on contradictory characters who are constantly unsure of their own motives and their personal destiny. In fact the Abbot's actions become much clearer if we reconstruct them as a series which plunges him progressively deeper into the deception which he is practising on himself:

(*a*) He heard 'the racket that the pair were creating. So that he might recognize the voices, he crept softly up to the door of the cell, stood there listening, and came to the definite conclusion that one of the voices was a woman's. His first impulse was to order the door to be opened.'[23] In fact the remainder of the story will suggest ulterior motives for this action. There is no explicit indication here of what for want of a better term we might call 'audio-voyeurism'; none the less, the tension of the passage ('*tutto* fu tentato di farsi aprire', my italics) conveys the extreme state of excitement which has beset the protagonist.

(*b*) After he has been listening at the door of the cell and rejected the temptation to open the door straight away: 'he then decided to deal with the matter differently and returned to his room, where he waited for the monk to come out.'[24] It is only the subsequent development of the story which will clarify the underlying motive of his behaviour.

(*c*) When the monk asks the Abbot for permission to go to the wood, 'The Abbot . . . was glad of the chance to find out more about the offence he had committed, and he gladly accepted the key and gave him ready permission.'[25] Obviously the Abbot is still acting in good faith at this point, yet the very sincerity of his authorization constitutes a further stage in his process of self-illusion.

(*d*) After the Abbot has wavered between two alternative lines of conduct: '. . . whether it would be better for him to open the man's cell in the presence of all the monks and let them bear witness of his disgrace . . . or first to hear the girl's account of the affair',[26] he decides to adopt the second: 'On reflecting that she might be a respectable woman or the daughter of a man of influence, not wishing to make the mistake of putting such a lady to shame by displaying her all to the monks . . .'[27] Here the process by which the Abbot has rationalized his behaviour and concealed his physical interest is brought to its conclusion. Now it remains for him to cross the point of no return.

(*e*) 'So he quietly made his way to the cell, opened the door, entered, and *locked the door behind him*.'[28] By now the character is almost past caring about providing a justification for his actions ('he . . . locked the door') and is beginning to reveal the latent motives that have underscored his whole treatment of the situation.

(*f*) After he has experienced 'the fleshly cravings'[29] which have so far lain dormant and unconfessed, the Abbot says to himself: 'Why not enjoy myself a little, when I have the opportunity?'[30]

and this constitutes his first open confession that he has been tempted into sin.

(*g*) Once he has decided to make love to the young woman, the Abbot says: 'It's always a good idea, in my opinion, to accept any gift that the Good Lord places in our path,'[31] which provides a pure utilitarian justification for his decision, despite the fact that his motives have undergone a clear volte-face in the course of the *novella*.

(*h*) The final touch in the process comes with the grandiose closing metaphor for the reversal of position:[32]

> He took her in his arms and kissed her a few times, then lowered himself on to the monk's little bed. But out of regard perhaps, for the weight of his dignity and the tender age of the girl, and not wishing to hurt her under an excessive load, he settled down beneath her instead of on top, and in this way he sported with her at considerable length.

This marks the culminating point of the friar's hypocrisy and subtly rationalized self-deception. But it also represents a further intensification of Boccaccio's aesthetic delight in combinatory manipulation of the plot. What we are left with is in fact a carefully constructed parameter of narrative points which set out to represent the way in which the Abbot conducts his self-deception. The line of psychological development which this parameter traces is certainly familiar to the great European novelists from Stendhal onwards who have used 'self-deceivers' in their books. Yet once again this comparison falls down. The mediaeval Abbot in Boccaccio is in fact constitutionally different from the more recent *heautonapatoumenoi* of the major European novel, because these latter heroes present the reader right from the outset with a justification for anticipating that they will evolve in a special way. At each stage of their tortuous *iter*, the reader is called upon to unravel for himself the complex knots inside which the characters have woven their desires and vacillations. In a sense the reader is invited to supply a continuous series of viable links between the possible future and the established past of a character. These links then provide a solid base upon which the deceptions that occur in the intermediate zone of present time can be anchored.

This is simply not the case with Boccaccio's Abbot: as a character he is immune to sudden changes or dynamic insights into behaviour which will occur later in his development. He is made of a totally different raw material. Above all, he lacks a line of development. He evolves as a character through a series of discrete contradictory moments rather than through a tortuous *iter*. He clearly moves from the moral indignation of the opening section, through a change of mind at the centre, to the closing forgiveness. But this line is depicted as a series of separate instances, in which one particular stage does not necessarily anticipate the following stage. The Abbot in fact comes alive exclusively in the narrative present. The dimensions of past and future have no relation to his present, and therefore he is incapable of psychological enrichment, since this would require by definition a system of anticipations and flashbacks. Initially the Abbot is a straight moralist. Later his indulgence of physical appetite is simplistically justified by the crudest of rationalizations. Also, the moment when he recognizes his error (this follows close on the collapse of his rationalization) is introduced inconsequentially as a manifestation of human waywardness. Hence the Abbot, no less than the other two characters in the *novella*, is ultimately non-psychological. As a fictional figure miming the existence of a real human being, he is no less inert than the monk and the country wench, though at first sight he seemed to 'improve' on them. At the end, they all become part of a functional scheme. Yet these narrative puppets succeed in conveying a deft moral statement.

These considerations have brought us to one final hypothesis: a fictional character cannot be clothed in a personal psychology if the narrative is synchronic. Characters only acquire a psychology in the course of diachronic development. For a character to be psychologically complex, the time-structure of the narrative must rely on a plurality of tenses. This hypothesis might be rephrased in the terms of linguistics: just as the individual sentence is determined by agreement of tenses, so any specific message that wishes to transmit psychological information must depend on a disagreement of tenses. This difference could be characterized by the opposition agreement/disagreement of tenses.

We can approach this theoretical problem with a practical example. In a fictional work there is a character A who turns to *B* and declares 'I love you'. Or maybe *A* can muster up a little more eloquence and say: 'It is impossible for me to live without you,' or indeed:

> Thou overheard'st ere I was ware,
> My true love's passion: therefore pardon me,
> And not impute this yielding to light love,
> Which the dark night has so discovered.

Taken by themselves, these sentences have precious little meaning from the psychological point of view. And narratively such statements merely serve to inform the reader of a plot development: namely, *A* loves *B*. *A* and *B* are qualified by this declaration, *A* as the loving agent and *B* as the person loved, but this hardly grants them psychological ramifications. When, however, in one of the most fascinating scenes from D. H. Lawrence's *The Rainbow*, Ann Brangwen simply says to Willie: 'Will, I love you, I love you, Will, I love you,'[33] the plain statement succeeds in conferring a deepened psychology on the two characters, the lover and the beloved, because the declaration has a basis in time. Or at any rate, its temporal basis is quantifiable since it is linked to a series of observations which have conducted both the fictional character and the reader to a discovery of love. In the case of *The Rainbow* the psychological dimension of the characters is guaranteed by the fact that Ann and Willie's feelings for each other stand in a diachronic relation. They develop sequentially from initial diffidence and mutual hostility to the erotic ritual which is played out in the pastoral moonlight scene. The psychological message is constituted by the present as well as the past, so that Ann's statement, 'I love you', assumes its full significance only by virtue of a deliberate *discordia temporum*. This grants the characters' actions a psychological validity which they could not otherwise acquire, and the same goes for the great love declaration by the heroine of *Romeo and Juliet*, whereas the characters in the *Decameron* are 'voyageurs sans bagages', deprived of a recollected past.

This sort of *décalage* contrasting two different moments in the character's fictional life-span is nearly always lacking in the *Decameron*, which is a work that lives and breathes, as I suggest elsewhere,[34] entirely in a narrative and grammatical present tense. The *Decameron* is inhabited by characters who become available for one single adventure, with the sole exception of Calandrino and his clowning friends,[35] whose periodic re-appearances are an unusual feature in the general strategy of the work.[36] The past of the *Decameron* character is restricted to a vague classificatory qualification: thus Agilulfo's wife is a 'beautiful . . . very intelligent and virtuous woman'.[37] Francesco Vergellesi 'was a very wealthy and judicious man, and he was also shrewd, but at the same time he was exceedingly mean'.[38] Beltramo di Rossiglione, the Bertram of *All's Well that Ends Well*, was 'of exceedingly handsome and pleasing appearance'.[39] The reader is rarely granted any more detailed information than this approximate label (the handsome young man, the mean gentleman, the beautiful and virtuous woman) which is stuck on to his name.

Their future is equally hazy, and could usually be condensed into a formula of the fairy-tale kind: 'and they lived happily ever after'. Beltramo: 'from that time forth, never failing to honour the Countess as his lawful wedded wife, he loved her and held her in the greatest esteem'.[40] Martuccio Gomito marries Gostanza: 'and they spent the rest of their lives in the tranquil and restful enjoyment of the love they bore one another'.[41] Even Gualtieri, the ambiguous hero in the last *novella* of the *Decameron*, after handing out such extraordinary treatment to his poor wife, 'lived long and contentedly with Griselda, never failing to honour her to the best of his ability'.[42] Alternatively, as in some of the stories of the Fourth Day, the characters' future is simply re-presented by two unhappy lovers sharing an eternal tenancy of the same tomb.[43] Between these opening and closing labels the actual episode stands as a single unit which has precedence over any demands of historical accuracy, psychological consistency or behavioural plausibility which we might be unwise enough to want to impose on it.

This is the puzzling factor which sets up an aesthetic gulf between the modern reader and the *Decameron*. We are all of us constructed out of bits and pieces of nineteenth-century fictional characters: these are our inescapable cultural heritage, even if our actual reading went no further than Enid Blyton. Inevitably we run our lives on parallel co-ordinates to those of the Dickens or Balzac hero, in terms of behaviour, reasoning, motivation, instinctive needs and mental constructs. It all turns out to be a kind of second-class copy of a nineteenth-century novel, i.e. the literary genre which was most obsessively concerned with the psychological credibility of the character. We can veer between consistency and inconsistency, we can follow a direct or a more tortuous psychological line (Julian Sorel and Raskolnikov need by no means be considered self-consistent), but ultimately we are still accustomed to picturing ourselves and the world, art and politics, all in an uncompromisingly diachronic line, that is to say, in terms of psychological feasibility.

When the modern reader has to come to grips with a work like the *Decameron*, which belongs to a narrative area with a completely different *raison d'être*, he feels disoriented and is tempted to look for something which cannot be found in the work, namely a familiar character fresh from the 500-plus pages of a tome written by the grandfather of his grandfathers. This also leads to the occasional insensitivity of criticism, which complains about the absence of narrative modes which Boccaccio neither intended nor wanted in the fabric of the *Decameron*.

Yet not all the *novelle* live exclusively in the present tense. In our analysis of the first *novella* we have seen how it was necessary to acquire information about the previous life history of the notary Ser Ciappelletto in order to relish his confession that much better. I insist on the word *relish* and not *understand*, since the writer is using the double perspective of the opening portrait and the subsequent confession to work on the psychology of the reader's process rather than fill out the figure of the protagonist. It is not that Ciappelletto becomes more subtle by means of this double perspective: we readers are the ones who are rendered subtler, and this leads to our refined enjoyment of the story.

There is another licentious story (*Decameron*, III, 1) which requires a doubling of the time perspective, the well-known story of Masetto (one of the less convincing episodes in Pasolini's recent film of the *Decameron*). Masetto, 'a young labourer, a big, strong fellow',[44] meets 'a funny little chap'[45] who had worked as a gardener in a convent but gave up his job because he was poorly paid by the Abbess and badly treated by the young nuns. Masetto pretends to agree with the silly remarks made by the little chap, but in fact begins to work out a plan so that he can well and truly cultivate the garden in the convent. He goes there pretending to be dumb, and is engaged by the aged steward as gardener. Once in the convent, he seduces and is in his turn seduced by all the nuns. Yet the *novella* does not follow up this diachronic arrangement of information to produce a psychological line. It does not expand the figure of Masetto by ascribing plans or reflections to him, or by adding further information about his personality: what it does is to give way to one of the most unrestrained examples of Boccaccio's combinative virtuosity. One might have expected that after Masetto's crafty plan had begun to bear its fruits and he was able to lie with one nun after the other, the story would have referred to the young gardener's private satisfaction or amusement at the success of the whole operation. Instead nothing of this sort happens: Boccaccio's main concern is at the combinative level.

The subsequent multiplication of his acts of fornication is based on a general ethical reflection on human nature which the author takes so much for granted that it admits of no further discussion (even an ignorant peasant like Masetto has understood it): the desires of the flesh are stronger than any moral or social law, and affect everyone indiscriminately, virtuous young men or scoundrels, chaste young maidens or girls of lascivious character, laymen and priests, serving girls and masters, countrywomen, young nuns and mothers superior, beggars and kings, princesses, hermits, sturdy young monks, pious abbots and solemn scholars. Having established this universal pattern of lust, all the author has to do is to follow the several manifestations of the law and the inevitable course of Masetto's conquests in order to fulfil his own lust for combinative ramifications.

At first the two young nuns invite Masetto into a hut, while the young man, who was only waiting 'for one of them to come and fetch him'[46] follows them in 'with idiotic cackles of laughter'[47] which are matched by the distant echo of the reader's slyer cackling. Meanwhile, a fellow nun tumbles to their game and confides in two other nuns in order to denounce the guilty ones to the Abbess. But then 'they changed their minds, and by common agreement with the other two, they took up shares in Massetto's holding'.[48] And that makes five. 'And they were joined by the other three at different times and in various circumstances.'[49] The author merely says 'in various circumstances'. Individual motives disappear completely: all that is involved is the combinative play. That makes eight. The only one left is the Abbess, and she will yield as soon as she gets an opportunity to admire Masetto's sexual organ from near at hand.

Clearly this is the real protagonist of the *novella*: not Masetto's brain (since the psychological dimension of the story is reduced to a minimum), but his member, which procures frequent coitus and generates 'a number of monklets'.[50] At the outset the Abbess 'was possibly under the impression that he had lost his tail as well as his tongue'.[51] Yet Masetto's 'tail' is certainly all there and Boccaccio plays on this fact considerably. First the two young nuns stop and stare ('cominciarono a riguardare').[52] The object of their interest is kept unspecified, for the verb 'riguardare', to stare, is left without a direct object. At the end of the story the Abbess will come across Masetto sleeping in the shadow of an almond-tree, with his tunic blown up over his stomach by the wind, so that he was 'all exposed. Finding herself alone, the lady stood staring at this spectacle.'[53] At this point the object of the verb has been stated: the organ on which the hungry gaze of the nuns has alighted[54] assumes the rôle of a protagonist, and forces the Abbess to act without delay:[55]

> She was seized by the same cravings to which her young charges had already succumbed. So, having roused Masetto she led him away to her room, where she kept him for several days, thus provoking bitter complaints from the nuns over the fact that the handyman had suspended work in the garden. Before sending him back to his own quarters she experienced over and over again ('provando e riprovando') that delicious feeling for which she had always reserved her most fierce disapproval.

Once again we have a case where plurality of reading approaches is invited. We ought to consider the different treatment which the Abbess on the one side and the eight younger nuns on the other receive from Masetto's industrious organ and the author's pen. In the case of the nuns, it is a hasty job in the hut, each one waiting her turn and no time wasted on it. Whereas, with the Abbess we have a prolonged operation, 'provando e riprovando', which goes on for days and days in an epic struggle which produces that 'delicious feeling' which the other nuns had speculated about on hearsay before experiencing Masetto,[56] and which they had verified after the experience.[57] 'The Abbess however, is the only one who experiences this delicious feeling over and over again to such a point of surfeit for the over-taxed gardener that 'his tongue-ligament breaks',[58] he pretends to be cured of the illness that caused his speech impediment and throws himself on the mercy of the Mother Superior, declaring his incapacity to satisfy the constitutional needs of nine women.

Now this difference of treatment might be explained in terms of age: the Abbess, being the oldest nun, is clearly the one who has fasted for the longest period away from the feast of love and now it is right that she should try to make up for lost time. Or it could be seen in social terms, corresponding to the difference in prestige and hierarchy between the nuns and their Superior: the latter is in a better position to organize things for herself than the younger nuns, and she can claim exclusive use of Masetto's organ to the disadvantage of these younger and equally famished subordinates. Or perhaps Masetto prefers the taste of mellower flesh and can perform prodigies with the Abbess which are out of the question when he is with his younger but inexperienced partners. These are perfectly respectable psychological queries, but they are all extraneous to the text. The *novella* tells us nothing about these possible considerations and seems to take no interest in such questions of human motivation.

A tactical rather than psychological interpretation, however, would take us in a different direction: first we would have a poor deaf-mute supposed to have 'lost his tail'; then there would be the 'staring' without any specific object; finally, when the real protagonist of the story comes on stage with the pimping help of the wind, the narrative gives way to a marathon of fornication. The motives for this final epic coitus involve psychological considerations, but the mind affected by them is not that of the character but quite simply the reader's. In fact the character's mind is put to shame by a comparison with his all-conquering member. By a tactical interpretation, therefore, one is talking in terms of special attention paid to the psychology of the reading process and the granting of correspondingly less attention to the psychology of the characters.

Their old steward had died a few days previously. And so, with Masetto's consent, they unanimously decided, now that they all knew what the others had been doing, to persuade the people living in the neighbourhood that after a prolonged period of speechlessness, his ability to talk had been miraculously restored by the nuns' prayers and the virtue of the saint after whom the convent was named, and they appointed him their new steward. They divided up his various functions among themselves in such a way that he was able to do them all justice. And although he fathered quite a number of monklets, it was all arranged so discreetly that nothing leaked out until after the death of the Abbess, by which time Masetto was getting on in years and simply wanted to retire to his village on a fat pension. Once his wishes became known, they were readily granted.[95]

The whole manner here is shockingly relaxed. The transformation of a pious convent into a centre of free love, the deliberate falsification of a miracle, the *accommodement*[60] with the celestial and civil authorities, the atmosphere of serene cohabitation in this extraordinary *ménage à dix*, the massive production of illegitimate offspring: all this is accepted without batting an eyelid, as the inevitable consequence of the combinative process of the narrative. Nor is there any trace here of a leering grin on the face of a lascivious old writer; perhaps there is just the faintest tinge of a smile in that phrase 'a number of monklets' ('assai monachin'), where the Italian word loses its final vowel ('monach*in*') in an apocopation which suggests that the word is almost withdrawn at the tip of the speaker's tongue. Nor is there any of the moralist's righteous indignation in the passage. The story simply stands as it has been told, the product of a psychological law (the universal fact of sexual desire which governs all human destiny) and the result of a compositional rule (the combinative technique which tends towards an exhaustive catalogue of all the possible permutations of coitus available to the characters).

But morality is lying in wait at the critical point, as the story comes into the last bend, where the relaxed style is precisely the element which makes the reader suspicious and goads him into action against his own tranquil acceptance of the story. Obviously something is wrong if all those disgraceful happenings can be recorded so impassively without the slightest hint of moral disapproval. It is up to the reader to work out the implications. The anti-clerical and anti-devotional stance of the *novella* (why does God need so many virgins?) comes out in Boccaccio's silence and in the undisturbed cadence of the closing paragraphs where the outrage has little to do with the facts as related but stems from lack of emotional tension in the narrative manner. There is an interesting parallel here with those scaring children's tales which come to their climactic effect with a complete lack of stylistic or narrative subtlety; 'So then along came the wolf, and gulp! – he gobbled up the little girl all in one mouthful.' On the other hand, the virulent anti-clericalism in the story of Tedaldo degli Elisei fails to move us because it is all explicitly stated, and therefore offers no manœuvring space for the reader. But the detached language of the closing paragraphs of Masetto subtly prompts us to feel a measure of indignation. The text can perhaps give the impression of being outrageously amoral; our reading, on the other hand, can even turn into an ethical meditation; the former does not exclude the latter.

D. H. Lawrence claimed in a somewhat ingenuous page that Boccaccio was a writer with a healthy open view of sexual activity, the exact opposite of the 'dirty little secret' which he was directing his polemical and moralistic fervour against in the essay *Pornography and so on*.[61] This line is close to Havelock Ellis, who has always maintained, with even more remarkable ingenuousness, that great literary masterpieces deal openly and objectively with sexual issues. Probably Havelock Ellis had a different list of literary masterpieces than I do, for mine would include: perversion, bestiality, incest, erotic sadism, moral and physical torture, the most unusual and remarkable sexual excesses, paederasty, paedophilia, gerontophilia, and so on and so forth. Whatever D. H. Lawrence would like to maintain, Boccaccio presents no exception to this pattern.

If we go through the *Decameron* systematically, what do we find? Day I, *novella* 4: a fat and probably senile abbot besports himself with a country wench, placing her on his chest so as not to crush her with his inordinate bulk; III, 1: a delightful example of multiple *ménage*, the untroubled cohabitation of one man and nine women; III, 6: a disguised rape, with the lover succeeding in bedding the woman he desires by pretending to be her husband; IV, 3: a case of indirect incest, with a man killing his own, and acquiring his brother's woman; V, 5: a man attempts to kidnap for sexual purposes a girl who turns out to be his sister; V, 10: a session *à trois* between a homosexual husband, his frustrated wife and a sturdy young lad; VII, 7: a sadistic female protagonist seems to derive erotic pleasure from terrorizing her lover and having her husband beaten; VII, 9: a wife and her lover indulge in congress under the disbelieving eyes of the husband; VIII, 7: the pleasures of love are heightened by the piquancy of physical torture inflicted on the hapless lover; VIII, 8: another case of coitus in the presence of the husband; IX, 6: two guests at an inn have coitus with the wife and daughter of the inn-keeper, all in the same room as the latter; IX, 10: another rapid sexual act under the eyes of the husband; X, 4: a clear case of necrophilia, where the unhappy lover, not content with merely kissing the face of the beloved woman who has been buried as if dead, begins to feel her breasts.

Of course, this is not a catalogue of *psychopathia sexualis*; yet it would be equally hard to fit it into Lawrence's scheme of healthy sexuality. The characters in the *Decameron* are thus no different from the real men in flesh and blood: they all bear witness to the infinite variety of human creation. The underlying morality of the whole *Decameron* is bound up with the complex sexuality of these *novelle*: it accepts all the ethical implications of our turbulent humanity in spite of the distorting focus of narrative devices.

Another example of 'healthy sexuality' is supposed by certain critics to be the *novella* of Alibech, III, 10, perhaps the most famous bawdy story in the *Decameron*. Here is a brief summary of its plot: Alibech, the beautiful fourteen-year-old daughter of a wealthy father (fourteen: one year younger than the canonical age of marriage in the *Decameron*), completely inexperienced in the facts of life, becomes infatuated with the ecstatic joys of Christian devotion and decides to withdraw into the desert of Tebaida in order to serve God better. A high-minded monk, alarmed by this new arrival at his solitary retreat, tries to get rid of her quickly by giving her herbs and wild fruit, and suggesting another place where there will be some other monk to teach her how to serve our Lord. Eventually, she arrives at the retreat of a young monk called Rustico, who decides to take her in 'to prove to himself that he possessed a will of iron'.[62] Inevitably temptations arise and the young man gives in to them 'after the first few assaults',[63] and forgets his devotions and self-chastisement enough to yield to the pleasure of relishing in his mind 'the youth and the beauty of the girl'[64] and subsequently to calculations as to how he might obtain his purpose without Alibech realizing 'how lecherous he was'.[65]

He tests out just how innocent and ingenuous she is with a series of cautious questions, and when this innocence is confirmed by her answers, Rustico decides to have his way with her 'with the pretext of serving God'.[66] After giving her full information on the Great Enemy, he suggests to her a novel way of replacing the Devil in Hell, 'di rimettere il diavolo in inferno'.[67] They both take off their clothes and at the moment of 'the resurrection of the flesh',[68] the hermit points out the place in her own body which contains 'Ninferno' (a popular corruption of the word for Hell, *Inferno*, with an obvious link to the term denoting a young girl, innocent maid, etc.: *ninfa*, 'nymph'). This is the place where the Devil should be banished, and the young girl, 'never having put a single devil into hell before',[69] at first feels some physical irritation, but after she has subdued the Devil's arrogance a number of times, she begins to enjoy this religious ceremony which involves so much incidental pleasure and urges the poor monk to ever more diligent devotions: 'Father, I came here to serve God, not to idle away my time. Let's go and put the devil back in Hell.'[70] Rustico, whose food consisted of herb-roots and water, is hardly capable of satisfying the novice's ravenous hunger for devotions and eventually 'this happened so infrequently that it was rather like chucking a bean into the mouth of a lion. . . .'[71] At the end of the *novella* the young girl returns home, where she soon discovers that it was hardly necessary to go as far as Tebaida to find someone capable of putting the Devil back in the *Ninferno*.

Now, according to Salinari, the sexual act in this *novella* is 'reduced to its natural dimensions, to those which make it at once a source of life and of joy'.[72] And Baratto insists: 'The metaphor of putting the Devil back in Hell stands for the sexual act seen in its primordial stage, the healthiest and most natural stage of all.'[73] Since we moderns are no longer primordial men, one supposes Baratto can suggest some alternative to the primitive congress of Rustico and Alibech for us! In actual fact this *novella* is in my opinion something far removed from the edifying myth of Golden Age erotics which the two critics cited above have detected.

There are at least three important points to establish in connection with *Decameron*, III, 10. The first is the precise parallelism set up between erotic ritual and religious ceremony, which is not so much based on a crudely obscene metaphor as on the writer's proposal of an unexpected analogy. Under this heading one should remember that the analogical connection of sex to religion, the physiological proximity of orgasm and mystic state, and the linguistic similarity of terms describing the genitals and the vocabulary of the Underworld are not, after all, such surprising phenomena to have to deal with in a mediaeval context. It is enough to think of Bernardus Silvestris;[74] or, staying in an area closer to Boccaccio, the mystic poet Jacopone da Todi,[75] where at times there is a quite remarkable merging of scatological into eschatological terms of reference. Hell was often located in the general area of feminine *trous*, as in the case of Rabelais's Sybil.[76] So Boccaccio's deliberately ironic recording of all the ceremonial in no way diminishes the seriousness of the *exemplum* he is giving. 'With the pretext of serving God',[77] one ends up in a situation where God is actually being served. The two young partners kneeling one in front of the other just before the sexual act, as if they were in joint adoration, present an extremely refined picture which has a certain affinity with the iconography of early religious painting.

Nor should we be shocked by the obscene metaphor, 'the resurrection of the flesh': just as the central myth of Christianity is based on a metaphor from eating and digesting, so this rather different myth is transformed into a metaphor concerned with the world of sexuality. The hermit's erect organ is, in a scriptural sense, possessed of the Devil, and there are various ways in which it may be exorcised: by fasting, vigils, mortification of the flesh, the more drastic remedy of Abelard, or taming its arrogant head in the fragrant 'Ninferno' of the nymph. This replacement of the Devil in Hell causes Rustico 'marvellous relief',[78] and there is a persuasive air of suggestion that it does actually provide God with 'incalculable service and pleasures'.[79] Not only this, but it was 'the most agreeable way of serving God'.[80] This latter closing phrase seals the gracefulness of the sexual act: their act of exorcism is 'greatly to His liking and pleasurable to the parties concerned, and a great deal of good can arise and flow in the process'.[81] Consequently the coitus in this story receives a divine blessing.

Indeed, the relationship between the two communicants is kept at a strictly religious level even during the act: 'This devil must certainly be a bad lot, Father, and a true enemy of God; for as well as plaguing mankind he even hurts Hell when he is driven back inside it.'[82] Of course this kind of literary touch shows deliberate irony on Boccaccio's part, but the writer still succeeds in persuading the reader subconsciously to review his automatic assumptions about sexual activity and religious observances. It is no accident, for example, that in this story more than anywhere else in the *Decameron* the author insists on the keen delights which sex can provide: for the man it is 'marvellous relief'; for the woman, 'dolce cosa' ('a sweet experience');[83] it gives 'so much pleasure and satisfaction'.[84] And again 'così volentieri come il Ninferno il riceve e tiene' ('as much as Hell enjoys receiving him and keeping him inside'):[85] and this last image, so persuasive and refined in the original, proves just how skilfully Boccaccio can handle the supposedly taboo areas of language.

According to my interpretation, the whole *novella* is constructed round the affinity of the obscene and the sacred, and this symbiosis should not be automatically dismissed as implausible or unproductive, even if the subsequent cultural history of Europe will witness an ever-widening gap between these two sections of human experience (at least up to Wilhelm Reich's eccentric theories).

A second observation must be made on this neglected *novella* (avidly read by everybody, analysed by very few), and this concerns the rigid symmetry of its two halves, which can be traced back to Boccaccio's combinative fondness for exhausting all the variations and organizing a neat geometrical reversal between separate units of a given plot (this has been commented on already in this and the preceding chapter). In the first section of the story we have Rustico attempting to persuade Alibech to make love: in the second part we have Alibech failing to persuade Rustico to do so. In the first part the 'Ninferno' is supposed to pacify the Devil's ardour; in the second part the Devil tries unsuccessfully to calm down the raging ardour of 'Ninferno'.[86] At first Rustico encourages Alibech to make her devotions, then later these rôles are reversed. This also satisfies the reader's instinctive delight in symmetry, since it helps to tone down the impression of sacrilege in what is going on by giving it a more *scientific* and inevitable-seeming sequence. In other words geometric order (the order which we are all taught to accept unquestioningly) serves to filter out our anguish at a possible outrage in what we are reading.

Third, it is interesting to note how little psychological motivation is at play in the story. If we compare it with La Fontaine's version (*Le diable en enfer*), some points may come to light; here is Rustico's comment when Alibech arrives at his hut:[87]

Comme il voulait être des plus parfaits,
Il dit en soi: Rustico, que sais-tu faire?
Veiller, prier, jeûner, porter la haïre?
Qu'est-ce cela? moins que rien; tous le font:
Mais d'être seul auprès de quelque belle
Sans la toucher, il n'est victoire telle:
Triomphes grands chez les anges en sont:
Méritons-les; retenons cette fille.
Si je résiste à chose si gentille,
J'atteins le comble, et me tire du pair.

(Since he wanted to become morally perfect / he said to himself: Rustico, what are the things you can do? / To keep vigils, pray, fast and wear the hair-shirt? / What does all that amount to? Next to nothing: everyone does it: / But to be unaccompanied, in the presence of a beautiful wench / without touching her body, that is certainly a victory over the flesh: / The recompense of this is great triumph among the angels: / Let us deserve such triumph, let us not send the girl away. / If I resist such a beautiful object, / I will reach the heights, and survive the struggle.)

Apart from La Fontaine's permanent interest in his *Contes* for scurrilous adventures, with a predilection for timid young girls being more or less forced to the act, in this particular story he also seems to be concerned with the psychology of the two participants. In the Boccaccio *novella* the idea of having the hermit try to put his chastity to the test is purely cursory ('being anxious to prove himself that he possessed a will of iron')[88] and equally quickly dismissed ('after the first few assaults finding himself out-manœuvred on all fronts, he laid down his arms and surrendered'),[89] whereas La Fontaine exploits this minor intuition and builds it up considerably, turning it into a struggle of the conscience which closes with a melodramatic renunciation of his vow all cast in the form of an 'Adieu': 'Adieu la haïre, adieu la discipline; / et puis voilà de ma dévotion' ('No more the hair-shirt, no more religious discipline; / an end to my devotion').[90]

Boccaccio will have none of this; he is unconcerned with what is going on in his totally imaginary hero's mind. What he is interested in is exploring the maximum possible permutations in the narrative game. When La Fontaine arrives at the point where the Devil is to be put back in 'Ninferno', he has Rustico slipping into her bed ('il se glisse dedans le lit')[91] and imposing his lust on the girl who is 'moitié forcée et moitié consentante / moitié voulant combattre ce désir / moitié n'osant, moitié peine et plaisir'[92] (which all sounds like a scene from a *comédie larmoyante*). So La Fontaine is involved in the banal reactions of that half-sized fictional construct that bears the name 'Alibech': he ignores the ritual playing-out of the scene in Boccaccio and can only treat the sexual coupling as a prefabricated literary *topos*.

Petronio, a critic who is particularly insensitive to this type of *novella*, has stated that Boccaccio treats the actual moment of sexual intercourse with a cursory touch that is unknown to our day and age.[93] But surely this is simply not true. It might be true to say that Boccaccio merely touches on the sexual act or passes it over in cases where he would have beeen unable to move outside a stylized *topos* and stage a specific happening which is poetically effective and impressive as a literary creation. This is why we have cursory references such as Rinaldo d'Esti and the widowed woman who both 'retired into her bedroom where they lost no time in getting into bed, and before the night was over they satisfied their longings repeatedly and in full measure'.[94] Or Alessandro degli Agolanti and the daughter of the King of England, who 'fell into each other's arms and for the rest of the night they disported of themselves to their great and mutual pleasure'.⁹⁵ Or Giannotto and La Spina 'began to taste amorous pleasure with each other'.⁹⁶

Boccaccio is quite the opposite of the average pornographer who uses every possible opportunity to offer detailed descriptions of the sexual organs and what they are up to. However, when he does get a proper chance to exploit what Petronio is pleased to call 'il momento dell' amplesso' at a poetic level, Boccaccio is not in the least bit coy about what is going on. In our *novella*, for instance, Alibech notices that certain something which is 'sticking out in front'⁹⁷ and when she has been given a lesson on the physio-theological connection linking the devil and her 'Ninferno', she takes part in the operation, which we then follow graphically, point by point. Thus, Boccaccio refers to the initial pain, the subsequent pleasure, the multiple repetition of the act, and so forth. We have already noted earlier in this chapter how Boccaccio chooses the precise and delicate observation 'come il Ninferno ... il riceve e tiene', 'as much as Hell enjoys receiving him and keeping him inside'.⁹⁸ This shows no trace whatsoever of reticence or prudishness: the sexual activity between Alibech and Rustico has been transformed into a unique event rather than a tired pornographic cliché.

We have a similar case in *Decameron*, IX, 10, the story of Donno Gianni di Barolo, a priest who offers to transform the wife of a poverty-striken peasant into a mare so that she can carry wares to the market by day and revert to her human body by night. The priest orders her to undress and stand on all fours like a horse. Then he starts casting his magic spells while touching various parts of the woman's body: 'These be fine mare's legs and fine mare's hooves',⁹⁹ 'This be a fine mare's breast',¹⁰⁰ and so he continues, gradually approaching more perilous zones of her anatomy. Obviously there comes a point when all that is left to make is her tail, so 'he lifted his skirt, took hold of the dibber that he did his planting with and stuck it straight in the appropriate furrow, saying: "And this be a fine mare's tail" '.¹⁰¹ With this inventive stroke, Boccaccio succeeds in redeeming the otherwise overwhelming obscenity by exploiting this absurd twist which he has introduced into it.

Again in *Decameron*, VII, 2, we have a story with a source n Apuleius¹⁰² where Boccaccio succeeds in bringing off a similar literary *coup* with the sexual act: Peronella, with her lover standing behind her, orders her husband to get into the tub which she pretends she has just sold to her young visitor. While the poor husband is busy inside the tub and his wife tells him all the places to clean and scrape in it, her lover takes her from behind as she blocks off the opening at the top of the jar and 'in quella guisa che negli ampi campi / gli sfrenati cavalli e d'amor caldi / le cavalle di Partia assaliscono / ad effetto recò il giovanil desiderio'[103] ('in the manner of a wild and hot-blooded stallion mounting a Parthian mare in the open fields, he satisfied his young man's passion').[104]

Obviously one doesn't have to go as far as Parthia[105] to see stallions adopting an approach from behind to mares in heat. But there are several elements which combine to convert what might have seemed like a squalid coupling with a tart into a mythical mating of male and female: we have the dominant rhythm of the three hendecasyllable lines concealed in the prose, the reference to the distant fabled country, the marvellous evocation of 'gli sfrenati cavalli e d'amore caldi', and the whole incongruousness of the preposterously detailed simile.

All Boccaccio's licentious *novelle* were imitated by La Fontaine in his *Contes*, and Croce made a brilliant comparison between the two versions of a single tale, insisting that the French poet lost the delicate touch of Boccaccio in the treatment of the most scandalous plots.[106] This judgment strikes me as true, since La Fontaine never succeeds in wiping the prurient leer off his face. He seems like a pander who distributes masturbatory delights with his lewd little tales; this makes him the opposite of the great erotic writer, who is always working to render his material unfamiliar and striking. None the less a collation of the Boccaccio source with its imitation in La Fontaine is often useful as an aid to understanding the aesthetics of the obscene, which is still one of the central issues in contemporary fiction.

La Fontaine's *Contes* are basically a *summa* of the whole of traditional licentious writing, with a wide selection of salacious adventures drawn from Athenaeus to Boccaccio, from Petronius to Rabelais, from Apuleius to Aretino. In this respect the *Contes* serve only too well to confirm the standard accusations of monotony, lack of inventiveness and a one-track mind which are made against the genre of licentious writing in literature. La

GWL

Fontaine provides an example of the infinite monotony of the obscene which Bédier mentions in his seminal study of the *Fabliaux*.[107] The French poet gives the impression that he is always telling the same story, based on the same elementary psychological principles. Invariably this story ends with a *déjà-vu* coitus: however different the build-up to the act, it always seems the same, trapped inside a conventional literary *topos* which closes the adventure with an organ x penetrating a cavity y to produce n pleasure, even though La Fontaine tries to redeem it with eloquent deificatory epithets.[108] Whether the subject is an abbess with a gardener, a princess with a pirate, or a chance meeting 'dans le fond des bois' with a shepherd girl, his erotic episodes go through a series of fixed stages until they reach their inevitable more or less voluptuous consummation.

La Fontaine denies his female characters the behavioural variety which at least he ascribes to his male figures: these women all react in the same way during the first approach of the male, who is always a predatory seducer type. Magdeleine, who is La Fontaine's version of Boccaccio's Comare Gemmata turned into a horse in *Decameron*, IX, 10, 'aimait mieux / demeurer femme, et juroit ses grands dieux / de ne souffrir un telle vergogne' ('preferred / to remain a woman and swore on all the Saints / not to submit to such a disgrace').[109] The valiant Bartolomea 'fit son devoir de pleurer / un demi-jour, tant qu'il se pût étendre: / Et Pagamin de la reconforter / Et notre Épouse à la fin de se rendre' ('dutifully wept / half a day, as much as she could manage; / Pagamin went on comforting her, / and our brave spouse at last surrendered herself').[110] Whereas in Boccaccio this same woman (*Decameron,* II, 10), who is kidnapped by a pirate from an impotent old husband, is easily persuaded[111] in the hands of the virile Paganino da Monaco. Even Alibech tries to curb the surging throb of her breasts ('sein qui pousse et repousse / certain corset en dépit d'Alibech, / qui tâche en vaine de lui clôre le bec' ('a breast which pushes and strains / the corset in spite of Alibech's / valiant efforts to muzzle it')[112] so as not to arouse Rustico before the ceremony which La Fontaine succeeds in making neither diabolic nor ritualistic, but simply rather dirty. Once the seduction is carried through, all La Fontaine's female figures indiscriminately are *lassatae sed non satiatae* and ask for a repeat performance: even the Magdeleine / Comare Gemmata figure begs Donno Gianni to come back another day when her husband is not there to complete her full metamorphosis into a mare.[113]

Once La Fontaine has settled the tiresome problem of female actions and motivations by reducing the woman to a behaviouristic model of almost Pavlovian crudeness (she starts all reticent and modest; she ends in heat and craving), all that is required is for the poet to play on the man's astuteness in conquering his reluctant bed-partner's favours. This reduces the narrative complexity of Boccaccio's stories to the straight vulgarity of prurient folk-tale.

The word is indeed 'prurient', rather than 'erotic', when La Fontaine covers over the most excessive *grossièretés* with a veil of euphemism or indirect reference (such as in the case of the *Tableau*[114] taken from Aretino: but why relate such stories at all if they make him feel ashamed?). His whole technique suggests a convent parlour where every gesture is accompanied by giggles and little hints. He indulges in evasive ploys; he may use an ostentatiously straightforward turn of phrase to disguise his embarrassment at the obscene subject; at times he seems to speak under his breath or offer little asides; he hesitates between Zerlina's 'will I or won't I?'; he seems to have a permanent rosy blush at all the scandals dripping from his pen. Obviously this means that La Fontaine's world is full of civilized rules and observances. The critic Lapp sees it as follows:[115]

> The *contes* appear to civilize sex. . . . What they refuse to do is to brutalize sex. The poet of the *contes* remains human and humane; his amorous fun-making involves partners with a civilized deference for one another, and if Alaciel and Hispal lack a sense of mystery, they never lack good manners. Even when the sex act in the *contes* represents war between the sexes, it is war fought according to the rules. So I believe that this quality is one reason why we must appreciate the *contes*, for theirs is a sexuality contemplated with the smile of reason.

Here the observations are convincing but the conclusion is unacceptable. For a literary treatment of the obscene, the smile of reason is simply not enough; at times we need a grin of delirium (witness all the great erotic writers, from Catullus onwards). 'Pour la création il faut un moment de délire' ('the requisite of creation is a moment of delirium'),[116] said Céline about another great erotic writer, Rabelais. If the battle of the sexes is waged according to the rules of social etiquette, it is bound to become a tedious experience. What is monotonous is not the obscene in itself, but obscenity when it is standardized in a single format; when sexual experience is reduced to an elementary physio-psychological model of stimulus and response with the narrative passively following the conventions of traditional *turpiloquium*. Even love stories can be boring if they are reduced to the standard terms of women's weeklies. Fortunately for us Boccaccio is not monotonous, for when he is obscene, he has the courage of his own obscenity.

The same kind of outrageous treatment which trangresses the traditional limits both of pornography and good manners, is to be found in *Decameron*, VIII, 7. This is the splendid story of the scholar and the widow, the longest *novella* in the *Decameron* and one which almost amounts to a short novel, with a proportional enrichment in the psychology of the characters. The protagonist of the story is a certain Rinieri, who had 'spent some years studying in Paris with the purpose, not of selling his knowledge for gain as many people do, but of learning the reasons and causes of things'.[117] Back in Florence, he falls madly in love with a beautiful widow, but she only has time for a younger man, her lover. The widow cruelly encourages the hopes of the scholar, and on a cold winter's night she has him summoned to her inner courtyard, where she repeatedly promises she will invite him into her house just as soon as her brother has left after paying an unexpected visit. With one excuse after another, the widow and her lover keep the scholar there for the whole night, in the snow, without any cover, freezing with cold while they besport themselves more indefatigably than usual, given the added excitement of the third party who is being made to suffer: 'Whereupon clasping her firmly to his bosom, her lover kissed her, not a thousand times, but more than a hundred thousands.'[118]

After the terrible night spent out in the cold, the scholar falls seriously ill, but, once he has recovered, he pretends he is still in love with his tormentress, in order to be able to devise a better revenge. His chance comes several months later, in the middle of the summer: the young widow has been jilted by her lover and plans to use what she imagines is the scholar's skill in the occult arts to regain her lost love. The scholar pretends to help her to cast a complex spell during the course of which she ends up naked at the top of a ruined tower, passing a whole day exposed to the heat of the midsummer sun after he has removed the ladder that led to the roof. When her maid finds her in the evening, this previously beautiful woman is '. . . more like a burnt log than a human form'.[119]

There have been two main lines of interpretation. The first tends to locate the story of the scholar and the widow in the tradition of mediaeval misogynous literature (this is extremely well summed up in Branca's note);[120] and a later work by Boccaccio himself, the *Corbaccio*,[121] shows him to be capable of indulging in rampant misogyny. The other general interpretation of the *novella* goes back to Sansovino[122] but has found considerable sympathy with modern critics:[123] it emphasizes the auto-biographical element lying just beneath the narrative surface of the story. Clearly the two approaches do not rule each other out: both can help towards an identification of the story's rôle and purpose, always providing that by autobiography we do not mean some rigid chronicling by the author of his private life, but simply a projection of personal emotions on a fictional setting. One thing is obvious: the impassioned defence of the intellectual and of 'the power of the pen'[124] ('you would have been so mortified by the things I had written that you would have put out your eyes rather than look upon yourself ever again'[125]) seems to reflect more than a theoretical view of literature; it shows strong signs of a direct influence by some dolorous past experience.

It is also worth noting that in this more than in any other *novella* of the *Decameron* there is an elaborate development of motivation and psychological structure in both of the main characters, so much so in fact that at times they appear to be playing a highly refined game of pressure and counter-pressures based on the secret shortcomings existing in the human psyche. Once the widow has been trapped on the roof of the sun-scorched tower, though tormented by heat, insects, thirst and a body racked with pain, she still has her wits and intelligence about her, and contrives to keep the scholar talking in a desperate game of entreaty and refusal, constantly trying to seek out a weak point that will save her in the murky depths of the man's blind rage. The woman exaggerates the suffering she has already gone through; invokes her frail femininity as compared with the strength of men: 'the eagle that conquers a dove has nothing to boast about',[126] calls on the love of God, pleads for her own good name, throws herself on his human compassion and magnanimity as a scholar. She reminds him of the beautiful body which he, 'not yet old',[127] had been so in love with, that body which '. . . brings sweetness, joy and solace to a man's youth'.[128] So she offers herself to him, declaring that she is willing to have him as 'my lover and my lord',[129] contrasting the present beauty of her body with what would become of it if she were forced to cast herself from the tower and be broken to pieces. She runs through all the modulations of prayer and supplication, begging for a drop of water, crying out for death, reminding the scholar of those dearest to him, especially the new woman whom he claims to have taken as a lover after his disappointment with the widow.

The whole section is a remarkable battle of wits which the woman is inevitably bound to lose, since every sentence she utters adds fuel to the sadistic enjoyment of the scholar. The more inhuman and outrageous his treatment of his victim becomes, the more pleasure he derives from standing round talking to her. At the outset he thought 'that the man to whom God should grant the favour of holding her naked in his arms could truly claim that he was in Paradise'.[130] Now, the pleasure which she never in fact gave him naked in his arms, she will give him naked on the tower. The woman speaks and cries; the scholar merely laughs. Not only are her prayers to no avail, they actually serve as a stimulus to heighten his enjoyment. Although the widow reminds him that he is not yet old, the scholar is faced by the fact that he is no longer a young man, so that his vendetta against the widow is not just a personal revenge on his own account, but a collective blow for his profession and his age-group against the arrogant potency of all young bloods:[131]

'You women are always falling in love with younger men, and yearning for them to love you in return, because of their fresher complexions and darker beards, their jaunty gait, their dancing and their jousting; but when a man is properly mature, he has put such matters as these behind him, and knows a thing or two that these young fellows have yet to learn. Moreover, because a young man will cover more miles in a single day, he seems to you a better rider. But whereas I admit that he will shake your skin-coat with greater vigour, the older man, being more experienced, has a better idea of where the fleas are lurking. Besides, a portion that is small, but delicately flavoured, is infinitely preferable to a larger one that has no taste at all. And a hard gallop will tire and weaken a man however young, whilst a gentle trot, though it may bring him somewhat later to the inn, will at least ensure that he is still in good fettle on arrival.'

This whole passage is stupendous and obscene: the extreme crudeness of some of the expressions is redeemed by the impassioned rhythm of the scholar's speech and the intense delicacy of phrases like 'il soavemente andare' ('the gentle movement'),[132] which seem to reflect an ideal experience of the author. And the psychological insight into the two protagonists is remarkably convincing, in that it sets out to catch and define the essential features and limits of masculinity and femininity as such. The framework is undoubtedly still that of the 'robust mediaeval tradition'[133] of misogynous literature, but the concrete achievement of the text is also misanthropic: nothing is sacred; no sentiment can survive the monstrous egocentricity by which both characters show that they have always been driven. Perhaps the only positive result is the pure play of human intelligence, their skill at rhetoric, life seen as a hard-fought chess game.

The preceding is one level of the text: but the text also points in different directions. For instance the *novella* may be intended, and can certainly be seen, as an obsessive geometric demonstration of the *contrappasso* ('making the punishment fit the crime') which Dante followed in his *Inferno*. For the scholar's revenge is strictly articulated in accordance with the standards adopted by God and Minos, the Infernal arbitrator, in sending sinful souls to their destined place of punishment. Thus it comes about that the details of the scholar's revenge appear to follow elementary psychological considerations, whereas in fact they may fit the rigid requirements of a whole structure of analogy and metaphor which Boccaccio seems to build up.

The device of *contrappasso*, in Boccaccio as well as Dante, follows not so much a system of justice as a linguistic or even geometric model. Even though the punishment must fit the crime, the 'object all sublime' of this infernal harmony is not an equitable distribution of crime and punishment: rather it consists in developing a fiendish metaphor, a play of words, a geometric pattern. In other words, I am arguing that it is not a personal vision of divine retribution which governs *contrappasso*, but a taste for metaphorical constructs and a love of symmetry: hence Paolo and Francesca in *Inferno* V are whirled about by the infernal storm simply because in the language there already exists the possibility of using metaphors like 'the storm of human passions', 'the hurricane of love', 'a tempest in the soul'. Again, in *Inferno* XXVIII, a character called Bertram de Born carries his head separated from his torso hanging from his hand like a lantern, because he separated fathers from sons.[134] In other words, his punishment is determined by the fact that the verb 'separate' ('partire') has a dual semantic value connoting both physical division and spiritual secession.

Thus in our *novella* the punishment is made to fit the crime by virtue of a rigid series of contrasted opposites. It is not just, as Baratto argues,[135] that we have an inexorable opposition between water and fire: in fact there is a methodical process by which the two positions are reversed in a pattern that is calculatedly Dantesque and incidentally strengthened by a series of unmistakable quotations from the *Divine Comedy* which help the reader to understand the deliberate game which Boccaccio is playing. We shall see that the *contrappasso* is not merely brought out by the way the widow is punished: it is also suggested by a number of lines from Dante half-concealed in Boccaccio's prose. The scholar had suffered the cold: now the woman shall suffer heat: 'I shall simply advise you, if you find yourself being scorched, to remember the freezing you gave me, and if you mix the hot with the cold, you will doubtless find the rays of the sun more bearable'.[136] The scholar had been trapped down below, at night time, in an enclosed courtyard; now the woman will be trapped up above, by day, on an exposed tower. The scholar's limbs had shrivelled and become livid; the woman's limbs will swell up and become purple. The widow used her maidservant to help to organize her dastardly joke; now the scholar will employ his own manservant at one point in his revenge. The only thing is that the perfect symmetrical reversal works to the woman's advantage in the case of their subsequent medication: 'My one great regret is that the illness I suffered on account of the cold required to be treated with stinking dung, whereas your own injuries, occasioned by the heat, can be treated with fragrant rose-water.'[137]

To show his readers the various stages in this use of *contrappasso* (which is another factor that serves to make the whole *novella* more of a literary construct and consequently less dependent on a banal source in the *vécu*), Boccaccio has sprinkled the language of the second half of the story with reminiscences from Dante. For example, at the top of the tower, 'there being not a breath of wind, the air was literally teeming with flies and gadflies which, settling in the fissures of her flesh, stung her . . . ferociously'.[138] In Dante's Anti-Inferno the cowardly are stung by gadflies and wasps:[139]

> Questi sciaurati, che mai non fur vivi,
> Erano ignudi, stimolati molto,
> Da mosconi e da vespe ch'eran ivi'

The woman sees the river: '. . . the Arno, whose inviting waters did nothing to lessen her thirst, but only made it worse.'[140] Mastro Adamo is in the same predicament in Dante:[141]

> Li ruscelletti che de' verdi colli
> Del Casentin discendon giuso in Arno,
> Faccendo i lor canali freddi e molli,

> Sempre mi stanno innanzi, e non indarno,
> Che l'imagine lor vie più m'asciuga
> Che 'l male ond'io nel volto mi discarno.

The woman's body seemed 'the ugliest thing in the world', 'la più brutta cosa del mondo';[142] Dante's Filippo Argenti is presented with the same adjective: 'Ma tu chi se', che sí se' fatto brutto?'[143] The woman calls for a glass of water to dampen her mouth 'which is so parched and dry that my tears will not suffice to bathe it' ('la bocca, alla quale non bastano le mie lagrime, tanta è l'asciugaggine e l'arsura la quale io v'ho dentro').[144] The word *arsura* recurs in the Mastro Adamo episode, when the forger says to Sinon: 'Tu hai l'arsura e 'l capo che ti dole.'[145] The woman 'aveva a gran divizia laccioli' ('was by no means deficient in guiles'):[146] this closely follows Dante's Ciampolo: 'Ond'ei, ch'avea lacciuoli a gran divizia.'[147]

It can hardly be an accident that there is such a large quantity of Dante reminiscences. Once again we are dealing with a subtle system of signals which instruct us on how to read the text. And every one of these signals points uncomprisingly towards a non-realistic representation: it moves us away from any expectation of a clumsy reproduction of reality towards an area of much more pronounced artistic detachment. One can sum up this approach by saying that Boccaccio's *livre* continually asks to be read as *livre* rather than an *exemple*.[148]

Before withdrawing to the top of the tower to recite the exorcism, the widow follows the scholar's instructions to bathe herself naked seven times in a river that runs nearby, while the man is in fact hidden behind some trees watching everything that takes place:[149]

> When the lady, in all her naked beauty, was passing within an arm's length of where he lay hidden, he could see her white form piercing the shades of the night, and as he gazed upon her bosom and the other parts of her body, perceiving how lovely they were and thinking to himself what was shortly to happen to them, he could not help feeling sorry for her. Moreover, being suddenly assailed by the desires of the flesh, which caused a recumbent part of his person to stand, he was strongly tempted to sally forth from his hiding-place, seize her in his arms, and take his pleasure of her. So that, what with his pity on the one hand and his lust on the other, he very nearly gave himself away. But when he remembered who he was, the wrong he had suffered, the reason for it, and the person who had inflicted it upon him, his indignation was rekindled, dispelling all his pity and fleshly desires, and, clinging to his resolve, he allowed her to proceed on her way.

This is surely one of the most intense and anguished moments of eroticism in the whole *Decameron*: it is beyond the limits of any form of 'civilized sex'. It teeters at the brink of delirium, banishing any notion of sexuality contemplated with the smile of reason. The white flesh of the woman which lights up the surrounding darkness and the precisely qualified erection (by no means glossed over, whatever the 'respectable' critics have tried to argue) urge the scholar towards a short sharp act of rape. But at the vital moment he is held back by other delights and responsibilities which remind him to taste the 'piacer serbato ai saggi'[150] rather than give way to the pleasure reserved for the lustful. Ultimately, however, the two different brands of pleasure seem to merge into one and the same, since the scholar's subsequent contemplation of the widow's physical disintegration, and the writer's description of her flesh stung by insects, scorched by 'the torrid heat of the floor beneath her feet'[151] and cooked to the point of agony by the midsummer sun, seem to reflect a vicious sadistic pleasure which is an end in itself. The *Decameron*, like so many great works of Western literature, is an outrageous text which holds out to the reader the promise of the forbidden pleasures of transgression.

Notes

1 Articles specifically devoted to erotic *novelle* are very sparse on the ground. The major monographs on the *Decameron* also give very little space to this problem. Pierre Poirier, *Boccace, moraliste de la chair*, Brussels, 1943, is hardly worth mentioning.

2 McW, p. 47. 'Intendo di raccontare cento novelle, o favole o parabole o istorie.' *Dec.*, *Proemio*, 13. See Baratto, 1970, p. 155.

3 McW, p. 90. '. . . farne venire tutte le legne' (*Dec.*, I, 4, 11).

4 McW, p. 91. '. . . non sopra il petto di lei salì, ma lei sopra il suo petto pose, e per lungo spazio con lei si trastullò' (*Dec.*, I, 4, 18).

5 My translation. '. . . che i monaci si debbano far dalle femine priemere, come da digiuni e da vigilie' (*Dec.*, I, 4, 21).

6 McW, p. 89.

> Per che, avendo udito che per li buoni consigli di Giannotto di Civigní Abraham aver l'anima salvata e Melchisedec per lo suo senno avere le sue ricchezze dagli agguati del Saladino difese, senza riprensione attender da voi, intendo di raccontar brievemente con che cautela un monaco il suo corpo da gravissima pena liberasse (*Dec.*, I, 4, 3).

7 *Dec.*, X, 6.

8 *Dec.*, VI, 2.

9 *Dec.*, VI, 4.

10 *Dec.*, VI, 7.

11 Anatole de Montaiglon and Gaston Raynaud, *Recueil général et complet des Fabliaux des XIIIe et XIVe siècles*, etc., Paris, 1883, vol. 3, p. 77.

12 *Novellino e Conti del Duecento*, ed. Sebastiano Lo Nigro, UTET, Turin, 1963, Novellino LIV, pp. 137–8.

13 McW, p. 709. 'Due giovani albergano con uno, dei quali l'uno va a giacere con la figliuola, e la moglie di lui disavvedutamente si giace con l'altro, quegli che era con la figliuola, si corica col padre di lei, e dicegli ogni cosa, credendo dire al compagno; fanno romore insieme; la donna, ravvedutasi, entra nel letto della figliola, e quindi con certe parole ogni cosa pacefica' (*Dec.*, IX, 6, 1).

14 Montaiglon and Raynaud, 1883, vol. 5, pp. 83ff. There is also a slightly different version, published by H. Varnhagen in *Englische Studien*, IX, 1886, pp. 241–6. The two versions have been printed facing each other in W. P. Bryand and G. Dempster, *Sources and Analogues of Chaucer's Canterbury Tales*, Routledge & Kegan Paul, London, 1958, pp. 126–47.

15 *Ibid.*, vol. 1, pp. 238ff.

16 In this *novella*, according to Branca (1970, p. 104) we have 'an exemplary combinatory development'. And Baratto (1970, p. 109): 'an almost geometric perfection'.

17 See Muscetta, 1965, p. 471.

18 McW, p. 714. '. . . incominciò a ridere e a farsi belle di lui e de' suoi sogni' (*Dec.*, IX, 6, 31).

19 McW, p. 89. '. . . assai bella' (*Dec.*, I, 4, 5).

20 McW, p. 91. 'La giovinetta, che non era di ferro nè di diamante, assai agevolmente si piegò ai piaceri dell'abate' (*Dec.*, I, 4, 18).

21 I have coined this word on the model of Terence's *heautontimoroumenos*, exploited by Baudelaire in a well-known poem.

22 L. Di Francia, *La IV novella del 'Decameron' e le sue fonti*, in *Miscellanea a Vittorio Cian*, Pisa, 1909, pp. 63–9.

23 McW, p. 90. '. . . lo schiamazzio che costoro insieme facevano e per conoscere meglio le voci, chetamente s'accostò all'uscio della cella ad ascoltare, e manifestamente conobbe che dentro a quella era femina, e tutto fu tentato di farsi aprire' (*Dec.*, I, 4, 7).

24 McW, p. 90. '. . . poi pensò di voler tenere in ciò altra maniera, e tornatosi alla sua camera, aspettò che il monaco fuori uscisse' (*Dec.*, I, 4, 7).

25 McW, pp. 90–1. 'L'abate, per potersi più pienamente informare del fallo commesso da costui . . . fu lieto di tale accidente, e volentier prese la chiave e similmente li diè licenzia' (*Dec.*, I, 4, 12).

26 McW, p. 91. '. . . o in presenza di tutti i monaci aprir la cella di costui e far loro vedere il suo difetto . . . o di voler prima da lei sentire come andata fosse la bisogna' (*Dec.*, I, 4, 13).

27 McW, p. 91. 'E pensando seco stesso che questa potrebbe essere tal femina o figliuola di tale uomo, che egli non le vorrebbe aver fatta quella vergogna d'averla a tutti i monaci fatta vedere' (*Dec.*, I, 4, 14).

28 McW, p. 91 (italics are mine). 'E chetamente andatosene alla cella, quella aprì ed entrò dentro, e l'uscio richiuse' (*Dec.*, I, 4, 14).

29 McW, p. 91. '. . . gli stimoli della carne' (*Dec.*, I, 4, 15).

30 McW, p. 91. 'Perchè non prendo io del piacere, quando io ne posso avere . . .' (*Dec.*, I, 4, 15).

31 McW, p. 91. 'Io estimo che egli sia gran senno a pigliarsi del bene, quando Domenedio ne manda altrui' (*Dec.*, I, 4, 16).

32 McW, p. 91 (I have slightly modified the translation at this point). 'Il quale, abbracciatala e basciatala più volte, in sul letticello del monaco salitosene, avendo forse riguardo al grave peso della sua dignità e alla tenera età della giovane, temendo forse di non offenderla per troppa gravezza, non sopra il petto di lei salí, ma lei sopra il suo petto pose, e per lungo spazio con lei si trastullò' (*Dec.*, I, 4, 18).

33 D. H. Lawrence, *The Rainbow*, Penguin, Harmondsworth, 1949, p. 130.

34 See G. Almansi, 'Lettura della novella di Bernabò e Zinevra (II, 9)', in *Studi sul Boccaccio*, vol. VII, 1973.

35 *Dec.*, VIII, 3; VIII, 6; VIII, 9; IX, 3; IX, 5.

36 See Russo, 1970, p. 245.

37 McW, pp. 241–2. '. . . bellissima donna, savia e onesta molto' (*Dec.*, III, 2, 4).

38 McW, p. 263. '. . . uomo molto ricco e savio e avveduto per altro, ma avarissimo senza modo' (*Dec.*, III, 5, 4).

39 McW, p. 305. '. . . bellissimo e piacevole' (*Dec.*, III, 9, 4).

40 McW, p. 314. '. . . e da quel dí innanzi lei sempre come sua sposa e moglie onorando, l'amò e sommamente ebbe cara' (*Dec.*, III, 9, 61).

41 McW, p. 423. '. . . e poi appresso con lei insieme in pace e in riposo lungamente goderono del loro amore' (*Dec.*, V, 2, 48).

42 McW, p. 824. '. . . con Griselda, onorandola sempre quanto più si potea, lungamente e consolato visse' (*Dec.*, X, 10, 67).

43 *Dec.*, IV, 1; IV, 8; IV, 9.

44 McW, p. 235. '. . . un giovane lavoratore forte e robusto' (*Dec.*, III, 1, 7).

45 My translation. '. . . un buon omicciolo' (*Dec.*, III. 1, 6). The word *omicciolo* conveys the idea of a slightly ridiculous caricature of a man.

46 McW, p. 239. '. . . se non l'esser preso dall'una di loro' (*Dec.*, III, 1, 31).

47 My translation. '. . . faccendo cotali risa sciocche' (*Dec.*, III, 1, 31).

48 McW, p. 239. '. . . mutato consiglio e con loro accordatesi, partefici divennero del podere di Masetto' (*Dec.*, III, 1, 33).

49 My translation. '. . . alle quali l'altre tre per diversi accidenti divenner compagne in vari tempi' (*Dec.*, III, 1, 33).

50 McW, p. 241 (I have slightly modified the translation) '. . . assai mona-chin' (*Dec.*, III, 1, 42).

51 McW, p. 237. '. . . estimava che egli cosí senza coda come senza favella fosse' (*Dec.*, III, 1, 20). This particular form of sexual allusion occurs frequently in the *Decameron*. In VII, 1, the wife of the bigoted Gianni Lotteringhi exorcises the pretended ghost (which consists of her lover who has come to the house to go to bed with her) with the following formula: 'Fantasima, fantasima, che di notte vai, a coda ritta ci venisti, a coda ritta te n'andrai' (*Dec.*, VII, 1, 27). This is neatly translated by McWilliam as 'Werewolf, werewolf, black as any crow. You come here with your tail erect, keep it up and go' (p. 526).

52 McW, p. 237 (*Dec.*, III, 1, 21).

53 McW, p. 239. '. . . stava tutto scoperto. La qual riguardando la donna, e sola vedendosi' (*Dec.*, III, 1, 34–5).

54 There is a painting by D. H. Lawrence on this subject, in *Paintings of D. H. Lawrence*, ed. M. Levy, with essays by M. T. Moore, J. Lindsay, R. H. Read, London, Cory Adams & Mackay, 1969, no. 14, p. 91.

55 McW, pp. 239–40 (I have made a slight modification to his translation).
In quel medesimo appetito cadde che caduto erano le sue monacelle; e destato Masetto, seco nella sua camera nel menò, dove parecchi giorni, con gran querimonia delle monache fatta che l'ortolano non venia a lavorar l'orto, il tenne, provando e riprovando quella dolcezza la qual essa prima all'altre solea biasimare (*Dec.*, III, 1, 35).

56 E io ho più volte a più donne, che a noi son venute, udito dire che tutte l'altre dolcezze del mondo sono una beffa a rispetto di quella quando la femina usa con l'uomo (*Dec.*, III, 1, 23).
Yet I have often heard it said, by several of the ladies who have come to visit us, that all other pleasures in the world are mere trifles by comparison with the one experienced by a woman when she goes with a man (McW, p 238).

57 McW, p. 239 '. . . bene era cosí dolce cosa' (*Dec.*, III, 1, 32).

58 My translation. '. . . rotto lo scilinguagnolo' (*Dec.*, III, 1, 36).

59 McW, pp. 240–1 (I have made one minor modification to the translation).
Ed essendo di quel dí morto il lor castaldo, di pari consentimento, apertosi fra tutte ciò che per addietro da tutte era stato fatto, con piacer di Masetto ordinarono che le genti circustanti credettero che, per le loro orazioni e per gli meriti del santo in cui intitolato era il munastero, a Masetto, stato lungamente mutolo, la favella fosse restituita, e lui castaldo fecero; e per sí fatta maniera le sue fatiche partirono, che egli le potè comportare. Nelle quali come che esso assai monachin generasse, pur sí discretamente procedette la cosa che niente se ne sentí so non dopo la morte della badessa, essendo già Masetto presso che vecchio e disideroso di tornarsi ricco a casa sua; la qual cosa saputa, di leggier gli fece venir fatto (*Dec.*, III, 1, 41–2).

60 Le Ciel défend, de vrai, certains contentements;
Mais on trouve avec lui des accommodements.
(Molière, *Tartuffe*, act IV, scene 5.) English translation: 'In truth Heaven forbids certain joys;/but one can always ask it to make a deal.'

61 'I find Jane Eyre verging towards pornography and Boccaccio seems to me always fresh and wholesome. . . . The fresh healthy naturalness of the Italian story-teller . . .' (D. H. Lawrence, *Pornography and so on*, Faber & Faber, London, 1936, pp. 22, 28. And again, see p. 30.)

62 McW, p. 315. '. . . per volere fare della sua fermezza una gran pruova' (*Dec.*, III, 10, 9).

63 McW, p. 315. '. . . senza troppi assalti' (*Dec.*, III, 10, 10).

64 My translation. '. . . di recarsi per la memoria la giovinezza e la bellezza di costei' (*Dec.*, III, 10, 10). The internal rhyme here is effective and suggestive.

65 My translation. '. . . lui come uomo dissoluto' (*Dec.*, III, 10, 10).

66 McW, p. 316. '. . . sotto spezie di servire a Dio' (*Dec.*, III, 10, 11).

67 *Dec.*, III, 10, 11.

68 McW, p. 316. '. . . la resurrezion della carne' (*Dec.*, III, 10, 12). According
to Branca this obscene metaphor derives from Apuleius, *Metamorphosis*,
II, 7; but in the Latin text we only have 'Staterunt et membra quae
iacebant ante', with no reference to the religious myth. But see *Dec.*,
VIII, 7, 67, and this chapter, p. 98.

69 McW, p. 317. '. . . che mai più non aveva in inferno messo diavolo
alcuno' (*Dec.*, III, 10, 22).

70 McW, p. 317. 'Padre mio, io son qui venuta per servire a Dio e non per
istare oziosa; andiamo a rimettere il diavolo in inferno' (*Dec.*, III, 10, 26).

71 McW, p. 318. '. . . ma sí era di rado, che altro non era che gittare una
fava in bocca al leone' (*Dec.*, III, 10, 30).

72 Salinari, 1963, p. 1274.

73 Baratto, 1970, p. 384.

74 See Bernardus Silvestris, *De Mundi Universitate* libri duo, ed. C. S.
Barach and J. Wrobel, Innsbruck, 1876.

75 Jacopone da Todi, 1230(?)–1306. His *Laudi* represent one of the most
intense moments of post-Franciscan mysticism in Italian poetry.

76 Virgil: '. . . horrendaeque procul secreta Sibyllae,/Antrum immane . . .'
(*Aen.* VI, 11–12). And Rabelais parodies this as follows:

> Ces parolles dictes, se retira en sa tesniere, et sus le perron de la
> porte se recoursa robbe, cotte ey chemise jusqu'a aux escelles, et
> leurs monstroit son cul.
>
> Panurge l'aperceut, et dist a Epsitemon: 'Par le sambre quoy de bois,
> voyla le trou de la Sibylle.' (*Le tiers livre des faicts et dicts heroiques du
> bon Pantagruel,* ch. 12).
>
> (Having said these words she withdrew to her den, and on the
> threshold she pulled gown, skirt and shirt up to her armpits and
> showed them her arse.
>
> Panurge glanced at it and said to Epsitemon: 'Pon my oath, lo and
> behold the Sybil's hole.')

77 McW, p. 316. '. . . sotto spezie di servire a Dio' (*Dec.*, III, 10, 11).

78 McW, p. 316. '. . . grandissima consolazione' (*Dec.*, III, 10, 18).

79 McW, pp. 316–17. '. . . grandissimo piacere e servigio' (*Dec.*, III, 10, 18).

80 McW, p. 319. '. . . il più piacevol servigio che a Dio si facesse' (*Dec.*,
III, 10, 35).

81 McW, p. 319. '. . . forte a grado a Dio e piacer delle parti, e molto bene
ne può nascere e seguire' (*Dec.*, III, 10, 35).

82 McW, p. 317. 'Per certo, padre mio, mala cosa dee essere questo diavolo,
e veramente nimico di Dio, che ancora al Ninferno, non che altrui, duole
quando egli v'è dentro rimesso' (*Dec.*, III, 10, 22). Note that she calls
him Father. Earlier she had called him simply Rustico (Dec., III, 10, 13).

83 My translation (*Dec.*, III, 10, 25).

84 McW, p. 317. '. . . tanto diletto e piacer' (*Dec.*, III, 10, 25).

85 McW, p. 317 (*Dec.*, III, 10, 27). The translation somehow spoils the
delicate image.

86 Per che tu farai bene che tu col tuo diavolo aiuti attutare la rabbia al
mio Ninferno, com'io col mio Ninferno ho aiutato a trarre la superbia
al tuo diavolo (*Dec.*, III, 10, 29).

Now that I have helped you with my Hell to subdue the pride of your devil, the least you can do is to get your devil to help me tame the fury of my Hell (McW, p. 318).

87 La Fontaine, *Contes et nouvelles en vers,* Garnier, Paris, 1961 (all quotations are taken from this edition). *Le Diable en enfer,* pp. 300–4. This quotation is at page 302.

88 McW, p. 315. '. . . per volere fare della sua fermezza una gran pruova' (Dec., III, 10, 9).

89 McW, p. 315. '. . . trovandosi di gran lunga ingannato da quelle, senza troppi assalti voltò le spalle e rendessi per vinto' (*Dec.,* III, 10, 10).

90 La Fontaine, 1963, p. 303.

91 *Ibid.*

92 *Ibid.*

93 Petronio, 1935, p. 42.

94 McW, p. 126. '. . . nella camera se n'andarono, e senza niuno indugio coricatisi, pienamente e molte volte, anzi che il giorno venisse, i lor desii adempierono' (*Dec.,* II, 2, 39).

95 McW, p. 133. '. . . e appresso insieme abbracciatosi, con gran piacere di ciascuna de le parti, quanto di quella notte restava, si sollazzarono' (*Dec.,* II, 3, 35).

96 My translation. '. . . a prendere amoroso piacere l'uno dell'altro incominciarono' (*Dec.,* II, 6, 37).

97 McW, p. 316. '. . . che cosí si pigne in fuori' (*Dec.,* III, 10, 13).

98 See note 85.

99 McW, p. 729. 'E queste sieno belle gambe e belli piedi di cavalla' (*Dec.,* IX, 10, 17).

100 McW, p. 729. 'E questo sia bel petto di cavalla' (*Dec.,* IX, 10, 18).

101 McW, p. 729. '. . . levata la camiscia e preso il piuolo col quale egli piantava gli uomini e prestamente nel solco per ciò fatto messolo, disse: "E questa sia bella coda di cavalla"' (*Dec.,* IX, 10, 18).

102 Apuleius, *Metamorphoses,* IX, 5. See L. Di Francia, 'Alcune novelle del Decameron illustrate nelle fonti', *Giornale Storico della Letteratura Italiana,* XLIV, 1904.

103 I have marked with strokes the division between the hendecasyllables which are concealed in the prose. The presence of these lines was shown by Branca in his edition of the *Decameron.*

104 *Dec.,* VII, 2, 34 (McW, p. 531).

105 See M. Pastore Stocchi, *Note e chiose interpretative.* 1. Le cavalle di *Partia* (Decameron, VII, 2, 34), in *Studi sul Boccaccio,* II, 1964, pp. 235–9.

106 Croce, 1967, pp. 86–7.

107 J. Bédier, *Les Fabliaux, études de littérature populaire et d'histoire littéraire du moyen âge,* sixth edition, Champion, Paris, 1964.

108 As an example: 'De grand plaisir notre amant s'extasie' (*Richard Minutolo,* in La Fontaine, 1963, p. 23).

109 La Fontaine, 1963, *La Jument du Compère Pierre,* p. 307.

110 *Ibid., Le Calendrier des Vieillards,* p. 105.

111 *Dec.,* II, 10, 15–16.

112 La Fontaine, 1963, pp. 302–3.

113 *Ibid.* p. 309.

114 *Ibid.* pp. 333–8.

115 J. C. Lapp, *The Esthetics of negligence; La Fontaine's Contes*, Cambridge University Press, 1971, pp. 172–3. See my review in *Studi sul Boccaccio*, VII, 1973, pp. 404–8.

116 L. F. Céline, 'Une Interview sur Gargantua et Pantagruel' in *Le Meilleur Livre du Mois*, reprinted in the special number of *La Herne* (no. 3, 1963) devoted to Céline.

117 McW, p. 621. '... avendo lungamente studiato a Parigi, non per vender poi la sua scienza a minuto, come molti fanno, ma per sapere la ragion delle cose e la cagion d'esse' (*Dec.*, VIII, 7, 5). This is a very interesting definition of a mediaeval *intellettuale*.

118 McW, p. 625. 'Per la qual cosa l'amante, abbracciandola, stretta, non che mille, ma più di centomilia la basciava' (*Dec.*, VIII, 7, 27). The Catullan source helps to make the point more obvious.

119 McW, p. 643. '... non corpo umano ma più tosto un cepperello in-arsicciato parere' (*Dec.*, VIII, 7, 140).

120 *Dec.*, VIII, 7, 1, Branca's footnote 1.

121 See G. Boccaccio, *Ameto, Lettere, Corbaccio*, ed. N. Bruscoli, Laterza, Bari, 1940.

122 Sansovino, 1543.

123 See Moravia, 1965, chapter on Boccaccio.

124 McW, p. 636. 'Le forze della penna' (*Dec.*, VIII, 7, 99).

125 McW, p. 636. 'Avrei scritto di te cose che ... di te stessa vergognandoti, per non poterti vedere t'avresti cavato gli occhi' (*Dec.*, VIII, 7, 100).

126 McW, p. 633. 'Niuna gloria è ad una aquila l'aver vinto una colomba' (*Dec.*, VIII, 7, 79).

127 McW, p. 636. '... e tu non se'vecchio' (*Dec.*, VIII, 7, 94).

128 McW, p. 636. '... che vaghezza trastullo e diletto è della giovanezza degli uomini' (*Dec.*, VIII, 7, 94).

129 McW, p. 635. '... per amadore e per signore' (*Dec.*, VIII, 7, 94).

130 McW, p. 622. '... colui potersi beato chiamare, al quale Iddio grazia facesse lei potere ignuda nelle braccia tenere' (*Dec.*, VIII, 7, 6).

131 McW, p. 637.
  'Voi v'andate innamorando e disiderate l'amor de' giovani, per ciò che alquanto con le carni più vive e con le barbe più nere gli vedete, e sopra sé andare e carolare e giostrare: le quali cose tutte ebber coloro che più alquanto attempati sono, e quel sanno che coloro hanno ad imparare. E oltre a ciò gli stimate miglior cavalieri e far di più miglia le lor giornate che gli uomini più maturi. Certo io confesso che essi con maggior forza scuotono i pilliccioni, ma gli attempati, sí come esperti, sanno meglio i luoghi dove stanno le pulci, e di gran lunga è da eleggere piuttosto il poco e saporito che il molto e insipido; e il trottar forte rompe e stanca altrui, quantunque sia giovane, dove il soavemente andare, ancora che alquanto più tardi altrui meni allo albergo, egli il vi conduce almen riposato' (*Dec.*, VIII, 7, 102–3).

132 There is no way of translating such an expression which indicates the *soavità* of the act.

Hwl

133 See Branca's footnote 2 at *Dec.*, VIII, 7, 1.
134 Perch' io parti cosí giunte persone,
Partito porto il mio cerebro, lasso!
Dal suo principio ch'è in questo troncone.
Cosí s'osserva in me lo contrappasso. (*Inferno*, XXVIII, 139–42.)
Because I parted those so joined I carry my brain, alas, parted from
its root in this trunk; thus is observed in me the retribution.
(Sinclair's translation, 1971, p. 353.)
135 Baratto, 1970, p. 151.
136 McW, p. 638. 'Ti dico che, se il sole ti comincia a scaldare, ricorditi del
freddo che tu a me facesti patire, e se con cotesto caldo il mescolerai,
senza fallo il sol sentirai temperato' (*Dec.*, VIII, 7, 108).
137 McW, p. 640. 'Di tanto mi dolgo forte, che la infermità del mio freddo
col caldo del letame puzzolente si convenne curare, ove quella del tuo
caldo col freddo della odorifera acqua rosa si curerà' (*Dec.*, VIII, 7, 126).
138 McW, p. 639. '. . . non faccendo punto di vento, v'erano mosche e
tafani in grandissima quantità abondanti, li quali, ponendolesi sopra le
carni aperte, sí fieramente la stimolavano' (*Dec.*, VIII, 7, 116).
139 *Inferno* III, 64–6. 'Those wretches, who never were alive, were naked
and sorely stung by hornets and wasps that were there' (Sinclair's
translation, 1971, p. 49). Also the verb, *stimolare*, is the same in both
Inferno and the *Decameron*.
140 McW, p. 639. '. . . Arno, il qual, porgendole desiderio delle sue acque,
non iscemava la sete ma l'accresceva' (*Dec.*, VIII, 7, 119).
141 *Inferno*, XXX, 64–9. 'The little streams that from the green hills of the
Casentino flow down to the Arno, making their channels cool and
moist, are always before me, and not in vain, for their image parches me
far more than the ill that wastes my features' (Sinclair's translation, 1971,
p. 373).
142 McW, p. 640 (*Dec.*, VIII, 7, 120).
143 *Inferno*, VIII, 36. 'But thou, who art thou that art become so foul?
(Sinclair's translation, 1971, p. 113).
144 McW, p. 640 (*Dec.*, VIII, 7, 123).
145 *Inferno*, XXX, 127. '. . . thou hast burning fever and aching head'
(Sinclair's translation, 1971. p. 377). The widow also has an 'aching
head' (*Dec.*, VIII, 7, 114).
146 *Dec.*, VIII, 7, 146 (McW, p. 644).
147 *Inferno*, XXII, 109. '. . . having great store of devices' (Sinclair's translation, 1971, p. 275).
148 See Chapter 1, pp. 3–4.
149 McW, p. 631.
E passandogli ella quasi allato cosí ignuda ed egli veggendo lei con
la bianchezza del suo corpo vincere le tenebre della notte, e appresso
riguardandole il petto e l'altre parti del corpo, e vedendole belle e seco
pensando quali infra piccol termine dovean divenire, sentí di lei
alcuna compassione; e d'altra parte lo stimolo della carne l'assalí
subitamente e fece tale in pié levare che si giaceva, e confortavalo
che egli da guato uscisse e lei andasse a prendere e il suo piacer ne

facesse: e vicin fu ad essere tra dall'uno e dall'altro vinto. Me nella memoria tornandosi chi egli era e qual fosse la 'ngiuria ricevuta e per che e da cui, e per ciò nello sdegno raccesosi, e la compassione e il carnale appetito cacciati, stette nel proponimento fermo, e lasciolla andare (*Dec.*, VIII, 7, 66–9).

150　L. Da Ponte, *Le Nozze di Figaro*, act I. 'Every man of Sense enjoys it', is Edward J. Dent's translation (Oxford University Press, 1937, p. 4).

151　McW, p. 640. '. . . e il fervor del battuto di sotto' (*Dec.*, VIII, 7, 120).

Four

The meaning of a storm

Let's take a character and call it Alpha. Alpha happens to be on a ship. The ship itself happens to be (though where else could it be?) in the middle of the sea. The sea is calm. The sky is clear.

So far everything is straight: the author wishes to communicate to us the fact that character Alpha is being transferred from one country to another by way of the sea: emigration, a pleasure cruise, a job with a shipping company. It could be any of those; or perhaps Alpha is a princess going to meet her future husband in a distant land.

The journey is uneventful. Nothing disturbs the serene and monotonous life that takes place on board the boat during a slow voyage under sail – steam engines had not yet been invented at the time of our story. The narrator has nothing in particular to tell us: Alpha's ship has already docked at a port in the country of destination.

Alternatively, we could take a different situation. The sky is becoming cloudy, the waves are swelling threateningly, the wind is freshening, the horizon is black, in the wind you can detect the plangent screeching of sea-gulls. In the next page the ship is in the clutch of the waves, the sailors are struggling to manage against the fury of the elements, the forward mast is split, the main mast bends under the force of the wind, the tiller is spinning round madly, etcetera.

Why? What's the purpose of telling us all this? Let's examine a few possible reasons.

First hypothesis: Alpha has departed from a point on the map which we can call A, and is directed towards a second point B. Instead, the fury of the elements diverts Alpha to a place called C. And here is where the real story is to begin. Alpha finds at place C a woman/man who changes the whole course of Alpha's life. Perhaps Alpha meets a hermit who converts him/her to Christianity: or a brother who has made a

fortune over the intervening twenty years in which they never
met.

Then again, a second hypothesis: Alpha has perhaps challenged
a divinity, Neptune for example, and is now being punished for
this *hubris*. Alternatively, the punishment could be less specific;
Alpha could be a sinner who must expiate guilt by passing
through the experience of a storm at sea.

Third hypothesis: the writer intends to eliminate Alpha from
the scene so that Beta can marry Gamma, and therefore has
Alpha die at sea in the course of a fierce tempest. If this is so,
then the tempest in question can be of fairly short duration:
when characters are planned to die off, little narrative time need
be wasted on them. You don't require any particular purple
passage about thunder and lightning, or breakers as high as a
house.

Our fourth hypothesis might be rather more elementary than
any of the preceding ones: the author is good at describing
storms and therefore unfailingly inserts a storm into each of his
works.

Fifth: we might suppose that the author wants to emphasize
one of Alpha's personal psychological traits; for example, he or
she easily becomes afraid, or is physically very daring. The
storm in the narrative provides the writer with an opportunity
to insert such details about Alpha. Therefore the following
description is going to be all about the person's reactions, and
have little to do with the fury of the elements which the character
has to react against.

Our sixth, and final, hypothesis about this literary situation of
an individual called Alpha in the middle of a stormy sea, reads as
follows: the story was becoming a little boring, so the narrator
wanted to liven things up with dramatic events.

Ah, the infinite monotony of literature.

Giovanni Boccaccio, alias Johannes Tranquillitatis, the sedentary
man secretly in love with adventure, according to a theory of
Alberto Moravia,[1] takes himself a nice handful of characters and
tosses them overboard into the sea. Let us see what he does with
them once they are in the water.

Landolfo Rufolo (*Decameron*, II, 4)

The next day, the wind changed quarter, and the two ships
hoisted their sails and set a westerly course. For the whole of
that day they made good progress, but in the evening a gale
began to blow, producing very heavy seas and separating the
two carracks from each other. By a stroke of ill-luck, the ship
in which the wretched, destitute Landolfo was travelling was
driven by the force of the gale on to the coast of the island
of Cephalonia, where she ran aground with a tremendous crash,
split wide open, and like a piece of glass being flung against a
wall, was smashed to smithereens. As is usually the case when
this happens, the sea was rapidly littered with an assortment of
floating planks, chests and merchandise. And although it was
pitch dark and there was a heavy swell, the poor wretches who
had survived the wreck, or those of them who could swim,
began to cling to whatever object happened to float across
their path. [2]

Not bad at all: the fatal sea is the cause first of the unfortunate
merchant's ruin, and then of his salvation. The sea which has
caused his shipwreck also provides him with the jewel case as
a raft. And this makeshift raft will ultimately serve to restore
the mercantile harmony which had been disturbed by Landolfo's
cruel losses. The whole circular story is concluded with a character who has re-acquired his wisdom in the course of his harrow-
ing vicissitudes. As a narrative component, the sea as it appears
in the passage that I have just quoted is rigorously functional,
an indispensable element of the plot together with the storm,
the sand-bank, the chests and the floating timbers; they are
what Tomashevsky calls *bound motifs*. [3] Possibly the only dispens-
able component of the situation is the ship itself, splitting open
and fragmenting like a piece of glass dashed against a brick wall.
This latter detail goes somewhat beyond a mere operative signal
in the text, and seems to emphasize, symbolically, with heightened
dramatic evidence the final crushing blow of Fate against the
unfortunate merchant of Ravello.

Bartolomea, wife of Ricciardo da Chinzica (*Decameron*, II, 10)

> And during their stay, in order to provide her with a little
> recreation, he arranged a day's fishing, he and the fishermen
> taking out one boat whilst she and some other ladies went along
> to watch from a second. But as he became absorbed in what he
> was doing, they drifted several miles out to sea almost before
> they realized what was happening.
> While their concentration was at its peak, a small galley
> came upon the scene commanded by Paganino da Mare, a
> notorious pirate of the time, who having caught sight of the
> two boats came sailing towards them. They turned and fled, but
> before they could reach safety, Paganino overtook the boat
> containing the women, and on catching sight of the fair lady,
> he disregarded everything else and took her aboard his galley
> before making off again under the very eyes of Messer
> Ricciardo, who had meanwhile reached the shore. 4

In this passage there is the particularly attractive *vignette* of
the boats drifting this way and that steered in any direction
the ladies wish to go. However, the sea is a missing element,
especially in the latter part of the quotation: in other words,
here one can say that the sea is an indistinct location where
it just so happens that a kidnapping is planned to occur. It
constitutes a spatial stage-direction, rather than a real literary
presence.

The three women from Marseille, daughters of N'Arnald Civada (*Decameron*, IV, 3)

> When the night finally arrived for them to go aboard the
> brigantine, the three sisters opened up a huge chest belonging
> to their father and took a large amount of money and jewellery
> from it, which they carried quietly away from the house
> according to plan. Their three lovers were waiting for them,
> and all six hurried aboard the brigantine, which immediately

weighed anchor and put out to sea. After an unbroken voyage, they arrived next evening in Genoa, where the new lovers enjoyed the first delectable fruits of their love.

Having taken on all the fresh provisions they needed, they put to sea again, making their way unimpeded from one port to the next until, a week later, they arrived in Crete. [5]

Here the adventure of the three girls and their eloping lovers need hardly have been by sea. The story would have changed little if the journey had taken place on the Orient Express. In this example the sea is again absent as a literary component.

Gerbino (*Decameron*, IV, 4)

Gerbino, who had caught sight of the lady as she stood on the ship's poop, looking infinitely more beautiful than he had pictured her, grew more inflamed with passion than ever before, and when the glove was produced he retorted that since there were no falcons around at that particular moment, the glove was superfluous, adding that if they refused to hand over the lady, they had better look to their weapons. Hostilities commenced without further ado, each side raining arrows and stones upon the other, and in this manner they fought for a long time, doing one another a fair amount of damage. In the end, finding that he was making little headway, Gerbino lowered a small boat that they had brought from Sardinia, set it on fire, and manœuvred it into a position alongside the ship with the aid of both of his galleys. Perceiving this, and knowing they were faced with the alternative of being roasted alive or surrendering, the Saracens brought the King's daughter up on deck from her cabin, where she had been giving vent to copious tears, and led her to the ship's prow. And having called upon Gerbino to witness the deed, they slaughtered her before his very eyes, whilst all the time she was screaming for help and pleading for mercy. They then cast her body into the sea with the words:

'Take her thus, for we are left with no choice but to let you have her in the form your treachery deserves.' [6]

Here the rôle of the sea is quite different. The sea is now a real physical divide between the two separated lovers. The woman is over on the other side of the water, and Gerbino's boarding attempt will arrive too late to save her. Thus the sea is merely space; it has become a symbol of distance and separation, though it could just as well have been replaced by a moat encircling a castle.

Cimone: the kidnapping of Iphigenia (*Decameron*, V, 1)

> Being thus resolved, he furtively enlisted the help of certain young nobles who were friends of his, made secret arrangements to fit out a ship with everything one needed for a naval battle, and put out to sea, where he hove to and waited for the vessel which was to convey Iphigenia to her husband in Rhodes. And after her husband's friends had been sumptuously entertained by her father, they escorted her aboard, pointed the ship's prow in the direction of Rhodes, and departed.
>
> On the following day, Cimone, who was very much on the alert, caught up with them in his own vessel, and standing on the prow, he hailed the crew of Iphigenia's ship in a loud voice:
>
> 'Lower your sails and heave to, or prepare to be overwhelmed and sunk!'
>
> Cimone's opponents had brought up weapons from below and were making ready to defend themselves, so he followed up his words by seizing a grappling-iron and hurling it on to the stern of the Rhodian ship as it was pulling swiftly away, thus bringing his bows hard up against the enemy's poop. Without waiting to be joined by his comrades, he leapt aboard the Rhodian's ship like a raging lion as though contemptuous of all opposition.[7]

The naval battle in the passage above is strictly functional to the *novella*. It serves to throw emphasis on Cimone's bravery. The sea is again an inert presence in the scene.

Cimone: a storm (*Decameron*, V, 1)

Scarcely four hours had elapsed since Cimone and the Rhodians
had parted company, when, with the approach of night, to
which Cimone was looking forward with a keener pleasure than
any he had ever experienced, an exceptionally violent storm
arose, filling the sky with dark clouds and turning the sea into a
raging cauldron. It thus became impossible for those aboard to
see what they were doing or steer a proper course, or to keep
their balance sufficiently long to perform their duties.

Needless to say, Cimone was greatly aggrieved by all this.
The gods had granted his desire, but only, it seemed, to fill
him with dread at the prospect of dying, which without
Iphigenia he would have faced with cheerful indifference. His
companions were equally woebegone, but the saddest one
of all was Iphigenia, who was shedding copious tears and
trembled with fear at every buffeting of the waves. Between
her tears she bitterly cursed Cimone's love and censured his
temerity, declaring that this alone had brought about the
raging tempest, though it could also have arisen because
Cimone's desire to marry her was contrary to the will of the
gods, who were determined, not only to deny him the fruits
of his presumptuous longing, but to make him witness her
demise before he, too, died a miserable death.

These laments she continued to pour forth, along with
others of still greater vehemence, until, with the wind blowing
fiercer all the time, the seamen at their wits' end, and everyone
ignorant of the course they were steering, they arrived at the
island of Rhodes. Not realizing where they were, they did
everything in their power to make a good landfall, and thus
prevent loss of life.

Fortune was kindly to their endeavours, and guided them
into a tiny bay, to which the Rhodians released by Cimone on
the previous day had brought their own vessel a little while
before.[8]

The storm is a conventional one, apparently serving at least
four of the literary purposes which I listed at the commencement
of this chapter. Cimone's ship is placed by the story-teller at the
mercy of the waves in order to: (*i*) oblige character Alpha

(Cimone) to go to harbour *C* (Rhodes) instead of harbour *B* (Crete); (*ii*) indicate the gods' hypothetical vengeance for the kidnapping carried out by Cimone (this at least is the interpretation of the storm which Iphigenia puts forward); (*iii*) clarify Iphigenia's real state of mind: she is not in love with Cimone and is instantly prepared to throw the blame for all her misfortunes onto him; and (*iv*) employ a dramatic scene to bring back to life an adventure which, having commenced with a splendid opening passage,[9] was becoming rather tedious. The storm in the *novella* of Cimone is, therefore, a model of the totally functional literary storm.

Gostanza (*Decameron*, V, 2)

And one night, she secretly left her father's house and made her way to the harbour, where she chanced upon a tiny fishing-boat, lying some distance away from the other vessels. Its owners having gone ashore just a little while earlier, the boat was still equipped with its mast, its sail and its oars. And since, like most of the women on the island, she had learnt the rudiments of seamanship, she stepped promptly aboard, rowed a little way out to sea, and hoisted the sail, after which she threw the oars and rudder overboard and placed herself entirely at the mercy of the wind. She calculated that one of two things would inevitably happen: either the boat, being without ballast or rudder, would capsize in the wind, or it would be driven aground somewhere and smashed to pieces. In either case she was certain to drown, for she would be unable to save herself even if she wanted to. So having wrapped a cloak round her head, she lay down, weeping, on the floor of the boat.

But her calculation proved quite wrong, for the wind blew so gently from the north that the sea was barely disturbed, the boat maintained an even keel, and towards evening on the following day she drifted ashore near a town called Susa, a hundred miles or so beyond Tunis.[10]

Here again the sea is an instrument of fate which drives those under sail off their intended course. From a stylistic point of view, however, it is just any old sea; hardly identifiable, little

differentiated and lacking in dramatic excitement. The key point
of the passage narrated comes where the woman is lying along
the bottom of the boat with her head wrapped in a cloak; she is
ignoring the sea which physically surrounds her.

Gian di Procida (*Decameron*, V, 6)

Not content with going from Procida to Ischia every day to
catch a glimpse of his beloved, Gianni would frequently make
the crossing by night, swimming there and back if no boat
was available, so that, even if he could see nothing else, he
could at least gaze upon the walls of her house. [11]

The descriptive writing here is all about an athletic challenge
to the valiant swimmer. Again one can say that the sea is missing
from the narrative scene.

If one treats the *novella* of Alatiel (with which I intend to deal
in the following pages) as an exception, then the seas in the
Decameron can be summed up as in my list above. The net
result is rather poor, surely, for such an adventure-orientated
writer as Moravia would have us believe Boccaccio to be. It
would almost seem as if the sea, traditionally the classic symbol
of human adventurousness, has little real interest for our
sedentary adventure-lover, Boccaccio. [12] The sea, in the *Decameron*,
is (and this is amply shown in my foregoing documentation) both
narratively and poetically inert. There is just one exception
(obviously, otherwise it would hardly have been worth my
trouble in starting to write this chapter), and this is the *novella*
of Alatiel, which, to paraphrase Osip Mandel'stam,[13] we could
call 'La più velica' ('the most nautical'; but *vela* means 'sail') of
Boccaccio's *novelle*.

Here, then, is a short synopsis of this rather complex story.
Alatiel is the exceedingly beautiful daughter of the Sultan of
Babylon. He sends her off to marry the King of Algarve, but
after her ship is wrecked she ends up in the hands of Pericone.
He falls in love with her beauty and seduces her, in spite of the
fact that she does not speak or understand his language. Next
Pericone's brother, Marato, falls in love with Alatiel, kills

Pericone and abducts the princess to a ship. The two owners of the ship also fall prey to her charm, kill Marato, and subsequently fight a duel for the possession of her person: one dies, the other is mortally wounded. She then falls into the hands of the Prince of Morea, who becomes her lover and protector. But the incautious prince makes the mistake of showing this beautiful mistress to the Duke of Athens, who immediately resolves on abducting her. He kills the Prince and, his hands still fouled with the murdered man's blood, enters her bed and possesses her. But their affair is also short-lived: the son of the Emperor of Constantinople yields to her fascination and takes her away from the Duke, only to lose her, after a while, to Osbech, King of the Turks. Next she becomes the mistress of Antioco, the King's retainer, who eventually dies; so she passes on to Antioco's friend, until she meets up with Antigono who was known in the court of her father.

She eventually succeeds in reaching her native land again, where she tells her father that she has spent all the years of her absence in a convent of pious, chaste, devout women, namely San Cresci in Valcava (*St Stiffen*, in the McWilliam translation, i.e. St Stiffen in the Hollow Valley, where the pun is self-explanatory). The end of the story shows Alatiel entering the bed of her destined husband, the King of Algarve, as a virgin, and convincing him that she is really so. 'Hence the saying: "A kissed mouth doesn't lose its freshness, for like the moon it always renews itself."'[14]

At the beginning of the *novella*, the Princess is embarking on a ship in order to meet her future husband in the distant land of Morocco:[15]

Finding the weather favourable, the ship's crew put on full sail, and for several days after leaving Alexandria the voyage was prosperous. But one day, when they had passed Sardinia and were looking forward to journey's end, they ran into a series of sudden squalls, each of which was exceptionally violent, and these gave the ship such a terrible buffeting that passengers and crew were convinced time and again that the end had come. But they had plenty of spirit, and by exerting all their skill and energy they survived the onslaught of the mountainous seas for two whole days. However, as night approached for the third time since the beginning of the storm, which showed no sign of relenting but on the contrary

was increasing in fury, they felt the ship foundering. Though
in fact they were not far from the coast of Majorca, they had
no idea where they were, because it was a dark night and the
sky was covered with thick black clouds, and hence it was
impossible to estimate their position either with the ship's
instruments or with the naked eye.

It now became a case of every man for himself, and there was
nothing for it but to launch a longboat, into which the ship's
officers leapt, preferring to put their trust in that rather than
in the crippled vessel. But they had no sooner abandoned ship
than every man aboard followed their example and leapt into
the longboat, undeterred by the fact that the earlier arrivals
were fighting them off with knives in their hands. Thus, in
trying to save their lives, they did the exact opposite; for the
longboat was not built for holding so many people in weather of
this sort and it sank, taking everybody with it.

Meanwhile, the ship itself, though torn open and almost
waterlogged ,was driven swiftly along by powerful winds until
eventually it ran aground on a beach on the island of Majorca.
By this time, the only people still aboard were the lady and her
female attendants, and they were all lying there like dead
creatures, paralysed with terror by the raging tempest. The
ship's impetus was so great that it thrust its way firmly into
the sand before coming to rest a mere stone's throw from the
shore, and since the wind was no longer able to move it, there
it remained for the rest of the night, to be pounded by the sea.

In the above passage we have a totally different sea on our
hands. About this much there can be no doubt. Like other seas
in the *Decameron*, this is a functional one, which serves to transport
the character to *C* (the isle of Majorca), rather than *B* (the kingdom
of Algarve, in Morocco), to which she was directed in the first
place. Unlike the other stories, this *novella* presents a sea that
goes beyond mere functionality and is laden with signs and
details which combine to suggest an apparent symbolic or
allusive system. To use Roland Barthes's terminology, we could
say that Alatiel's sea is also a sea *indiciel*.[16] It follows a metaphorical line of narrative which takes us back to models that are
considerably more complex, or at least significantly different
from the purely informative and operational code.

The sea in Alatiel's *novella* not only keeps us in touch with the geographical displacements and misadventures of the heroine: it actually tells us something else; it invites us to move towards a different decoding of the data provided by the story. Boccaccio's marine information does not simply refer the reader back to other elements in the narrative along the sequential and metonymic chain of the story. They also refer on to a subtler level, independent from, and alien to, the mere sequence of events that make up its plot. From an informational standpoint, one is entitled to feel that this is sea as opposed to land. One knows that it is a voyageable sea, a space that can be crossed and not just a point on a line, a place where the journey happened to stop. But there is also a sensation of the sea as an untamable creature, an element outside human control, a tormented sea which succeeds in throwing haywire the planned crossing of the heroine.

Yet the reader is being presented with a redundancy of data, and the narrative becomes somewhat overpowering, if the act of reading is to be conducted on a purely functional plane. For Alatiel's sea is also an infinite sea; it is a literary stretch of salt water, in which ships have to by-pass Dantesque isles, Maiolica, Sardegna, moving towards the fabled Morocco.[17] It is a sea whose storms have little to do with the *Decameron*'s conventional presentation of the elements in upheaval, but articulated into a dramatic struggle of men against the forces of destiny. This is a supernatural sea beaten incessantly by a high wind that goes on for days and days; mysterious, dark and pitch-black, a sea where men can no longer guess where they are, and navigational aids have become useless. This is also a providential, judgment-passing sea: it condemns to death those cowardly sailors who came to knife-blows in order to secure themselves a place on the lifeboat. It is a teasing sea, which destroys those sailors that left the ship to save their lives and preserves the women who stayed on the ship in expectation of their death. Most important of all, we are dealing with an active sea: it makes the ship race 'velocissimamente', so much so that after having struck against the shore of the island, the ship is rushing forward so furiously that 'quasi tutta si ficcò nella rena, vicino al lito forse una gittata di pietra'.[18] We shall meet further references to the speed and fury of the sea in other marine sections of the *novella*.

Now it seems that we are in a position to ask ourselves the real question: Why all these details about the sea? Why the extravagant redundancy, why the mysteriousness of the messages concerning the sea? Why has Boccaccio chosen to give us such an ambiguous and complex sea, when all he needed narratively was a modest little storm sufficient to divert the ship in such a way that the character Alpha landed at point *C* instead of *B*, at the isle of Majorca instead of Morocco, which was Alatiel's original destination? The sea in Cimone's *novella* (*Decameron*, V, 1), which fulfils an analogous function, is not at all like the sea in Alatiel's *novella*: a storm rises and that particular boat ends up at Rhodes, despite all the crew's efforts to the contrary. And there was an end to it.

Perhaps it will be instructive for us to follow this special sea through the subsequent developments of the plot in which it has already played so conspicuous a part. Alatiel becomes the lover of Pericone; Marato, Pericone's brother, kills him, kidnaps the woman, and takes her off by a ship on which 'the ship's crew, taking advantage of a strong and favourable wind, cast off and sailed swiftly away'.[19] The success of Marato's criminal plan is carried off by these triumphant notes at the end of a paragraph of narrative. Now it is the turn of others to fall for Alatiel, and the two owners of the ship:[20]

> found that Marato kept a close watch on her. But one day,
> when the ship was sailing along like the wind and Marato was
> standing on the stern facing seaward without the least suspicion
> of their intentions, . . .

they push Marato into the sea. But why should the ship have been going 'a vela velocissimamente'?[21] At a functional level, this information is redundant. Evidently we are again faced by a passage where we shall need to use a different deciphering key, one which will enable us to unravel the various extra-functional elements which we are meeting in the *novella*.

Again, the window from which the Prince of Morea looks out 'overlooked a cluster of houses that had been laid in ruins by the violence of the sea. It was but rarely, if ever, that anybody went there.'[22] These ruined houses are an important component of the story, because they justify the curious way in which the madman discovers the corpses (besides, this scene could be viewed as an indirect way of increasing the horror and fascination of the double murder). But why are the houses represented as destroyed 'dall'impeto del mare' ('by the violence of the sea')? Surely this is designed to maintain the story's permanent thorough-bass, the deafening roar of breakers and storms which acts as a kind of musical accompaniment to the unleashing of human passions all round the figure of Alatiel.

And even here, the adventures of the young woman and the sea are not over: Costanzio, the Emperor of Constantinople's son, kidnaps Alatiel in the Duke of Athens's garden, causes her to embark on a boat, and turns to the sailors without delay: 'Constant ordered them to cast off and start rowing. And the sailors, not so much rowing as flying, just before dawn on the following day arrived at Aegina.'[23] Now why should he be described as in all this hurry? The Duke is a good distance away, and is not pursuing them at this point. Other kidnappers in the *Decameron* (Paganino in II, 10 and Cimone in V, 1, for example) don't behave like this at all. So here, too, the hyperbole ('non vogando ma volando') suggests that there is another reason for the comment, a reason outside the informative code of the text. Both Marato's ship, adverbially qualified with *velocissimamente*, and Costanzio's sailors' *non vogando ma volando*, are evidently symbolic, rather than purely functional factors.

The sea recurs just once more, in this *novella*, when the Princess offers her father an odd metaphorical version of her vicissitudes. She says: 'Father, some twenty days after my departure, our ship was disabled by a raging tempest, and ran aground at night on the shores of the western Mediterranean, near a place called Aiguesmortes.'[24] From this beach of Aiguesmortes, *Aguamorta*, the four authoritative knights are supposed to have taken her to the monastery of San Cresci in Valcava, where Alatiel alleges that she passed her period of enforced exile in chastity. Now, if we have an 'Aguamorta', a dead water, perhaps we shall also get an 'Acquaviva'?

My intention has been clear from the outset. I was looking for a way of proving the presence of a symbolic line running through the whole *novella*. How far this type of q.e.d. will be acceptable in the field of exact sciences is quite another question. As far as the juridical canons of the arts take us (and these must surely be both a science of the *dedans*, as well as the *dehors*, and therefore accept the promptings of an inner experience), up to now the results of my experiment seem to be quite satisfying. Only a symbolic system, present and active in the *novella*, could possibly account for the plethora of unusual, eccentric and extravagant elements which accompany the various descriptions of sea and storm that Alatiel has to pass through. Over and apart from this proof, we shall also try to hazard an identification of the verbal elements that convey the symbolic message within a specific semantic area which we shall define with the composite term sea/wind.

However, this can only be the last step of our interpretative *iter*. From this point onwards, it is all a question of working hypotheses and variations on a theme. It could be that we do, in fact, have a binary symbolic system that links the a-sexualized world of Aguamorta with the sexualized world of Aquaviva, the living water, the sea. But a more exact symbolic distribution of these various elements would be entirely arbitrary. Sea and wind cannot symbolize anything precise and identifiable. We can hardly set up an equation of the kind: sea $= x$; wind $= y$. This latter could only exist in the well-ordered labyrinth of an allegory structure; certainly not in the chaotic crater of symbolic constructs. The category sea/wind in this *novella* (and in this one only) creates a symbolic combine, a puzzle, by definition insoluble and unparaphrasable, trapped inside a closed system of allusions and suggestions.

Let us take a celebrated example of a storm in literature which is at once *fonctionnel* and *indiciel*: the storm in the third act of *King Lear*. At one level this storm is rigidly functional in that it serves: (*i*) to emphasize the cruelty of Goneril and Regan; (*ii*) to quicken Lear on the path to total madness; (*iii*) to render more dramatic his meeting with Edgar; (*iv*) to make the figure of the old King more pitiful; (*v*) to heighten the loyalty of the Fool and of Kent; and so on. However, the text cannot be taken so much *à la lettre*. Lear's storm is just as much *indiciel*:

(*i*) The storm involves the pathetic fallacy: it is the external projection of the rage and fury that are boiling inside the King's heart.

(*ii*) The storm is a wounded and vengeful humanity which is bursting out in an explosion of anguished hatred of woman, against maternity and against the feminineness of the world:

'And thou, all-shaking thunder,/strike flat the thick rotundity o'th'world!'[25]

(*iii*) The storm is humanity devouring itself 'like monsters of the deep!'[26]

(*iv*) The storm is an astrological message, a sign of ill times boded by the sun and moon eclipses; *ergo* it is a condemnation of Edmund's scepticism, since he refused to believe in celestial portents.[27]

(*v*) The storm=King Lear. His challenge to the storm is a challenge to himself, a manifestation of *odium sui*, and the opening phrase: 'Blow winds, and crack your cheeks!'[28] which plays on the amphibological value of 'crack', stands for Lear's desire to tear himself and his flesh asunder.

One could go further along this line of interpretation, but what purpose would it serve? Possible interpretations of a given episode in literature are infinite, and ultimately all valid. And ultimately all useless. King Lear's storm is decodeable, but incomprehensible. There is no way of arriving at a global interpretation capable of delivering to us, wrapped up neatly inside a formula, both the storm and the fascination of that particular storm. All one can do is to suggest associative groupings that throw a little more light on the actual scene in the text.

The grouping sea/wind in the *novella* of Alatiel is not dissimilar. It constitutes a symbolic montage of somewhat more problematic decoding, but incomprehensible to the same degree and unparaphrasable like all works of poetry.[29] All we can allow ourselves to do is to establish the presence of a number of constants, and suggest various possible links between the metonymic *chaînes* and the metaphoric *chaînes* which are involved in the composite picture. The *velicità*, the sailingness of the *novella*, seems to propose, side by side with the sea wind, the presence of another wind which troubles human souls who have been overwhelmed by the extraordinary physical beauty of Alatiel. The Princess, locked inside the prison of non-communication (she does not speak the language of her various lovers), arouses mute and unstated passions in men which can only be exemplified in a literary context by a system of extra-human co-ordinates. This projects Man's instincts up on to the screen of a partially anthropomorphized world of nature. The fascinating association *visage/paysage* (which I have elsewhere treated as the 'sexualization of nature'[30] – in our *novella* it is enough to think of the name of the convent where Alatiel claims that she was in retreat), actually becomes a complex metaphorical conglomeration binding together the human world (woman, man, instinct, love, anxiousness, passion, fury, lust, attractiveness, penetration, alarm, self-destruction, oblivion, orgasm, etc.) with a humanized natural world (sea, wind, storm, ship, land penetrated by a ship, land destroyed by the sea, sails, flying, speed, and so forth). It is in this anguished and fascinating symbolic puzzle that we can identify, in my view, the most suggestive motif in the *novella*. It is a *novella* which relates two parallel adventures: marine passions and human passions; the elements let loose and instincts unbridled; flying and orgasms.

For Alatiel is not 'a beautiful woman'. She is a superhuman figure; mythic, or at least closely related to a myth. Even her linguistic isolation can be read as an ambivalent sign, both *fonctionnel* and *indiciel*. On the one hand, her complete ignorance of West European languages is convincing from a narrative standpoint, and serves to give special emphasis to the gesticulations of the characters, especially during the first seduction (Alatiel and Pericone). Yet her non-communication is also *indiciel* in the story; it constitutes a sign standing for Alatiel's isolation, which is due to her superhuman features. Any mating with a mythic character must take place in silence, because there can exist no dialogue, no normative vocabulary, for the relationship between man and myth. Vittore Branca, though conscious of this *novella*'s fascination, has insisted on the human dimensions of its protagonist by declaring that 'the theme of beauty as the prime cause of all misfortunes, and consequently Alatiel's tragic interpretation of her own beauty' is 'the most fascinating aspect of this *novella*'.[31] However, Branca's interpretation pays too little attention to the hyperbolic and exaggerated connotations which follow Alatiel around in all her adventures. Alatiel, 'according to everybody who had set eyes on her, was the most beautiful woman to be found anywhere on earth.'[32] This pre-eminence of Alatiel projects her, as a character, towards a superior form of life right from the initial description of her physical attributes.

The epithets and adverbs that are generated by her loveliness all happen to be in the superlative: *sommamente, smisuratamente, ardentissimamente*, and so on. All is excessive, unmeasurable, de-humanized in the *novella*. The story's impact hardly resides in Alatiel's anguished consciousness of her disastrous beauty (an allure that drags her to misfortune and her numerous lovers to their death), but rather in the very superlativeness of the beauty and therefore of the pleasure which she offers the male world. This 'maraviglioso piacere'[33] poetically justifies her lovers' deaths. They seem to be repeating the zoological phenomenon of the male bees who burn up their existence in a fatal coitus with the queen-bee. The deaths which constellate Alatiel's catastrophic erotic career are not merely dramatic or pitiable, but in fact sacred deaths: her men died for the faith. The uniqueness and superlativeness of the whole experience can only be sealed by their death. If a single lover survived, it would trivialize the adventure and reduce Alatiel to the rôle of *femme fatale*, or *belle dame sans merci*, or just a vulgar consumer of men. Alatiel's lovers die, and as they die, they enshrine the loved woman, who becomes a priestess of Eros, not a nymphomaniac.

This is the right moment to move from a mythic to a psychological level. Surely certain experiences are bound to be terminal, and must perforce close off a cycle of human life. In everyday life, these climactic turning-points can assume different aspects: a changed attitude towards life, an abdication, an unexpressed or unconscious vow, the opening of a fresh chapter, departure, exile, becoming an itinerant, etc. In literature, and especially in non-*intimiste* types of writing, the field of choice is considerably more restricted. The terminal experience must be sealed with a clamorous occurrence, a dramatic farewell (remember the *Addio* in opera) or a death.

Perhaps no writer better than Racine has succeeded in conveying the feeling that certain experiences can have no future, only a past. I am thinking of the farewell words of Bérénice to Antiochus in the last scene of the tragedy:[34]

> Prince, après cet adieu, vous jugez bien vous même
> Que je ne consens pas de quitter ce que j'aime
> Pour aller loin de Rome écouter d'autres vœux.

> Prince, after this farewell you can see for yourself/that I cannot consent to abandon the one I love/and leave Rome far behind in order to listen to other vows.

This example is taken from a play where eroticism exists only at the 'impure' state, filtered down through a series of social and dramatic conventions. The *novella* of Alatiel, which has a more direct and uncontaminated eroticism, is supposed to convey to a reader a hallowed conception of the sexual act. In order for this to be so, the characters who perform it must not only vanish from the stage after the ultimate decisive experience of their existence; they must die. They must destroy their very lives, by disappearing 'with a bang and not with a whimper'. For one of her men, a post-Alatiel life is literarily inconceivable in the moral climate of the *Cento novelle*. That which follows after ecstasy, after the sighting of God, after the burning experience of hallowed eroticism—these potential *post-scripta* could form subject-matter for an *intimiste* text or for a romantic poem of nostalgia, but not for a text completely immersed in the present tense such as the *Decameron*. 'Il maraviglioso piacere' which Alatiel's lovers experience marks their sentence of death. The mythic halo of the woman determines their death; their death endorses the mythic essence of the woman as a character in the story.

Love in *Decameron*, II, 7, is on the one hand oblivion, on the other is death. Oblivion: one should think of the bulging sentence 'ella, già con lui *dimestica*tasi, Pericone *dimentica*to avea',[35] where the phonetic similarity between the two key verbs underlines the cognate nature of the two experiences: to get to know one man = to forget the preceding man.

Death in this *novella* is pre-eminently violent and blood-stained. This latter fact ties up in turn with another feature of the story's eroticism: in Alatiel, love is transgression, mindless and crazy subversion of those moral values which regulate contemporary society. One by one all the privileged tenets of an ethically balanced world are attacked and shattered by the 'focoso amore'; 'his blazing passion gaining the upper hand over his sense of honour'.[36] This is the cardinal phrase of the whole *novella*. Nothing can withstand the onrush of the senses. Alatiel's vow of chastity and her verbal promise, the 'gentle'[37] nature of Pericone, the kinship ties which link Marato to his brother, the professional honour of the two ship-owners, the sacredness of the guest-host relationship for the Duke of Athens, the latter's nobility of birth, Costanzio's ties of friendship with his sister's family, Antioco's devotion to his master, his venerable old age, the friendship of

The meaning of a storm   127

Antioco's favourite companion, his respect towards his expired
friend: the whole pack of cards of human duty and decency
tumbles down when faced by love, which becomes a powerful
and iconoclastic deity.

In *Decameron*, II, 7, to use some of Georges Bataille's concepts,[38]
Eros is violence, violation, outrage. All the deaths, killing,
strangling, rape and violence that take place in the *novella* are not
only parallel to the notations concerning Alatiel's fatal charm:
they are an integral part of the myth of her charm. The killings
are sacred, part of a religious ceremony. Hence the blood with
which the Duke of Athens fouls his hands in the first horrifying
sexual embrace is holy blood.[39]

Notes

1 Alberto Moravia, 1965, chapter on Boccaccio.
2 McW, p. 138.

> Il dí seguente, mutatosi il vento, le cocche ver ponente venendo far
> vela, e tutto quel dí prosperamente vennero al loro viaggio; ma nel
> fare della sera si mise un vento tempestoso, il qual faccendo i mari
> altissimi, divise le due cocche l'una dall'altra. E per forza di questo
> vento addivenne che quella sopra la quale era il misero e povero
> Landolfo, con grandissimo impeto di sopra all'isola di Cifalonia
> percosse in una secca, e non altramenti che un vetro percosso ad un
> muro tutta s'aperse e si stritolò: di che i miseri dolenti che sopra quella
> erano, essendo già il mare tutto pieno di mercatantie che notavano e di
> casse e di tavole, come in cosí fatti casi suole avvenire, quantunque
> oscurissima notte fosse e il mar grossissimo e gonfiato, notando
> quelli che notar sapevano, s'incominciarono ad appiccare a quelle cose
> che per ventura loro si paravan davanti(*Dec.*, II, 4, 16-17).

3 See Todorov, 1966. And also see Baratto, 1970, p. 138.
4 McW, p. 222.

> E quivi standosi, per darle alcuna consolazione, fece un giorno pescare,
> e sopra due barchette, egli in su una co' pescatori ed ella in su un'altra
> con altre donne, andarono a vedere; e tirandogli il diletto, parecchi
> miglia, quasi senza accorgersene n'andarono infra mare.
>
> E mentre che essi più attenti stavano a riguardare, subito una galeotta
> di Paganin da Mare, allora molto famoso corsale, sopravenne, e
> vedute le barche, si dirizzò a loro; le quali non poteron sí tosto fuggire,
> che Paganin non giugnesse quella ove eran le donne: nella quale
> veggendo la bella donna, senza altro volerne, quella, veggendo messer
> Ricciardo che già era in terra, sopra la sua galeotta posta, andò via
> (*Dec.*, II, 10, 12-13).

5 McW, p. 356-7.

> Per che, venuta la notte che salire sopra la saettia dovevano, le tre

sorelle, aperto un gran cassone del padre loro, di quello grandissima
quantità di denari e di gioie trassono, e con esse di casa tutte e tre
tacitamente uscite, secondo l'ordine dato, li lor tre amanti che
l'aspettavano trovarono: con li quali senza alcuno indugio sopra la
saettia montate, dier de' remi in acqua e andar via, e senza punto
rattenersi in alcuno luogo, la seguente sera giunsero a Genova, dove i
novelli amanti gioia e piacere primieramente presero del loro
amore.

E rinfrescatisi di ciò che avean bisogno, andaron via, e d'un porto in
uno altro, anzi che l'ottavo dí fosse, senza alcuno impedimento
pervennero in Creta (*Dec.*, IV, 3, 18–19).

6 McW, pp. 364–5.

Gerbino, il qual sopra la poppa della nave veduta aveva la donna
troppo più bella assai che egli seco non estimava, infiammato più che
prima, al mostrar del guanto rispose che quivi non avea falconi al
presente perchè guanto v'avesse luogo; e per ciò, ove dar non volesser
la donna, a ricevere la battaglia s'apprestassero. La qual senza più
attendere, a saettare e a gittar pietre l'un verso l'altro fieramente
incominciarono, e lungamente con danno di ciascuna delle parti in
tal guisa combatterono. Ultimamente, veggendosi Gerbino poco
util fare, preso un legnetto che di Sardigna menato aveano, e in quel
messo fuoco, con amendue le galee quello accostò alla nave. Il che
veggendo i saracini e conoscendo sé di necessità o doversi arrendere o
morire, fatto sopra coverta la figliuola del re venire, che sotto coverta
piagnea, e quella menata alla proda della nave e chiamato il Gerbino,
presente agli occhi suoi lei gridante mercé e aiuto svenarono, e in mar
gittandola dissono:

'Togli, noi la ti diamo qual noi possiamo e chente la tua fede l'ha
meritata' (*Dec.*, IV, 4, 21–3).

7 McW, p. 410.

E cosí detto, tacitamente alquanti nobili giovani richiesti, che suoi
amici erano, e fatto segretamente un legno armare con ogni cosa
opportuna a battaglia navale, si mise in mare, attendendo il legno
sopra il quale Efigenia trasportata doveva essere in Rodi al suo marito.
La quale, dopo molto onor fatto dal padre di lei agli amici del marito,
entrata in mare, verso Rodi dirizzaron la proda e andar via.

Cimone, il qual non dormiva, il dí seguente col suo legno gli
sopraggiunse e d'in su la proda a quegli che sopra il legno d'Efigenia
erano forte gridò:

'Arrestatevi, calate le vele, o voi aspettate d'esser vinti e sommersi in
mare.'

Gli avversari di Cimone avevano l'armi tratte sopra coverta e di
difendersi s'apparecchiavano: per che Cimone, dopo le parole preso un
rampicone di ferro, quello sopra la poppa de'rodiani, che via andavano
forte, gittò, e quella alla proda del suo legno per forza congiunse; e
fiero come un leone, senza altro seguito d'alcuno aspettare, sopra la
nave de' rodian saltò, quasi tutti per niente gli avesse (*Dec.*, V,
1, 26–8).

8 McW, p. 411–12.

Egli non erano ancora quattro ore compiute poi che Cimone li
rodiani aveva lasciati, quando, sopravegnente la notte, la quale
Cimone più piacevole che alcuna altra sentita giammai aspettava, con
essa insieme surse un tempo fierissimo e tempestoso, il quale il cielo di
nuvoli e 'l mare di pestilenziosi venti riempiè; per la qual cosa né
poteva alcun veder che si fare o dove andarsi, né ancora sopra la nave
tenersi a dovere fare alcun servigio.

Quanto Cimone di ciò si dolesse non è da domandare. Egli pareva che
gl' iddii gli avessero conceduto il suo disio acciò che più noia gli fosse
il morire, del quale senza esso prima si sarebbe poco curato. Dolevansi
similmente i suoi compagni, ma sopra tutti si doleva Efigenia, forte
piangendo e ogni percossa dell'onda temendo: e nel suo pianto
aspramente maladiceva l'amor di Cimone e biasimava il suo ardire,
affermando per niuna altra cosa quella tempestosa fortuna esser nata,
se non perché gl' iddii non volevano che colui, il quale lei contra li lor
piaceri voleva aver per isposa, potesse del suo presuntuoso disiderio
godere, ma vedendo lei prima morire, egli appresso miseramente morisse.

Con così fatti lamenti e con maggiori, non sappiendo che farsi i
marinari, divenendo ognora il vento più forte, senza sapere o conoscere
dove s'andassero, vicini all'isola di Rodi pervennero; nè conoscendo
per ciò che Rodi si fosse quella, con ogni ingegno, per campar le
persone, si sforzarono di dovere in essa pigliar terra, se si potesse.

Alla qual cosa la fortuna fu favorevole, e loro perdusse in un piccolo
seno di mare, nel quale poco avanti a loro li rodiani stati da Cimon
lasciati erano colla lor nave pervenuti (*Dec.*, V, 1, 37–41).

9 The vision of beautiful Iphigenia asleep, which transforms the imbecile
Cimone into a noble and wise young man. This scene is well known
through the famous painting by Rubens, now in Vienna.

10 McW, pp. 418–19.

E uscita segretamente una notte di casa il padre e al porto venutasene,
trovò per ventura alquanto separata dall'altre navi una navicella di
pescatori, la quale, per ciò che pure allora smontati n'erano i signori di
quella, d'albero e di vela e di remi la trovò fornita. Sopra la quale
prestamente montata e co' remi alquanto in mar tiratasi, ammaestrata
alquanto dell'arte marinaresca, sí come generalmente tutte le femine in
quella isola sono, fece vela e gittò via i remi e il timone, e al vento
tutta si commise; avvisando dover di necessità avvenire o che il vento
barca senza carico e senza governator rivolgesse, o ad alcuno scoglio
la percotesse e rompesse, di che ella, eziandio se campar volesse, non
potesse, ma di necessità annegasse; e avviluppatasi la testa in un
mantello, nel fondo della barca piagnendo si mise a giacere.

Ma tutto altramenti addivenne che ella avvisato non avea: per ciò
che, essendo quel vento che traeva, tramontana, e questo assai soave, e
non essendo quasi mare e ben reggente la barca, il seguente dí alla
notte che su montata v'era, in sul vespro ben cento miglia sopra
Tunisi ad una piaggia vicina ad una città chiamata Susa ne la portò
(*Dec.*, V, 2, 10–13).

11 McW, p. 444.
    Il quale, non che il giorno da Procida ad usare ad Ischia per vederla venisse, ma già molte volte di notte, non avendo trovata barca, da Procida infino ad Ischia notando era andato, per poter vedere, se altro non potesse, almeno le mura della sua casa (*Dec.*, V, 6, 5).

12 The anonymous English translator of the 1620 edition (according to H. G. Wright, John Florio) filled out all the nautical descriptions of the *Decameron* with saltier sailor terminology. H. G. Wright writes, in *The first English translation of the Decameron (1620)* (Uppsala, 1953): 'One has the impression that the translator has a special interest in the sea. Although the *Decameron* does not afford much scope for descriptions of the sea. . . . when Chynon stands "aloft on the decke" and cries to his enemies "Stroke your sayles, or else determine to be sunke in the Sea", his words appear to breathe the translator's own spirit and to reflect the staunch courage of the Elizabethan seamen' (p. 16).

13 '*Inferno*, XXVI is the most sailorly [*velica*] of Dante's cantos.' Osip Mandel'stam, *Discorso su Dante*, in *La quarta prosa*, De Donato, Bari, 1967, p. 150. But see Baratto, 1970, p. 101.

14 McW, p. 191. 'Bocca basciata non perde ventura, anzi rinnuova come fa la luna' (*Dec.*, II, 7, 122).

15 McW, p. 170–1.
    I marinari, come videro il tempo ben disposto, diedero le vele a' venti e del porto d'Alessandria si partirono e più giorni felicemente navigarono: e già avendo la Sardigna passata, parendo loro alla fine del loro cammino esser vicini, si levarono subitamente un giorno diversi venti, li quali, essendo ciascuno oltre modo impetuoso, sí faticarono la nave dove la donna era e' marinari, che più volte per perduti si tennero. Ma pure, come valenti uomini, ogni arte e ogni forza operando, essendo da infinito mare combattuti, due dí si sostennero; e surgendo già dalla tempesta cominciata la terza notte, e quella non cessando ma crescendo tutta fiata, non sappiendo essi dove si fossero né potendolo per estimazion marinesca comprendere né per vista, per ciò oscurissimo di nuvoli e di buia notte era il cielo, essendo essi non guari sopra Maiolica, sentirono la nave sdruscire.
    Per la qual cosa, non veggendovi alcun rimedio al loro scampo, avendo a mente ciascun se medesimo e non altrui, in mare gittarono un paliscalmo, e sopra quello più tosto di fidarsi disponendo che sopra la isdruscita nave, si gittarono i padroni; a' quali appresso or l'uno or l'altro di quanti uomini erano nella nave, quantunque quelli che prima nel paliscalmo eran discesi colle coltella in mano il contradicessero, tutti si gittarono, e credendosi la morte fuggire, in quella incapparono: per ciò che, non potendone per la contrarietà del tempo tanti reggere il paliscalmo, andato sotto, tutti quanti perirono.
    E la nave, che da impetuoso vento era sospinta, quantunque sdruscita fosse e già presso che piena d'acqua, non essendovi su rimasa altra persona che la donna e le sue femine (e quelle tutte per la tempesta del mare e per la paura vinte su per quella quasi morte giacevano), velocissimamente correndo, in una piaggia dell' isola di Maiolica

percosse; e fu tanta e sí grande la foga di quella, che quasi tutta si
ficcò nella rena, vicina al lito forse una gittata di pietra: e quivi dal
mar combattuta, la notte, senza poter più dal vento esser mossa, si
stette (*Dec.*, II, 7, 10–13).

16 Barthes, 1966, pp. 1–27. For a fuller discussion of the terms *fonctionnel*
and *indiciel*, see my *Il ciclo della scommessa*, Bulzoni, Rome, 1975.

17 Both islands and the country of destination, Morocco, immediately
recall episodes from the *Inferno*:

Tra l'isola di Cipri e di Maiolica
non vide mai sí gran fallo Nettuno,
non da pirati, non da gente argolica. (*Inferno*, XXVIII, 82–4)
Between the islands of Cyprus and
Majorca Neptune never saw so great
a crime, not of pirates
nor of men of Greece (Sinclair's translation).

And in the celebrated episode of Ulysses, his ship came close to 'Morocco,
e l'isola de' Sardi' (See *Inferno*, XXVI, 104).

18 I quote from the original Italian to indicate the full force of the expression
'si ficcò nella rena'. McWilliam's translation: 'The ship's impetus was so
great that it thrust its way firmly into the sand before coming to rest a
mere stone's throw from the shore . . .' (p. 171). But see Baratto, 1970,
p. 140.

19 McW, p. 175. 'I marinari, avendo buon vento e fresco, fecero vela al
lor viaggio' (*Dec.*, II, 7, 36).

20 McW, p. 176.

E veggendola molto da Marato guardata, e per ciò alla loro intenzione
impediti, andando un dí a vela velocissimamente la nave, e Marato
standosi sopra la poppa e verso il mare riguardando, e di niuna cosa da
loro guardandosi (*Dec.*, II, 7, 40).

21 It is impossible to convey both the impact of the superlative adverb,
velocissimamente, and the reinforced significance of the alliteration, *vela*
*velo*cissimamente.

22 McW, p. 178. 'guardava sopra certe case dall'impeto del mare fatte
cadere, nelle quali rade volte o non mai andava persona' (*Dec.*, II, 7, 54).

23 I have here slightly altered the McWilliam translation to convey the
exceptional force of the expression *non vogando ma volando*. 'Costanzio . . .
comandò che de' remi dessero in acqua e andasser via. Li quali non vogando ma volando, quasi in sul dí del seguente giorno ad Egina pervennero' (*Dec.*, II, 7, 74).

24 McW, p. 188. 'Padre mio, forse il ventesimo giorno dopo la mia partita
da voi, per fiera tempesta la nostra nave, sdruscita, percosse a certe
piaggie là in ponente, vicine d'un luogo chiamato Aguamorta una
notte' (*Dec.*, II, 7, 106).

25 *King Lear*, III, 2, 6–7.

26 *King Lear*, IV, 2, 48–50.

27 *King Lear*, I, 2, 107–8, and Edmund's monologue in I, 2, 124–40.

28 *King Lear*, III, 2, 1.

29 'Wherever paraphrase is possible, the bedsheets are not crumpled;

poetry has not spent the night in that place', Osip Mandel'stam, *La quarta prosa*, De Donato, Bari, 1967, p. 127.

30　G. Almansi, *La géante di Baudelaire*, in *Il Verri*, 28, 1968.

31　Branca, 1970, footnote 3 at *Dec.*, II, 7, 7. Neither can I agree with the interpretation of Baratto, who believes that Alatiel does not exist as a character: 'She is the events that occur to her' (Baratto, 1970, p. 96). This view ignores the mythic dimension of the princess.

32　McW, p. 170. '. . . la più bella femmina che si vedesse in quei tempi nel mondo' (*Dec.*, II, 7, 9).

33　*Dec.*, II, 7, 80. McWilliam's translation, 'a very happy time', fails to carry the full force of the original. But any translation would fall short of the Italian, since there is no English word that exactly corresponds to the Italian *maraviglioso*.

34　Racine, *Bérénice*, Act V, scene 7.

35　*Dec.*, II, 7, 37. I have to use the Italian text to convey how close the two words are phonetically. McWilliam's translation: 'she soon returned his affection and forgot all about Pericone' (p. 175).

36　McW, p. 178. '. . . pesando più il suo focoso amore che la sua onestà' (*Dec.*, II, 7, 51).

37　'Un gentile uomo il cui nome era Pericon da Visalgo' (*Dec.*, II, 7, 17).

38　See mainly Georges Bataille, *L'Érotisme*, Éditions de Minuit, Paris, 1957.

39　For a different interpretation of this *novella*, see the recent volume by C. Segre, *Le strutture e il tempo*, Einaudi, Turin, 1974, chapter 4, pp, 145–59.

Five

Passion and metaphor

Here is an outline of the plot of the first *novella* of the Fourth Day. Tancredi, Prince of Salerno, has a deep affection for his daughter, Ghismonda. So at first he is slow to arrange a marriage for her. Later, when she returns to her father's palace as a widow at a still youthful age, he unwisely postpones any arrangements for her to re-marry. Ghismonda feels that she is left with no alternative but to take herself a lover, and after carefully reviewing all the young men who attend the palace, she fixes her choice on Guiscardo, who is a brave and noble-spirited young man, but of low social rank. The princess invites Guiscardo to come to her bedchamber by passing along a secret passage which leads to an open cavern in the mountainside. Thus the young pair become lovers, but their relationship is found out by Tancredi, who has Guiscardo killed, and his heart cut out of his body. The Prince then sends the heart as a present to his daughter. Ghismonda reacts with considerable strength of spirit: she bathes the heart with her tears and then adds to it a potion of poisonous herbs which she has prepared. Lifting to her lips a cup which contains the blood from her lover's heart, her own tears and the poison, she commits a noble suicide by draining this gruesome beverage.

This *novella* is one of the most famous in the *Decameron*. It has been constantly translated, re-adapted, set to poetry and dramatized for the stage; critics have shown an unflagging interest in it, and its diffusion has been exceptional in terms of its social, cultural and geographical ramifications.[1] Almost all the major Boccaccio scholars of the twentieth century have attempted a critical analysis of the story, and it is interesting to note their striking range of disagreement as to how it should be read. This wide variety of conclusions should initially dispose us to investigate the possibility that there are several different narrative levels co-existing in the *novella*, and perhaps to suspect that this is an intentional plurality of meaning and interpretation on Boccaccio's part, one which he was inclined to introduce in other major stories. In this connection it is enough to think of the *novella* of Griselda (*Decameron*, X, 10) where the polyvalence of the text suggests that it is a deliberate, one might even say malicious, product of Boccaccio's authorial strategy.

Yet if we are going to accept the supposition that there is a genuine, a well-intentioned obscurity in the text, then we shall be obliged to consider how the difficulty of the *novella* can be reconciled with its extreme success. Luigi Russo posed the question in his *Letture critiche del Decameron*, trying to identify the reasons which had led to its striking diffusion, but the solution he arrived at is hardly acceptable: [2]

> I have called the *novella* poetic/oratorical: oratorical because the general tone, as in Ghismonda's long speech to her father, is towards an abstract defence of the flesh. Oratory generalizes a motif, while poetry always renders it more individual, and arrives at the universal by going *via* the contingent. This explains the story's immense success, because the man in the street understands oratory much better than poetry.

Quite apart from the too rigid distinction after the manner of Croce,[3] Russo's hypothesis seems to be contradicted by the fact that the story did not spread merely to a popular readership, but in fact reached widely varied social and cultural *milieux*, from the humanistic circles of the Italian fifteenth century to late Renaissance Spain and the English world of the seventeenth and eighteenth centuries. In any case, Russo's view of Ghismonda's great tragic speech as oratorical is quite unacceptable to me.

Indeed, there is surely a case for seeing the exceptional success of the story as being in part due to the fascinating ambiguities which lurk inside it. Its essence is unclear and non-explicit. It is bound up in a dense web of allusive references to an underlying sphere of instinct and motivation. Although this narrative substratum is constantly on the point of emerging at the surface level of the story, it is never in fact unequivocally defined or communicated to the reader. Hence one can surely see it as the exact opposite of an oratorical poetic mode, since oratory must by definition convey an explicit message and eliminate margins of doubt.

Now if obscurity or unclearness or opaqueness[4] is to be one of the salient features of the *novella*, the critic's task is to isolate the equivocal element in it and attempt to circumscribe the fictional area which falls inside this ambiguity of artistic intention and effect. One could start by dividing the *novella* up into two distinct narrative zones. The first of these is bathed in light; it is open, self-explanatory, compact and coherent in tone, containing at its very centre a protagonist who 'moves through the story with pride and self-confidence, the aristocratic and solitary figure of Ghismonda'.[5] The second is a zone of darker and circuitous effects, comprising an area of ill-defined lines and dominated by an equally forceful antagonist, despite his essential incoherence as a fictional human being: Tancredi.

In Russo's view, Tancredi is the bare outline of a character or a failed character: it can be said that he is 'a mere expedient of the narrative which ensures the continuity of the plot'.[6] Subsequently Getto performed a clear reversal of this interpretation. He redeemed Tancredi the character from Russo's heavily negative judgment and counter-proposed him as the successful figure of an inept and vacillating individual, a kind of 'character without character', one who is untrained in that very art of living[7] which Ghismonda can be seen to have triumphantly incarnated. Certainly this interpretation comes close to the dynamic core of the character in the plot, but it is still not completely satisfying, because it fails to justify or explain a whole gamut of decisions and feelings, entertained by Tancredi, which contradict the view that he is inept and indecisive, and ultimately a man who dabbles in cruelty rather than being deliberately wicked.

The formula 'character without character' was doubtless a brilliant and serviceable notion; yet its key-word 'character' has a plurality of possible meanings, and reflects the basic imprecision and hence inadequacy of current psychological usage. 'Without character', for example, could once upon a time have stood for a valid classification, but in a contemporary context it merely becomes a moralizing judgment. The truth of the matter is that no quick formula can really solve the question of such a self-contradictory character as Tancredi, with his brusque changes from decisive action to cringing and melodramatic gestures which resemble a pathological state of mental confusion bordering on madness. Muscetta sums up this side of him as a 'swirl of puerile weakness and senile cruelty'.[8]

We are inclined to adopt a different kind of interpretation

(originally put forward in a flash of critical intuition by Moravia in his article on Boccaccio)[9] and look for a continuous unspoken current of incestuous sentiments. This seems to be the only critical direction which restores Tancredi to a fully-rounded character, unlocking him from a fragmentary series of irreconcilable gestures. Drawing on this fresh psychological and narrative insight, the critic Muscetta has redefined the figure of Tancredi and presented him as the 'real protagonist' of the *novella*, seeing him as a modern dramatic hero, with an almost Shakespearean touch, and arguing that his story is the first in the *Decameron* to present the theme of passionate love.[10]

None the less, incestuous feeling as such has no definable location in the text of the *novella*. One cannot point to a given *locus* and say 'herein lies incest'. One could almost state with deliberate paradox that the incest element lies outside the *novella*, yet that the text is still a continuous invitation to the reader to accomplish the intuitive act of extrapolating incest from it. And yet this intuitive act in turn is not indispensable to an understanding or even feeling for the story (which points to one of the strangest paradoxes of art): for the suggestion and fascination of the non-expressed seem to suffice by themselves to create the magic spell which causes the reader to be gripped by the story. Nor is it right to conclude, as Muscetta does,[11] that Boccaccio never steps across the dividing-line between the implicit and the explicit in handling this incestuous sentiment. If this were so, then it would presuppose that the reader reaches a different level of emotional immersion in the story than the author does. It would imply that the reader makes a step which is taboo and crosses the fatal threshold while the author himself stops at the brink. Perhaps we may propose a different solution: Boccaccio has drawn the reader into a ploy of silence.

If we separate the two main characters so that they lose their reciprocal relationship to each other, we are bound to destroy their plausibility and end up with an improbable pair. Tancredi and Ghismonda can only be considered each as a function of the other. On the one side we have Tancredi, an ambiguous figure as we have already described him, but impressive as a literary portrait of such vacillations, and incoherent because of a series of internal contradiction in his own soul, not by virtue of some human weakness or the author's supposed inadequacy as an

artist. On the other side we have the fully-articulated figure of
Ghismonda, who can express herself by word or action, until
her intransigence reaches the point of self-destruction. She is
therefore irreparably pitted against her father, who is resourceless
in word and deed.

Tancredi's actions and responses germinate in an obscure area
somewhere between his conscious and instinctive self. This
condemns him to inarticulacy and incoherence. Getto is certainly
right to see in Ghismonda marked skills in the art of life and in
Tancredi a corresponding inability. This may be a satisfactory
and even conclusive summary of the princess, but for Tancredi it
can only be a preliminary step towards the modulation of a set
of motives which Boccaccio has partially hinted at for us within
the limitations of his own ethical stance. Had he made an explicit
statement of the incest theme, he would have been obliged to
pass on to a consideration of its moral implications (perhaps
even an examination of his own conscience as voyeuristic com-
poser of such a scene), and this could hardly be debated inside the
narrative tissue of the *Decameron*.[12]

Yet the abyss of unconfessed feelings lies open in front of
each one of us, writers and readers. It is up to us to plumb its
implications or to enjoy the fascinating giddiness which comes
from looking down beyond the forbidden threshold. Once again
we are dealing with the 'open work', which requires the reader's
collaboration, whether it be conscious or unconscious.

The mutual dependence of Tancredi and Ghismonda is
underlined right from the early paragraphs of the *novella*:[13]

> Tancredi, Prince of Salerno, was a most benevolent ruler,
> and kindly of disposition, except for the fact that in his old age
> he sullied his hands with the blood of passion. In all his life he
> had but a single child, a daughter, and it would have been
> better for him if he had never had any at all.
>
> He was as passionately fond of this daughter as any father
> who has ever lived, and being unable to bring himself to part
> with her. . . .

Tancredi is described in relation to his daughter and his love for
her. The only item in the quotation which is extraneous to this
relationship with Ghismonda, 'benevolent ruler, and of kindly
disposition' is immediately drawn back into the father-daughter

Kwl

rapport by the first conditional clause in the passage. Getto rightly notes that the structure of the whole sentence, depending on the two uses of the particle 'se' ('if') already seems to reflect the essential key to Tancredi's character, namely his tortuous line of conduct.[14] One could add that these two 'se' subordinate the figure of the father to that of his daughter. Boccaccio is hinting that the father would be perfectly humane if . . . , he would be perfectly happy if. . . . The daughter is already, at her very first appearance in the story, a figure that conditions the personality of the father. Thus the father is in a sense *victime* before he turns into *bourreau*. And even at this point we are aware of the writer's insistence on the excessiveness (is he saying, the abnormality?) of his love for Ghismonda: he was 'passionately fond of this daughter'. We feel the writer's emphasis once more when Tancredi is reluctant to give her in marriage: 'being unable to bring himself to part with her, he refused to marry her off'; again, at the point where her short-lived husband, the Duke of Capova, has died: 'her father was so devoted to her that he was in no hurry to make her a second marriage'.[15]

The section of the story described above covers less than one page, three paragraphs out of the sixty-two[16] which make up the text of the *novella* in Branca's edition of the *Decameron*. After these three paragraphs, the father practically disappears from Boccaccio's narrative for the rest of the first part of the story, which goes up to the conclusion of the young pair's courtship emphasized by the reference to their oft-repeated sexual contact. In this extremely short narrative section, the first page of the *novella*, the predominance of the theme of excessive paternal love can hardly be due to mere chance: the story-teller repeatedly jokes with ironic malice about it. Within the economy of the story it only seems justifiable as a stylistic device which has the specific purpose of influencing the reader not by virtue of the meaning of the various sentences, but by way of the very repetition itself.

We should notice *en passant* how in this opening page of the *novella*, which is so important for the artistic formation of the fictional figure of Tancredi, the real emphasis is all on his rôle as loving father. There is really little evidence of 'aristocratic prejudice' or 'genteel atmosphere', which have been suggested by Petronio[17] and Di Pino[18] respectively, to try to account for Tancredi's subsequent behaviour. Even in the second half of the *novella* we shall see that these class prejudices are presented in highly ambiguous form and are actually contradicted by other elements in the narrative.

The time has come to look at the love intrigue between Guiscardo and Ghismonda, which goes forward with the complicity of the cavern inside the mountain. Once again it is useful to refer to Getto's exemplary study, where there are a number of interesting observations on the page dealing with the cavern, which he considers 'one of the most fascinating and memorable images of the entire *Decameron*'.[19] First of all, Getto notes how the mythico-historical treatment of the cavern contributes to the persuasiveness of the *scenario*: 'By means of this temporal perspective the secret passage to the cavern is rendered even more distant, and the whole effect is to heighten the atmosphere of jealously guarded secrecy which the whole *novella* lives and breathes.'[20] Hence Getto argues that the *scenario* responds to a narrative requirement, and that its function is dramatic rather than ornamental:[21]

> This *scenario* is simply devised to allow the two lovers a chance to meet, and the meeting must be such as to fulfil their need for secrecy and at the same time keep their energy and sense of initiative occupied. There we are dealing with a non-decorative *scenario*, one which we can describe as 'active'. It is a *scenario* as part of the action.

If we stay close to Getto's terms, we can interpret his argument as saying that the setting in the cavern has an activating effect on the characters, and that it contributes to their meeting without actually determining the atmosphere which surrounds the first contact between the two lovers. But the activating effect of the cavern does not just work on Guiscardo and Ghismonda, but on their readers, beginning with Getto himself, who recognized the fascination and memorableness of the scene. The critic insists on the secrecy of action in the story, on the obsessive repetition of adverbs and sentences suggesting circumspect and covert movements. This brings him to posit a 'poetry of action', of a stealthy action inherent in the secrecy of the plot. Finally when Getto quite correctly identifies the culminating point in Guiscardo's descent by rope to the cavern, he states in terms which are not quite specific enough, that the action 'exudes a sense of enterprise, passion and the fascination of adventure'. [22]

The problem still stands: what exactly creates this fascination? Clearly not Guiscardo's spirit of enterprise, because this goes no further than the standard sense of initiative in any strong and healthy young man who is 'full of amorous longings'. The actual events seem insufficient to account for the brilliance of this particular episode in the *novella*. Hence it becomes necessary to go beyond the scenario in its functional rôle (the *scenario-azione*) and attempt to decipher its overwhelming effect both on the characters involved and ourselves as readers.

This is the kind of direction Muscetta seems to be moving in, when he talks about the transfiguration of a cavern open on the mountain slope 'into a mysterious erotic stage-setting'. [23] Here the adjective 'erotic' can only mean: inherently capable of arousing thoughts concerning the act of love. Hence we are obliged to move on into the difficult no-man's-land between aesthetics and psychology. We must tackle the problem openly: if the setting is erotic (and even Getto's position could allow this definition), precisely what does its eroticism consist of, and where is it to be found? Perhaps it lies in our eroticized perception of it, which amounts to an instinctive reaction to a scene which becomes erotic in the reader, whereas it is not so in the text? Yet this hypothesis does not solve the problem as to how there can be a transition from the non-eroticism of the scene to the eroticism of the reader's perception of that scene. Unless this question can be answered, the formula 'erotic stage-setting' would seem to have no sense.

We have reached the following *impasse*: on the one hand we are determined to retain the idea of an erotic *scenario* because we cannot help being convinced that there is something relevant in Muscetta's observation. On the other hand, however, we are unable to find a logical justification for it. To escape from the vicious circle I should like to advance a tentative hypothesis. [24] After the two young lovers have consummated their relationship, this is how Boccaccio closes the scene: [25]

> During the night, Guiscardo climbed back up the rope, made his way out through the aperture by which he had entered, and returned home. And now that he was conversant with the route, he began to make regular use of it.

Now it is clear that Boccaccio is not interested in Guiscardo's repeated descent into the cave, but in the repeated intercourse implied by it. So the descent becomes an indirect reference to the sexual act, a signal to remind us that the route leads fatally to Ghismonda's bedchamber. Here it is a short step on to the hypothesis that Guiscardo's descent is not only an indirect reference but a straight metaphor for the sexual act, which in turn provides a new interpretation of the episode.

However, it is hardly wise to look for an exact *correspondance* between all the elements of the signifier (natural surroundings, topography, action, the clothes that Guiscardo puts on, the plant growth on the rock wall, etc.) and the various possible components of the sexual entity which has been signified by it. This kind of detailed comparison can only be made in openly pornographic compositions, in the manner, for example, of Hogarth's *Cottage*, where each single part of the landscape matches a corresponding item in a woman's anatomy, until the point where her uterus houses the idyllic cottage itself.[26] We could even go so far as to say that in order to avoid being pornographic it is not enough for a symbolic construction to be autonomous and self-justifying (Hogarth's engraving already meets these conditions): it must also be non-systematic in its sexual allusion, just as the imagery of doors, locks and keys in fairy-tales has a frequent but not inevitable erotic charge. In this kind of representation it is essential that innocent expressions be jumbled together with ambiguous hinting and lubricious suggestion, so that the total symbolic construction is asymmetrical and unplanned in appearance.

If we accept the above premises, we shall find that this particular episode in the *novella* is not lacking in ambivalent details that could be harnessed specifically to a sexual interpretation of the whole scene. The cavern had been used 'at some remote period of the past'[27] (perhaps this hints at Ghismonda's first marriage?). Now, as for the cavern, hardly anybody remembered that it was still there; but 'Love has reminded the enamoured lady of its existence' (the return of sexual interest after her widowhood?). The way into the cavern is by 'a secret staircase . . . but the way was barred by a massive door'. Ghismonda struggles for 'several days' against this barred gate, using all her wiles (her hesitation before embarking on the act of adultery?). On the side of the mountain there happens to be a *spiraglio* ('shaft'), which 'was almost entirely covered by weeds and brambles'. And it is through this fissure in the rock that Guiscardo lets himself down with the help of a rope, which he hitches on 'to a stout bush that had taken root at the mouth of the opening'. He wears 'a suit of leather to protect himself from the brambles'.[28]

Quite obviously all these details do admit of a coherent internal explanation: they could correspond to the geological and botanical facts of Guiscardo's arrival at the love nest. They even admit of the plausible realistic detail noted by Muscetta concerning the open caves in the mountainside that really do exist in the country around Salerno.[29] But as a narrative function they serve to explain the cavern, and not the subtle fascination that the cavern exerts on us. Indeed, the cavern in the latter sense seems to assume a rôle as objective correlative for a normally covert human experience. The only difficulty in interpretation arises from the rather wide gap between the sign and its referent. Now, in the finale of Ionesco's *Jacques ou la soumission*, for example, the two lovers describe the gallop of a horse with its mane on fire.[30] In this case it is fairly easy for us to accept the scene as a transposition into fabulous terms of the lovers' sexual passion, because the gap between the two terms of comparison is considerably shorter. In the case of *Decameron* IV, 1, the gulf between mineral/vegetable world and human experience is much wider; at least in Hogarth's composition the gulf is easier to cross because the reference is so immediate and unequivocal. Also, Boccaccio's collaboration in setting up the possible comparison of cavern and sexual receptacle is hinted and ambiguous.

Following on this scene Tancredi makes what Getto calls an 'unforgettable'[31] reappearance on the stage by his becoming an unseen witness of 'what Guiscardo and his daughter were doing' (this latter verb is deliberately brutal): 'From time to time, Prince Tancredi was in the habit of going alone to visit his daughter, with whom he would stay and converse for a while in her chamber and then go away'[32] '. . . without anyone hearing or noticing': the intimacy of Tancredi's relationship with his daughter is conveyed by Boccaccio in purely indirect terms of movement and manner: he is 'all by himself', 'unseen', 'unheard', and so on. On the day in question, Tancredi's procedure is to enter the bedroom, go up next to his daughter's bed and sit

down on a 'low stool'; there he 'rested his head against the side
of the bed, drew the curtain round his body as though to conceal
himself there on purpose, and fell asleep'.[33]

This seems in absolute terms a superb model of an unconfessed love sentiment. The old man who falls asleep with his
head leant against the empty bed of his daughter suggests a
whole area of unconscious personal feelings. And this aura of
secrecy invests all the participants in the narrative set-up, both
fictional character, writer and readers, without in any way dimin-
ishing the poignant sensuality of the tableau. It brings us to one
of the highest points in Boccaccio's art, a scene where ambiguity
of feeling and expression is brought to an extreme limit of
tension without actually upsetting the flow of the narrative.
What is achieved on the page is brought off despite the opposite
flow of two quite separate artistic requirements. On the one
hand Boccaccio allows free rein to the expansion of a lyrical
moment and a plurality of possible psychological implications,
resulting in the intensely emotional effect of the whole picture.
On the other hand the author must respect the tight logical
progression of his narrative, resulting in an impressive balancing
act which preserves the overall economy of the text.

The story proceeds with Guiscardo and Ghismonda entering
the bedroom where Tancredi has already fallen asleep:[34]

> They then went to bed in the usual way; but whilst they were
> playing and cavorting together, Tancredi chanced to wake up,
> and heard and saw [here the polysyndeton is cruelly effective]
> what Guiscardo and his daughter were doing. The sight filled
> him with dismay, and at first he wanted to cry out to them, but
> then he decided to hold his peace and, if possible, remain
> hidden, so that he could carry out, with greater prudence and
> less detriment to his honour, the plan of action that had
> already taken shape in his mind.

This passage is particularly subtle. The banal excuse which
Tancredi provides himself[35] for staying to watch the ensuing
sexual act is also the narrator's device for keeping him where he is
and guiding him towards his subsequent course of behaviour.

But the voyeuristic self-indulgence of which the character
himself seems unaware, and which the author cannot express
explicitly, must still be recognized if we are not to deny the

fundamental premisses of the scene, which were established when Tancredi fell asleep with his head leaning against his daughter's bed. Nor is it going too far to see Boccaccio skilfully transferring the arousal of the voyeur from an excitement at what he has seen to his physical gymnastics after the dramatic sight: 'And Tancredi though he was getting on in years, clambered through a window and lowered himself into the garden.'[36]

In fact there is nothing in the plot to justify these movements in rational terms; Tancredi is accustomed to coming and going freely from his daughter's bedroom, and this habit is taken up again in the next scene: '. . . paid his usual call upon his daughter in her chamber. And having locked the door behind him. . . .'[37] Tancredi's leap from the window is not a requirement of the action, but an indirect representation in external and behaviouristic terms of the character's physical arousal.

A similar example of delayed reaction by the aggrieved party in a sexual intrigue can be found in the *novella* about the heart of the lover which is served up and eaten at table (*Decameron*, IV, 9). Here is the outline of the story. The Count of Rossiglione discovers that his wife has become the lover of his best friend, the Count of Guardastagno, so he has the latter killed, the heart drawn out of the dead body and then serves up the heart as a meal to his adulterous wife, pretending that it is the heart of a wild boar. Hearing the real truth after she has finished eating, the wife declares that she will never add any more food on top of the eminently noble dish which she has just consumed. She gets up from the table, walks back to an open window and throws herself out to her death in the castle courtyard far below.

This story seems a reverse or mirror image of the *novella* of Ghismonda[38] by virtue of their respective positions as opening and closing stories in the Fourth Day,[39] and the significant substitution of husband for father as the aggrieved male who repeats the theme of the heart served up or presented to the woman in love. In IV, 9, after the macabre banquet, Rossiglione gives an account of how he has revenged himself and also reveals the linguistic motif on which the *vendetta* had been constructed by the final tragic pun on the verb *piacere*: 'I am not surprised to find that you liked it dead, because when it was alive you liked it better than anything else in the whole world.'[40] Probably this image is derived from Seneca's *Thyestes*.[41] The final section of this tragedy is conspicuous for a series of macabre conceits and amphibologies based on erotic/gastronomic *doubles entendres*. There is a constant play on love for one's family and love for the flesh of the family; on possession by physical embrace and possession by incorporation in the digestive tract:

Hic esse natos crede in amplexu patris.
Hi sunt eruntque; nulla pars prolis tuae
Tibi subtrahetur. Ora quae exoptas dabo
Totumque turba iam sua implebo patrem.
Satiaberis, ne metue. Nunc mixti meis
Iucunda mensae sacra iuvenilis colunt;
Sed accientur.

(Be sure that here, in their father's bosom, are thy sons;
– here now, and here shall be; no one of thy children shall
be taken from thee. The faces which thou desirest will I
give, and wholly with his family will I fill the sire. Thou
shalt be satisfied, have no fear of that. Just now, in company,
at the children's table, they are sharing the joyful feast; but I
will summon them.)

. . . Iam accipe hos potius libens
Diu expetitos – nulla per fratrem est mora:
Fruere, osculare, divide amplexus tribus.

(Now, rather, take these with joy, whom thou hast so
long desired. Thy brother delays thee not; enjoy them,
kiss them, divide thy embraces 'mongst the three.)[43]

. . . Quidquid e natis tuis
Superest habes, quodcumque nun superest habes.

(Whatever of thy sons is left, thou hast; whatever
is not left, thou hast.)[44]

This taste for verbal *agudezas* even seems to infect the ill-starred victim of the operation, who rounds off the sequence of puns with this final infelicitous word-play:[45]

Genitor en natos premo
Premorque natis.

(Lo, I, the father, overwhelm my sons, and by my sons
am overwhelmed.)

The Seneca source for the Boccaccio episode, whether direct or indirect, seems convincing. But subsequent development of the story shows Boccaccio reversing the dramatic treatment in the Seneca passage, for the woman's reaction to Rossiglione's statement is surprisingly cool and self-controlled: 'On hearing this, the lady was silent for a while', [46] and after her husband has told her the full facts: 'You can only imagine the anguish suffered by the lady on hearing such tidings of Cabestanh, whom she loved more dearly than anything else in the world. But after a while [dopo alquanto] she said. . . .' [47] Seneca had described the upheaval of the stomach against the dreadful ingestion with a wealth of detail:

Quis hic tumultus viscera exigitat mea?
Quid tremuit intus? Sentio impatiens onus
Meumque gemitu non meo pectus gemit?

(What is this tumult that disturbs my vitals? What trembles in me? I feel a load that will not suffer me, and my breast groans with a groaning that is not mine.) [48]

Volvunturque intus viscera et clusum nefas
Sine exitu luctatur et quaerit fugam.

(Their flesh is turning round within me, and my imprisoned crime struggles vainly to come forth and seeks way of escape.) [49]

whereas in Boccaccio the whole reaction is summed up by two pregnant hesitations: 'Alquanto stette' and 'dopo alquanto'. The Italian writer refuses to admit a single element that might exteriorize the conflict which is taking place inside the horrified victim of the trick ('se dolorosa fu'), so as not to disturb the heroic dignity of the woman's sudden decision to take her life by walking backwards towards a window. If she does have any reaction against the unwitting anthropophagy, it seems to take place immediately *after* her death: 'The window was situated high above the ground, so that the lady was not only killed by her fall but her body came apart in pieces.' [50] Here the woman's *disfacimento*, which is superfluous to the strict economy of the *novella*, can only serve as a device conveying (after the event) the internal laceration which destroys all the fibres of her being (the verb *disfare*) at the moment when she learns precisely what she had swallowed. Once again we are dealing here, as in the case of the Ghismonda story, with a perfect narrative mechanism which works both ways: either for a reader who is fully aware of the particular stylistic procedure which has been adopted, or for the reader who is unaware of it but nevertheless registers the hidden impact of such unexpected twists in the plot. Tancredi's descent from the window or the *disfacimento* of Rossiglione's wife's body are both incidents which transmit an emotional charge that preserves their dramatic effect at either a rational or instinctive level of interpretation.

Despite the immense variety of characters in the *Decameron*, the differing types of figure (noblemen, merchants, young lovers male and female, peasants, craftsmen, fathers, mother and so on) all present a number of recurring features which give the work its essential sociological unity and save the *Cento novelle* from being broken up into a series of unco-ordinated vignettes. In this bourgeois world morality is no fixed point of reference, but rather a self-adjusting scale of values which changes to fit the differing situation and social rank of the characters.

A fairly frequent situation in the *Decameron*, for example, is that of fathers faced by the discovery of their daughter's fornication. Yet their reactions are widely varied, ranging from the salacious acceptance of Lizio da Valbona (in V, 4) to the ruthless vendetta pursued by Amerigo (V, 7), with intermediate stages represented by Andreola's father (IV, 6) and Currado Malaspina (II, 6). However, in all these cases there is one constant element; fornication and adultery are only apparently condemned as they relate to the inflexible canons of religious morality. In actual fact the degree of guilt is measured simply in accordance with the socio-economic standing of the man and woman in question. In other words, they are judged by the flexible canons of mercantile morality.

Tancredi's behaviour in the second section of our *novella* might appear to fall inside the pattern of outraged fathers. But in point of fact he does not react like a Boccaccesque father but as a man gripped by pangs of jealousy. This jealousy grows on Tancredi until it has all the marks of an overwhelming guilty passion. His madness even goes beyond the terms of a 'character without character' who might be unable to put his society's moral principles into practice in his personal life because of some basic inadequacy at the level of *l'arte di vivere*. Tancredi's is the madness of a man at conflict with himself, no longer capable of understanding what is going on inside him and desperate to rationalize his instincts and behaviour.

When he criticizes Ghismonda for having chosen as her lover a 'youth of exceedingly base condition', this reproof bears all the appearance of a flimsy pretext devised by Tancredi to justify his subsequent cruelty both in his own eyes and those of others. The insincerity of his criticism on this count is borne out by the contradictions in his behaviour. At the moment when he invokes aristocratic principles, his actions represent the opposite of those principles. The author's emphasis rings mercilessly and deliberately down on the weakness and emotional frailty of Tancredi: 'his eyes filled with tears and he said to her . . .'[51] '. . . and so saying, he lowered his gaze and began to wail as though he were a child who had been soundly beaten.'[52] Boccaccio's insistence on these details is not so much designed to indicate that faint-heartedness is the psychological key to the character (because elsewhere Tancredi is obviously fully ruthless in his tactics and far from vacillating), but rather to point out the logical weakness of the reproof which Tancredi has had recourse to, and to show that his complaints allegedly arising from offended aristocratic pride are self-invalidating at the very moment when he produces this type of argument against his daughter. Thus the question of principle which De Sanctis saw as the dominant motif in this and other *novelle*[53] only has a negative function here. The ambiguous and self-contradictory way in which Boccaccio presents the issue constitutes an invitation to the reader to ignore these superficial pretexts which Tancredi has alleged.

Thus Ghismonda's answer to the accusations is itself a clear condemnation of Tancredi's essential insincerity, and should not be read just as an oratorical defence of the demands of the flesh. Muscetta takes the view that 'Ghismonda proclaims that all men are equal when faced by passion, so the emphasis falls not on the purging nature of love, but on the carnality of all human creatures'.[54] This is the intellectual logic of Ghismonda's speech, although its dramatic tension is due to the emotional force of the partly concealed references to the true nature of Tancredi's relationship with her. Her opening word to her father is 'Tancredi' and not 'father'.[55] When she compares her own vigorous youthful sexuality to Tancredi's senile impotence, she is not merely making an abstract defence of the values of those who are young in body and spirit; she is in fact adopting a stance of outrageous flirtatiousness. She is sniping across the brutal competitive relationship that holds between a man and a woman who are in conflict at the sexual level:[56]

> 'You are of flesh and blood, Tancredi, and it should have been obvious to you that the daughter you fathered was also made of flesh and blood, and not of stone or iron. Although you are now an old man, you should have remembered, indeed you should still remember, the nature and power of the laws of youth. And although much of your own youth was spent in pursuit of military glory, you should none the less have realized how the old and the young are alike affected by living in comfort and idleness.

> As I have said, since you were the person who fathered me, I am made of flesh and blood like yourself. Moreover, I am still a young woman. And for both of these reasons, I am full of amorous longings, intensified beyond belief by my marriage, which enabled me to discover the marvellous joy that comes from their fulfilment. As I was incapable of resisting these forces, I made up my mind, being a woman in the prime of life, to follow the path along which they were and I fell in love.'

By this point the father-daughter relationship has disappeared. Ghismonda is challenging her antagonist at the practical level of sexual and amorous potency. She declares that 'concupiscevole disiderio' ('the amorous longings') exist in old people just as much as in young people, but their fulfilment is prevented by old age. After a few more clauses dealing with her appropriate choice of lover, Ghismonda harps back with cruel exactness on the *punctum dolens*: 'di lui lungamente goduta sono del mio disio' ('I have long been enjoying the gratification of my desires.')[57] And at the end of her speech she delivers the final clinching insult: 'Now get you hence to shed your tears among the women.'[58] This is what gives rise to Tancredi's heartlessness, for he matches her cruel insults with equally cruel acts, while still rationalizing his line of behaviour ('he would cool her ardent passion by taking revenge on her paramour'). [59]

Thus his cutting out the heart from Guiscardo's body becomes the sadistic projection of an old man's desire to castrate his youthful rival. This is why the tragic conclusion of the affair is not determined by the impossibility of a love relationship between two members of widely different social class, but is inevitably bound up with the specific rôle of the real protagonists, father and daughter, who move fatally through a series of linked reactions to the final disaster. In this connection Muscetta is right to mention Shakespeare: [60] as it mounts to a preordained catastrophe, Ghismonda's tragedy is far closer to *Othello* than to other *novelle* in the *Decameron* or contemporary stories which deal with the theme of a daughter who commits fornication.

If we are prepared to read the dialogue between Tancredi and Ghismonda as a direct clash between a man and a woman on the sexual level, despite the fact that it is disguised as a daughter's rebellion against the moral standards and social respectability of her father, we are also bound to revise our opinion about the symbolic significance of the heart in the final section. Clearly Guiscardo's heart acquires a multiplicity of meanings, and the successive handling and passing around of the bleeding organ hardly arouses a sense of horror because it merely represents a nodal complex of symbols; it becomes the meeting-point for a varied but not irreconcilable set of symbolic effects. Ghismonda states that for her the heart is the 'dear sweet vessel of all my joys'. [61] In other words it is the resting-place of love in all its manifestations whether physical or spiritual. It is also the dwelling-place of the soul: [62]

> 'I shall see that my soul is united with that other soul which you kept in your loving care. How could I wish for a better or surer companion as I set forth towards the unknown? I feel certain that his soul still lingers here.'

Tancredi, on the other hand, resembles Messer Guiglielmo Rossiglione in seeing the heart as pre-eminently an organ to be torn out and away. For both of them it is the vital physical component without which a Guiscardo (or Guiglielmo Guardastagno) must lose all human faculties. Over and above all these *correspondances*, however, the heart has a supreme function

in the close of the story: it is the justification, even the
subject, of the final play on words which fixes the pattern
of the last page far more effectively than the psychology of
the characters. The two significant passages are built round
the statement of the 'most trusted servant'[62] to Ghismonda:
'Your father sends you this to comfort you in the loss of
your dearest possession, just as you have comforted him
in the loss of his';[64] with the corresponding reply from
Ghismonda: 'Nothing less splendid than a golden sepulchre
would have suited so noble a heart; in this respect, my father
has acted wisely.'[65] Ghismonda's remark conditions her subsequent actions. The young woman transfers the play of words
from the level of language to the level of deed. She lives out
the metaphor which father and daughter have set up.[66] This
makes her washing of the heart into what amounts to a religious
ceremony because it actualizes the metaphor into a normative
mode of behaviour, as with transubstantiation in the Holy
Communion.

There is surely no need to accept Muscetta's view that Ghismonda's bathing the organ with her tears is an act 'which purifies
all the macabre elements of the situation'.[67] There is nothing
macabre about it because by this stage in the *novella* everything
takes place at the level of metaphor; in the same way there is
nothing macabre about the wine drunk in lieu of blood at
Communion. The emotional properties of Boccaccio's scene
have little to do with an expansive sentimental heroism, but
simply derive from Ghismonda's extreme intellectual coherence
and choice of phraseology. Her sacrifice is not a victory of the
spirit, but a triumph of the word.

The finale of Rossiglione's *novella* runs on parallel lines:[68]

On observing that his lady had finished it down to the last
morsel, the knight said:
   'What did you think of that, madam?'
   'In good faith, my lord,' replied the lady, 'I liked it very
much.'
   'So help me God,' exclaimed the knight, 'I do believe you
did. But I am not surprised to find that you liked it dead,
because when it was alive you liked it better than anything else
in the whole world.'

Again in this *novella* the woman who has lost her lover is prepared to accept the linguistic challenge of the situation: 'But God forbid that any other food should pass my lips now that I have partaken of such excellent fare as the heart of so gallant and courteous a knight as Guillaume de Cabestanh.'[69] Both Ghismonda and Guiglielmo Rossiglione's wife commit suicide as an act which is not so much the psychological consequence of preceding events as the necessary and logical outcome of their metaphor.

Notes

1 There is a vast literature on this subject: J. Zupita, 'Die mittelenglischen Bearbeitungen der Erzählung Boccaccios von Ghismonda und Guiscardo', *Litteraturblatt für germanische und romanische Philologie*, XIII (1892), p. 412; F. J. Child, *The English and Scottish Popular Ballads*, Boston, 1894, V, pp. 29–38; A. Belloni, *Frammenti di critica letteraria*, Milan, 1903; C. B. Bourland, 'Boccaccio and the Decameron in Castilian and Catalan literature', *Revue Hispanique*, XII, 1905; J. W. Cunliffe, 'Gismond of Salern', *PMLA*, XXI (1906), f. 2; A. C. Lee, *The Decameron: its Sources and Analogues*, London, 1909; B. Zumbini, 'La novella di Ghismonda', *Biblioteca degli Studiosi*, Naples, I (1909); C. Lombardozzi, *La novella boccaccesca di Ghismonda e la sua fortuna nel teatro italiano*, Studio editoriale moderno, Catania, 1928; J. Raith, *Boccaccio in der englischen Literatur von Chaucer bis Painters Palace of Pleasure*, Munich, 1936; H. G. Wright (ed.), *Early English versions of the Tales of Guiscardo and Ghismonda and Titus and Gisippus from the Decameron*, London, 1937, EETS, Orig. Ser. 205; N. Orsini, *Studi sul Rinascimento Italiano in Inghilterra*, Sansoni, Florence, 1937; H. G. Wright, *Boccaccio in England from Chaucer to Tennyson*, University of London, Athlone Press, 1957.

2 Russo, 1970, p. 162.

3 The typical Crocean distinction between *poesia* and *non-poesia*.

4 I borrow the concept of *opaqueness* from an interesting article by M. Pagnini, 'Interpretazione di "*Autumn Refrain*" di Wallace Stevens: con qualche considerazione sulla poetica e sulla critica', now in his *Critica della funzionalità*, Einaudi, Turin, 1970. According to Pagnini the opaqueness of a text hinders the natural tendency of the reader to reach directly for the *signifié*, involving him in the process of the *signifiant* and forcing him to become more aware of, and responsive to, the formal value of the work.

5 'Si muove, con tremenda sicurezza, aristocratica e sola, la figura di Ghismonda' (Muscetta, 1965, p. 412).

6 Russo, 1970, p. 162.

7 *L'arte di vivere*, the art of living, is, according to Getto's interpretation, the main concern of Boccaccio in the *Decameron*. The characters stand or fall according to their mastery of this subtle art.

8 Muscetta, 1965, p. 412.

9 Moravia, 1965, chapter on Boccaccio.

10 Muscetta, 1965, p. 412.

11 *Ibid.*, p. 413.

12 In spite of the great variety of amorous activities in the *Decameron*, the theme of incest is very rare. We find a hint of unintentional incest in V, 5. In IV, 3 there is a love-relationship with a sister-in-law. For a curious incestuous interpretation of the last *novella* of the *Decameron*, see O. Rank, 'Der Sinn der Griseldafabel', *Imago*, I, 1912; later published in *Der Kunstler und andere Beitrage*, Internationaler Psychoanalytische Verlag, Vienna,1925.

13 McW, p. 332.

> 'Tancredi, principe di Salerno, fu signore assai umano e di benigno ingegno, se egli nello amoroso sangue nella sua vecchiezza non s' avesse le mani bruttate; il quale in tutto lo spazio della sua vita non ebbe che una figliuola, e più felice sarebbe stato se quella avuta non avesse.
> Costei fu dal padre tanto teneramente amata, quanto alcuna altra figliuola da padre fosse giammai: e per questo tenero amore . . .'
> (*Dec.*, IV, 1, 3–4).

14 Getto, 1958, p. 100.

15 McW, p. 332. '. . . non sapiendola da se partire, non la maritava. . . . Il padre, per l'amore che egli le portava, poca cura si dava di più maritarla' (*Dec.*, IV, 1, 4–5).

16 I refer to the division by *comma* in the edition by Branca from which I take all quotations from the *Decameron*.

17 Petronio, 1935, p. 79.

18 Di Pino, 1957, p. 227.

19 Getto, 1958, p. 104.

20 *Ibid.*

21 *Ibid.*

22 *Ibid.*, p. 105.

23 Muscetta, 1965, p. 412.

24 The first suggestion to analyse the sexual symbolism of the scene came from my friend Harry McWilliam, whose translation of the *Decameron* into English I use constantly for the purposes of this book.

25 McW, p. 334.

> Guiscardo poi la notte vegnente su per la sua fune salendo, per lo spiraglio donde era entrato se n'uscí fuori e tornossi a casa; e avendo questo cammino appreso, più volte poi in processo di tempo vi ritornò (*Dec.*, IV, 1, 14).

26 See *Hogarth's Graphic Works*, compiled and with a commentary by Ronald Paulson, Yale University Press, New Haven and London, 1956, vol. 2, The Engravings, III, ill. 333.

27 McW, p. 333. '. . . di lunghissimi tempi davanti fatta' (*Dec.*, IV, 1, 9).

28 McW, pp. 333–4. '. . . quasi da pruni e da erbe di sopra natevi era riturato . . . e se vestito d'un cuoio che da' pruni il difendesse . . . e accomandato ben l'uno de' capi della fune ad un forte bronco che nella bocca dello spiraglio era nato . . .' (*Dec.*, IV, 1, 9–12).

LWL

I have not found other symbolic constructs of this kind in the *Decameron*. There are of course geographical and toponomastic notations which are a metaphor for anatomical details: the *Val Cava* in the novella of Alatiel (II, 7), the *Monte Nero* in the introduction to the Sixth Day; but these obscene metaphors are much closer to the precise *correspondances* of Hogarth's cottage than to the vague symbolism of the *novella* of Ghismonda. In the *novella* of Agilulf (III, 2) the *torchietto* and the *bacchetta* (the torch and the stick) can be interpreted as veiled phallic symbols, although here the problem is of a different nature. But see *Corbaccio* (G. Boccaccio, *Opere minori*, Salani, Florence, 1964, pp. 681–2).

29 Muscetta, 1965, p. 412.

30 E. Ionesco, *Théâtre I*, Gallimard, Paris, 1954, pp. 117ff.

31 Getto, 1958, p. 106.

32 McW, p. 334. 'Era usato Tancredi di venirsene alcuna volta tutto solo nella camera della figliuola, e quivi con lei dimorarsi e ragionare alquanto, e poi partirsi' (*Dec.*, IV, 1, 16).

33 McW, p. 335. '. . . e appoggiato il capo al letto e tirata sopra sé la cortina, quasi come se studiosamente si fosse nascoso, quivi s'addormentò' (*Dec.*, IV, 1, 17).

34 McW, *ibid.*

Andatisene in su 'l letto, sí come usati erano, e insieme scherzando e sollazzandosi, avvenne che Tancredi si svegliò, e sentí e vide ciò che Guiscardo e la figliuola facevano: e dolente di ciò oltre modo, prima gli volle sgridare, poi prese partito di tacersi e di starsi nascoso, se egli potesse, per potere più cautamente fare e con minore sua vergogna quello che già gli era caduto nell'animo di dover fare (*Dec.*, IV, 1, 18–19).

35 Again a somewhat risky hypothesis. 'Autre victime de la lettre: le personnage, objet d'une créance à la fois excessive et dérisoire, il n'a jamais le droit de s'abuser sur lui-même, sur ses sentiments; l'alibi est une catégorie inconnue du vraisemblable critique' (R. Barthes, *Critique et vérité*, série *Tel Quel*, Éditions du Seuil, Paris, 1966, p. 21).

36 McW, p. 335. 'Della quale Tancredi, ancora che vecchio fosse, da una finestra di quella si calò nel giardino . . .' (*Dec.*, IV, 1, 21). See Muscetta, 1965, p. 413.

37 McW, p. 336. '. . . secondo la sua usanza nella camera n'andò della figliola, dove fattalasi chiamare e serratosi dentro con lei . . .' (*Dec.*, IV, 1,25).

38 The Fourth Day forms an intricate network of symmetries, parallelisms and contrasts, which have not yet been fully explored by Boccaccio criticism. I will only mention the most singular coincidences:

(*a*) The symmetrical position of *novelle* 1, 5 and 9, in which the murder is performed by father, brothers and husband respectively.

(*b*) The way in which Frate Alberto chooses the object of his love in the *novella* which comes immediately after the story of Tancredi seems to be a parody of the criteria used by Ghismonda for the selection of her lover: 'Friar Alberto had sensed immediately that she was something of a half-wit, and realizing that she was ripe for the picking, he fell passionately in love with her there and then' (McW, p. 345).

(c) The tenth *novella* can be considered a parody of all the tragic *novelle* which preceded it in the course of the Day (see Branca, 1970, pp. 124–).7

(d) People belonging to different social classes fall in love in analogous yet subtly varied ways.

The best example of a structural study of one Day of the *Decameron* is provided by Cesare Segre, 'Funzioni, opposizioni e simmetrie nella giornata VII del Decameron', *Studi sul Boccaccio*, VI, 1971, pp. 81–108.

39 The tenth story stands aside from the others, in so far as it is not bound to follow the topic set for the Day.

40 McW, p. 391 'Nè me ne meraviglio se morto v'è piaciuto ciò che vivo più che altra cosa vi piacque' (*Dec.*, IV, 9, 20).

41 'Seneca is Boccaccio's only real discovery in those years and his Fiammetta is striking confirmation of this fact.' (A. E. Quaglio, *Le chiose all'Elegia di Madonna Fiammetta*, Università di Padova, Pubblicazioni della Facoltà di Lettere e Filosofia, vol. II, Cedam, Padua, 1957, p. 48). The *Elegia di Madonna Fiammetta* shows several Seneca sources. One can usefully consult V. Russo, 'Il senso del tragico nel "Decameron"', *Filologia e Letteratura*, XI, 1965, 1, pp. 29–83 (on Seneca, pp. 58–65 and 73–4).

42 Seneca, *Thyestes*, ll. 976–82. All quotations from Seneca come from the following edition: L. *Annei Senecae Tragediae*, ed. Fridericus Leo, vol. 2, Berolini, apud Weidmannos, 1963. English translations from *Seneca's Tragedies with an English translation* by F. J. Miller, in two volumes, Loeb Classical Library, London and New York, Heinemann and Putnam's Sons, vol. 2.

43 *Ibid.*, ll. 1021–3.

44 *Ibid.*, ll. 1030–1.

45 *Ibid.*, ll. 1050–1.

46 McW, p. 391. 'La donna, udito questo, alquanto stette' (*Dec.*, IV, 9, 21).

47 McW, ibid. 'La donna udendo questo di colui cui ella più che altra cosa amava, se dolorosa fu non è da domandare; e dopo alquanto disse . . .' (*Dec.*, IV, 9, 23).

48 *Thyestes*, ll. 999–1001.

49 *Ibid.*, ll. 1041–2.

50 McW, p. 391. 'La finestra era molto alta da terra, per che, come la donna cadde, non solamente morí, ma quasi tutta si disfece' (*Dec.*, IV, 9, 24).

51 McW, p. 336. 'Piangendo le cominciò a dire . . .' (*Dec.*, IV, 1, 25).

52 McW, *ibid.* '. . . questo detto bassò il viso, piangendo sí forte come farebbe un fanciul ben battuto' (*Dec.*, IV, 1, 29).

53 De Sanctis, 1949, vol. 1, p. 326.

54 Muscetta, 1965, p. 414.

55 In Alfieri's tragedy, *Mirra*, which derives from the famous account of the incestuous love of a daughter for her father in Ovid's *Metamorphoses* (Book X, ll. 298–502), the heroine of the play calls her father by name: 'È ver: Ciniro meco/inesorabil sia' (Act 5, ll. 217–18). Quite the opposite of Lolita, who comes out with the superb and atrocious 'Dad'.

56 McW, p. 337.
    Esser ti dovea, Tancredi, manifesto, essendo tu di carne, aver generata
    figliuola di carne e non di pietra o di ferro; e ricordarti dovevi e dei,
    quantunque tu ora sia vecchio, chenti e quali e con che forza vengano
    le leggi della giovanezza: e come che tu, uomo, in parte ne' tuoi
    migliori anni nell'armi esercitato ti sii, non dovevi di meno conoscere
    quello che gli ozi e le dilicatezze possano ne' vecchi non che ne'
    giovani.
    Sono adunque, sí come da te generata, di carne, e sí poco vivuta, che
    ancor son giovane; e per l'una cosa e per l'altra piena di concupiscibile
    desiderio, al quale maravigliosissime forze hanno date l'aver già, per
    essere stata maritata, conosciuto qual piacer sia a cosí fatto disidero dar
    compimento. Alle quali forze non potendo io resistere, a seguir
    quello a che elle mi tiravano, sí come giovane e femina, mi disposi e
    innamoràmi (*Dec.*, IV, 1, 33–5).

57 *Dec.*, IV, 1, 37; McW, p. 338. I give both the Italian and English text
    to emphasize the rôle of *lungamente* in the original sentence.

58 McW, p. 339. 'Or via, va con le femine a spander le lagrime tue' (*Dec.*,
    IV, 1, 45).

59 McW, p. 339. '... pensò con gli altrui danni raffreddare il suo fervente
    amore (*Dec.*, IV, 1, 46).

60 Muscetta, 1965, p. 415. But see also Bonfantini: 'Ghismonda's frenzied
    tirade to her father is heart-rending ... like some of the most passionate
    and fascinating speeches uttered by certain Shakespearean characters in
    the throes of despair' (M. Bonfantini, 'Boccaccio e il Decameron', in
    Pegaso, 1930, pp. 13–28).

61 McW, p. 340. '... dolcissimo albergo di tutti i miei piaceri' (*Dec.*, IV, 1,
    51).

62 McW, p. 340.
    Senza alcuno indugio farò che la mia anima si congiugnerà con
    quella, adoperandol tu, che tu già cotanto cara guardasti. E con qual
    compagnia ne potre'io andar più contenta o meglio sicura a' luoghi
    non conosciuti che con lei? Io son certa che ella è ancor quicentro
    (*Dec.*, IV, 1,53–4).

63 McW, p. 339. '... un suo segretissimo famigliare' (*Dec*, IV, 1, 47).

64 McW, p. 339. 'Il tuo padre ti manda questo per consolarti di quella cosa
    che tu più ami, come tu hai lui consolato di ciò che egli più amava'
    (*Dec.*, IV, 1, 47).

65 McW, p. 340. 'Non si conveniva sepoltura men degna che d'oro a
    cosí fatto cuore chente questo è: discretamente in ciò ha il mio padre
    adoperato' (*Dec.*, IV, 1, 49).

66 A similar literal enactment of the metaphor, but with a somewhat
    ludicrous result, is in Tasso's *Gerusalemme Liberata*. Tancredi, having
    killed Clorinda, fails to understand why his eyes are now tearless when
    they contemplate her wounds:
        Asciutte le mirate? or corra, dove
        Nega d'andare il pianto il sangue mio. –
        Qui tronca le parole; e, come il move

Suo disperato di morir desio,
Squarcia le fasce e le ferite; e piove
Da le sue piaghe essacerbate un rio. (*Gerusalemme Liberata,* xii, 83).

Fairfax's translation fails to convey this pun:
But thither now run forth my guilty blood,
Whither my plaints, my sorrows cannot wend. –
He said no more; but, as his passion wood
Enforced him, he 'gan to tear and rend
His hair, his face, his wounds; a purple flood
Did from each side in rolling streams descend . . .

(T. Tasso, *Jerusalem Delivered,* The Edward Fairfax translation newly introduced by Roberto Weiss, London, Centaur Press, 1962).

67 Muscetta, 1965, p. 415.

68 McW, pp. 390–1.

Come il cavaliere ebbe veduto che la donna tutto l'ebbe mangiato, disse:

'Donna, chente v'è paruta questa vivanda?'
La donna rispose: 'Monsignore, in buona fè ella m'è piaciuta molto.'
'Se m'aiti Iddio,' disse il cavaliere 'io il vi credo nè me ne maraviglio se morto v'è piaciuto ciò che vivo più che altra cosa vi piacque' (*Dec.,* IV, 9, 18–20).

69 McW, p. 391. 'Ma unque a Dio non piaccia che sopra a cosí nobil vivanda, come è stata quella del cuore d'un cosí valoroso e cosí cortese cavaliere come Messer Guiglielmo Guardastagno fu, mai altra vivanda vada!' (*Dec.,* IV, 9, 23).

Dec.	GIOVANNI BOCCACCIO, *Decameron*, ed. Vittore Branca, Le Monnier, Florence, 1956.
McW	GIOVANNI BOCCACCIO, *Decameron*, translated with an introduction by G. H. McWilliam, Penguin, Harmondsworth, 1972.
Auerbach, 1953	ERICH AUERBACH, *Mimesis*, Doubleday, New York, 1953.
Baratto, 1970	MARIO BARATTO, *Realtà e stile nel Decameron*, Neri Pozza Editore, Venice, 1970.
Barthes, 1966	ROLAND BARTHES, 'Introduction à l'analyse structurelle des récits', *Communications*, no. 8, 1966.
Branca, 1970	VITTORE BRANCA, *Boccaccio Medioevale*, Sansoni, Florence, 1970 (first edition, 1965).
Cottino-Jones, 1968	MARGA COTTINO-JONES, *An anatomy of Boccaccio's style*, Editrice Cymba, Naples, 1968.
Croce, 1967	B. CROCE, *Poesia popolare e poesia d'arte*, Laterza, Bari, 1967 (1st ed. 1933).
Dante, *Inferno*	DANTE ALIGHIERI, *La Commedia secondo l'antica vulgata*, ed. Giorgio Petrocchi, vol. 2, *Inferno*, Mondadori, Milan, 1966.
Dante, *Inferno* (English, Sinclair's translation)	DANTE ALIGHIERI, *The Divine Comedy*, Italian text with translation and comment by John D. Sinclair, vol. I, *Inferno*, Oxford University Press, London, Oxford, New York, 1971 (first edition, 1939).
Dante, *Purgatorio*	DANTE ALIGHIERI, *La Commedia secondo l'antica vulgata*, ed. Giorgio Petrocchi, vol. 3, *Purgatorio*, Mondadori, Milan, 1967.
Dante *Purgatorio* (English, Sinclair's translation)	DANTE ALIGHIERI, *The Divine Comedy*, Italian text with translation and comment by John D. Sinclair, vol. 2, *Purgatorio*, Oxford University Press, London, Oxford, New York, 1971 (first edition, 1939).
Dante, *Paradiso*	DANTE ALIGHIERI, *La Commedia secondo l'antica vulgata*, ed. Giorgio Petrocchi, vol. 3, *Paradiso*, Mondadori, Milan, 1968.
Dante, *Paradiso* (English, Sinclair's translation)	DANTE ALIGHIERI, *The Divine Comedy*, Italian text with translation and comment by John D. Sinclair, vol. 3, *Paradiso*, Oxford University Press, London, Oxford, New York, 1971 (first edition, 1939).
De Sanctis, 1949	FRANCESCO DE SANCTIS, *Storia della letteratura Italiana*, ed. Benedetto Croce, fourth edition, 2 vols, Laterza, Bari, 1949.

, ... *as an End. A Defence of Humanism. Literary, Social and Political Essays*, Secker & Warburg, London, 1965.

Muscetta, 1965   EMILIO CECCHI, NATALINO SAPEGNO (eds), *Storia della letteratura italiana*, vol. *Il Trecento*, chapter on *Boccaccio e i novellieri* by Carlo Muscetta, Garzanti, Milan, 1965.

Padoan, 1964   GIORGIO PADOAN, 'Mondo aristocratico e mondo comunale nell'ideologia e nell'arte di Giovanni Boccaccio', *Studi sul Boccaccio*, II, 1964, pp. 81–216.

Petronio, 1935   GIUSEPPE PETRONIO, *Il Decameron, Saggio Critico*, Laterza, Bari, 1935.

Russo, 1970   LUIGI RUSSO, *Letture critiche del Decameron*, Laterza, Bari, 1970 (first edition 1956).

Salinari, 1963   GIOVANNI BOCCACCIO, *Decameron*, with introduction by Carlo Salinari, Laterza, Bari, 1963.

Sansovino, 1543   F. SANSOVINO, *Lettere sopra le dieci giornate del Decamerone*, Venice, 1543.

Scaglione, 1963   ALDO SCAGLIONE, *Nature and love in the late Middle Ages*, University of California Press, Berkeley and Los Angeles, 1963.

Seneca, 1963   L. ANNEI SENECAE *Tragoediae*, ed. Fridericus Leo, vol. 2, Weidmann, Berlin, 1963.

Shakespeare, *King Lear*, Arden Edition, 1961   WILLIAM SHAKESPEARE, *King Lear*, edited by K. Muir, Methuen, London, 1961 (first edition, 1952).

Todorov, 1966   *Théorie de la littérature, textes des formalistes russes réunis*, ed. and trans. Tzvetan Todorov. Preface by Roman Jakobson, Éditions du Seuil, Paris, 1966.

Todorov, 1969   TVETAN TODOROV, *Grammaire du Décameron*, Mouton, The Hague, Paris, 1969.

Index

Numbers in bold indicate the pages devoted to that particular *novella*.

Abelard 84
Abraham (*Dec.*, I, 2) 51, 64, 99
Adamo, Mastro (Dante, *Inferno*
   XXX) 97
Adriano (*Dec.*, IX, 6) 66
Aegina 121, 131
Agilulfo (*Dec.*, III, 2) 75, 154
Aguamorta 121, 122, 131
Alatiel 116–27, 132, 154
Alberichi (Dante, *Paradiso*, XVI) 17
Alberto, Frate (*Dec.*, IV, 2) 154
Aleman, M. 57
   Guzman de Alfarache 57
Alessandro (*Dec.*, II, 3) 87
Alexandria 117, 130
Alfieri, V. 155
   Mirra 155
Algarve 116–18
Alibech (*Dec.*, II, 7) 63, 64, 82–8, 90
Almansi, G. 101, 132
Amerigo (*Dec.*, V, 7) 147
Andreola (*Dec.*, IV, 6) 147
Andreuccio (*Dec.*, II, 5) 34, 35, 63
Antigono (*Dec.*, II, 7) 117
Antiochus (Racine, *Bérénice*) 125
Antioco (*Dec.*, II, 7) 117, 126, 127
Apuleius 88, 89, 103, 104
Aretino 89, 91
Aristotle 38, 59
Arno 97, 106
Athenaeus 89
Athens 117, 121, 126, 127
Auerbach, E. 34, 57, 59, 60, 159

Babylon 116
Balzac, H. de 75
Baratto, M. 17, 57, 59, 60, 83, 84,
   96, 99, 100, 103, 106, 127, 130–2,
   159

Barilli, R. 55
Barth, J. 61
Barthes, R. 118, 131, 154, 159
Bartolomea (*Dec.*, II, 10) 90, 111
Bataille, G. 127, 132
Baudelaire, C. 100, 132
Beatrice (*Dec.*, VII, 7) 38, 39
Bédier, J. 90, 104
Bellarmino, Cardinal 25
Belloni, A. 152
Beltramo (*Dec.*, III, 9) 75
Benvenuto da Imola 59
Bergamino (*Dec.*, I, 7) 52
Bernabò (*Dec.*, II, 9) 101
Bertram de Born (Dante, *Inferno*,
   XXVIII) 96
Blyton, E. 75
Boccaccio, G. vii, 3, 4, 6–9, 11, 12,
   16, 20, 22–7, 29–32, 34, 39, 40,
   43, 44, 46, 49, 51, 52, 54, 63–6,
   68, 69, 72, 76–8, 81, 84, 85,
   87–93, 95–9, 101, 102, 104, 105,
   109, 116, 119, 120, 127, 133, 134,
   136–8, 140–4, 146–8, 151–6,
   159, 160
   Corbaccio 93, 105, 154
   Decameron vii, 3–15, 18, 20–30,
      33, 37–9, 41, 47, 55, 56, 63–6,
      69, 74–6, 81, 82, 85, 92, 93, 98,
      99, 101, 104, 106, 116, 118,
      119, 121, 126, 130, 133, 136–9,
      147, 150, 152–6, 159, 160
   Proemio 56, 63, 99
   Introduction 11
   DAY ONE 51, 52
   Novella 1 4, 13, 15, **24–55**,
      56–64
   Novella 2 33, 51, 52, 58, 63,
      64, 99

Boccaccio, G.
Decameron—cont.
Novella 3 51, 52, 62–4, 99
Novella 4 33, 51, 52, 58, **63–6,
69–76**, 81, 99–101
Novella 5 33, 34, 51, 52, 58
Novella 6 34, 51, 52, 58
Novella 7 52
Novella 8 52, 53
Novella 9 53, 54
Novella 10 52
DAY TWO
Novella 1 54, 62
Novella 2 87, 104
Novella 3 87, 88, 104
Novella 4 110, 127
Novella 5 34, 35, 63
Novella 6 88, 104, 147
Novella 7 **116–27**, 130–2, 154
Novella 9 101
Novella 10 90, 104, 111, 121,
127
DAY THREE
Novella 1 60, 64, **76–81**, 101,
102
Novella 2 75, 101, 154
Novella 5 75, 101
Novella 6 82
Novella 7 39, 59, 81
Novella 9 75, 101
Novella 10 63, 64, **82–8**, 90,
102–4
DAY FOUR 75, 144, 154, 155
Introduction 24
Novella 1 101, **133–52**, 153–6
Novella 2 154
Novella 3 82, 111, 112, 128,
153
Novella 4 112, 113, 128
Novella 5 154
Novella 6 147
Novella 8 101
Novella 9 101, **144–7**, 151, 152,
154, 155, 157
Novella 10 155
DAY FIVE 16
Novella 1 113–15, 120, 121,
128–30

Novella 2 75, 101, 115, 116,
129
Novella 4 147
Novella 5 82, 153
Novella 6 116, 130
Novella 7 147
Novella 8 39, 59
Novella 9 **15–18**
Novella 10 82
DAY SIX 20, 21
Introduction 154
Novella 1 **20–3**, 28, 32, 55, 56,
62
Novella 2 21, 55, 65, 99
Novella 4 65, 99
Novella 7 65, 99
Novella 9 55
Novella 10 27, 38, 53, 57, 59,
62
Conclusion 12
DAY SEVEN 155
Novella 1 101
Novella 2 **88–9**, 104
Novella 7 **38–9**, 59, 82
Novella 9 15, 82
DAY EIGHT
Novella 3 101
Novella 6 101
Novella 7 82, **92–9**, 103, 105–7
Novella 8 82
Novella 9 101
DAY NINE
Novella 2 64, 65
Novella 3 101
Novella 5 101
Novella 6 **66–9**, 82, 100
Novella 10 82, **88**, 90, 91, 104
DAY TEN 10, 13, 18
Novella 3 15
Novella 4 82
Novella 6 65, 99
Novella 8 15
Novella 10 4, 13, 26, 29, 30,
32, 37, 75, 101, 134, 153
Elegia di Madonna Fiammetta 155
Bologna 38, 39, 59
Bonfantini, M. 156
Boniface VIII, Pope 21, 31, 58

Borges, J. L. 19, 55
Borghini, V. 25
Bourland, C. B. 152
Bovary, Emma 40
Boves, Jean de 66, 67
Branca, V. 17, 29, 34, 37, 41, 52,
54–6, 58–60, 62, 93, 100, 103–6,
124, 132, 138, 153, 155, 159
Brangwen, Ann (D. H. Lawrence,
The Rainbow) 74
Bruscoli, N. 105
Bryand, W. P. 100
Burgundy 24, 27, 31, 32, 40

Cacciaguida (Dante, Paradiso) 17
Calandrino (Dec.) 75
Camus, A. 35
Can Grande (Dec., I, 7) 52
Canterbury, 100
Capaneo (Dante, Inferno, XIV) 27, 57
Capua 138
Carducci, G. 17
Carlo (King Charles of Anjou)
(Dec., X, 6) 65
Carroll, Lewis 6
Catellini (Dante, Paradiso, XVI) 17
Catullus 39, 91, 105
Cecchi, E. 160
Céline, L. F. 91, 92, 105
Cellini, B. 14
Cephalonia 110, 127
Cepperello (Dec., I, 1) 4, 13, 15,
24–38, 40–58, 60–3, 76
Certaldo 53, 62
Charles the Stateless (Dec., I, 1) 31, 58
Chaucer, G. 66, 68, 100, 152
Chichibio (Dec., VI, 4) 65
Child, F. J. 152
Christopher Robin 8, 9
Ciampolo (Dante, Inferno) 98
Cian, V. 100
Cimone (Dec., V, 1) 113–15, 120,
121, 128–30
Ciniro (Alfieri, Mirra) 155
Cipolla (Dec., VI, 10) 27, 38, 53, 57,
62
Cisti (Dec. VI, 2) 21, 55, 65
Clorinda (Tasso, Gerusalemme) 156

Constantinople 117, 121
Coppo (Dec., V, 9) 16–18
Costanzio (Dec., II, 7) 117, 121, 126,
131
Cottino-Jones, M. 56, 57, 61, 62,
159
Crete 112, 115, 128
Crews, F. 8, 17
Croce, B. 27, 56, 57, 89, 104, 134,
152, 159
Cunliffe, J. W. 156
Currado Malaspina (Dec., II, 6) 147
Cyprus 52, 131

Dante 1–4, 17, 20, 34, 35, 38, 47,
61, 95–8, 119, 130, 159
Divine Comedy 1–5, 7, 20, 26, 34,
35, 59, 96, 159
Inferno 7, 20, 27, 34, 35, 38, 47,
48, 57, 59, 61, 95–8, 106,
130, 131, 159
Purgatorio 20, 45, 61, 159
Paradiso 3, 17, 159
Da Ponte, L. 107
De Michelis, C. 56
Dempster, G. 100
De Sanctis, F. 25, 27, 50, 57, 62,
148, 155, 159
Dickens, C. 75
Di Francia, L. 70, 100, 104
Dioneo (Dec.) 17
Di Pino, L. 138, 153, 160
Dostoevsky, F. 35, 76

Ecclesiastes 38, 59
Edgar (King Lear) 122
Edmund (King Lear) 123, 132
Egano (Dec., VII, 7) 38, 39
Ellis, Havelock 81
England 134
Epsitemon (Rabelais, Le tiers livre)
103
Europe 85

Fairfax, E. 157
Fassò, L. 60, 160
Federico degli Alberighi (Dec., V,
9) 15–18

Fiammetta (*Dec.*) 16, 17
Filippa (*Dec.*, VI, 7) 65
Filippi (Dante, *Paradiso*, XVI) 17
Filippo degli Alberighi (*Dec.*, V, 9)
16, 18
Filippo Argenti (Dante, *Inferno*,
VIII) 97
Flaubert, G. 40
Florence 5, 7, 10, 11, 17, 18, 20, 22,
24, 26, 31, 40, 92
Florio, J. 130
France 31, 32, 41, 51, 52, 58
Francesca (Dante, *Inferno*, V) 96
Francesco Vergellesi (*Dec.*, III, 5) 75
Francis, St 103

Gargantua (Rabelais) 30, 105
Gascony 52
Gemmata (*Dec.*, IX, 10) 90
Genet, J. 56
Genoa 112, 128
Gerbino (*Dec.*, IV, 4) 112, 113, 128
Getto, G. 17, 21–3, 31, 45, 55–8, 60,
61, 135, 137–40, 142, 152–4, 160
Ghismonda (*Dec.*, IV, 1) 133–9,
141, 143, 144, 147–52, 154, 156
Gianni di Barolo (*Dec.*, IX, 10) 88,
90
Gianni Lotteringhi (*Dec.*, VII, 1)
101
Gianni da Procida (*Dec.*, V, 6) 116,
130
Giannotto (*Dec.*, II, 6) 88
Giannotto da Civigni (*Dec.*, I, 2)
51, 64, 99
Giovanna (*Dec.*, V, 9) 15
Gisippo (*Dec.*, X, 8) 15, 152
Gombert (*fabliau* by Jean de Boves)
66, 67
Goneril (*King Lear*) 122
Gostanza (*Dec.*, V, 2) 75, 115
Greci (Dante, *Paradiso*, XVI) 17
Greece 131
Grimaldi (*Dec.*, I, 8) 52
Griselda (*Dec.*, X, 10) 4, 13, 26, 29,
30, 32, 37, 75, 101, 134, 153
Gualtieri (*Dec.*, X, 10) 75
Guccio (*Dec.*, VI, 10) 38

Guglielmo Borsiere (*Dec.*, I, 8) 52
Guiglielmo di Guardastagno (*Dec.*,
IV, 9) 144, 146, 150, 152, 157
Guiglielmo di Rossiglione (*Dec.*,
IV, 9) 144, 146, 147, 150–2
Guiscardo (*Dec.*, IV, 1) 133, 139–44,
146, 147, 150–2, 154

Hogarth, W. 141, 142, 153, 154

Ionesco, E. 142, 154
Iphigenia (*Dec.*, V, 1) 113–15, 128,
129
Ischia 116, 130
Italy 2, 32, 41, 63

Jacopone da Todi 84, 103
Jakobson, R. 160
Jane Eyre 102
Job 37, 59
Judas 25, 26, 29, 37, 38

Kent (*King Lear*) 122

La Fontaine, J. de 86, 87, 89–91,
104, 105, 160
Landolfo Rufolo (*Dec.*, II, 4) 110,
127
Lapp, J. C. 91, 105
Lawrence, St 53
Lawrence, D. H. 74, 81, 82, 101, 102
Pornography and so on 81, 102
The Rainbow 74, 101
Lee, A. C. 152
Leo, F. 155
Lizio da Valbona (*Dec.*, V, 4) 147
Lodovico (*Dec.*, VII, 7) 38, 39
Lolita (Nabokov) 155
Lombardozzi, C. 152
Lombardy 41, 60
Lo Nigro, S. 100

Machiavelli, N. 68
MacLuhan, M. 14
McWilliam, H. vii, 101, 153, 159
Magritte, R. 5
Majorca 118–20, 130, 131
Mandel'stam, O. 116, 130, 132

Manganelli, G. 61
Marato (*Dec.*, II, 7) 116, 117, 120, 121, 126, 131
Mark, St 37
Marseille 111
Martellino (*Dec.*, II, 1) 54
Martuccio Gomito (*Dec.*, V, 2) 75
Masetto (*Dec.*, III, 1) 60, 64, 76–81, 101, 102
Matthew, St 37
Mediterranean 7, 9, 11, 121
Melchisedek 51, 64, 99
Merry, B. 61
Miller, F. J. 155
Milne, A. A. 8, 17
   Winnie the Pooh 8–10, 17
Minos (Dante, *Inferno*, III) 95
Molière 102
   Tartuffe 102
Momigliano, Attilio 46, 56, 61, 160
Monferrato 51
Montaiglon, A. de 99, 100
Morato, O. 25
Moravia, A. 105, 109, 116, 127, 136, 153, 160
Morea 117, 120
Morocco 117–20, 131
Muir, K. 160
Muscetta, C. 21, 49, 55, 62, 100, 135, 136, 140, 142, 148, 150–7, 160
Musciatto (*Dec.*, I, 1) 31, 32, 40, 57

Naples 7, 34
N'Arnald Civada (*Dec.*, IV, 3) 111
Nastagio (*Dec.*, V, 9) 39
Nathan (*Dec.*, X, 3) 15
Neptune 109, 131
Nero, Emperor 27
Nicostrato (*Dec.*, VII, 9) 15

Oretta (*Dec.*, VI, 1) 20–3, 32, 56
Ormanni (Dante, *Paradiso*, XVI) 17
Orsini, N. 152
Osbech (*Dec.*, II, 7) 117
Ovid 155

Padoan, G. 51–4, 56, 60, 62, 160

Paganino (*Dec.*, II, 10) 90, 111, 121, 127
Pagnini, M. 152
Painter, W. 152
Panfilo (*Dec.*) 30, 47, 50, 52, 62
Pantagruel (Rabelais) 103
Panurge (Rabelais) 103
Paolo (Dante, *Inferno*, V) 96
Paris 92, 105
Parthia 89, 104
Pasolini, P. P. 76
Pastore Stocchi, M. 104
Paulson, R. 153
Pavlov 91
Peckham, M. 18
Pericone (*Dec.*, II, 7) 116, 117, 120, 124, 126, 132
Peronella (*Dec.*, VII, 2) 89
Perugia 34
Petrocchi, G. 159
Petronio, G. 87, 88, 104, 138, 153, 160
Petronius Arbiter 89
Picasso, P. 28
Pinocchio 6
Pinuccio (*Dec.*, IX, 6) 66, 68
Plato 30
Poe, E. A. 24
Poirier, P. 99
Prato 31, 50, 54
Procida 116, 130

Quaglio, A. E. 155

Rabelais, F. 30, 36, 57, 84, 89, 92, 103
Racine, J. 125, 132
   Bérénice 125, 132
Raith, J. 152
Rank, O. 153
Raskolnikov 35, 76
Ravello 110
Raynaud, G. 99, 100
Regan (*King Lear*) 122
Reich, W. 85
Rhodes 113–15, 120, 128, 129
Ricciardo da Chinzica (*Dec.*, II, 10) 111, 127
Richard Minutolo (*Dec.*, III, 6) 104

Rinaldo d'Esti (*Dec.*, II, 2) 87
Rinieri (*Dec.*, VIII, 7) 92
Rome 51, 125
Rubens, P. P. 129
Rudel, J. 38
Rufa Bononiensis 39
Russo, L. 17, 57, 59–61, 101, 134,
    135, 152, 160
Russo, V. 155
Rustico (*Dec.*, III, 10) 64, 83–8, 90,
    103

Saladin (*Dec.*, I, 3) 51, 64, 99
Salerno 133, 137, 142, 153
Salinari, C. 83, 103, 160
Salviati, L. 25
Sanguineti, E. 160
Sansovino, L. 93, 105, 160
Sapegno, N. 160
Sardinia 112, 117, 119, 128, 130,
    131
Sartre, J.-P. 56
Scaglione, A. 62, 160
Segre, C. 132, 155
Seneca 38, 59, 144–6, 155, 160
    Thyestes 144–6, 155
Shakespeare, W. 136, 150, 156, 160
    All's Well 75
    King Lear 122, 123, 131, 132, 160
    Othello 150
    Romeo and Juliet 74
Silvestris, B. 84, 103
Sinclair, J. D. 17, 18, 35, 59, 61,
    106, 131, 159
Sinon (Dante, *Inferno*, XXX) 97
Sklovsky, V. 7
Sollers, P. 1–3, 17
Solomon 38, 59
Spain 134
Spina (*Dec.*, II, 6) 88

Stendhal 72, 76
Stevens, W. 152
Susa 115, 129

Tancredi ('Tasso, *Gerusalemme*) 156
Tancredi (*Dec.*, IV, 1) 133, 135–8,
    142–4, 147–50, 153, 154, 156
Tasso, T. 156, 157
    Gerusalemme 156, 157
Tebaida 82, 83
Tedaldo (*Dec.*, III, 7) 39, 81
Tennyson, A. 152
Terence 100
Thebes 57
Tito (*Dec.*, X, 8) 15, 152
Todorov, T. 55, 127, 160
Tolstoy, L. 7
Tomashevsky, B. 110
Tunis 115, 129
Tuscany 31, 58

Ughi (Dante, *Paradiso*, XVI) 17
Ulysses (Dante, *Inferno*, XXVI) 131

Vanni Fucci (Dante, *Inferno*, XXIV)
    27, 34, 35,
Varnhagen, H. 100
Vienna 129
Virgil 103
    Aeneid 103
Voltaire, F. M. A. de 25

Weiss, R. 157
Wright, H. G. 130, 152

Zerlina 91
Zinevra (*Dec.*, II, 9) 101
Zumbini, B. 152
Zupita, J. 152